D1584302

THE DOLPHIN GUIDE TO HAWAII

PATRICK D. HAZARD first became fascinated with Hawaii when he went there as director of the Institute of American Studies at the East-West Center of the University of Hawaii. He received the Ph.D. in American Culture from Western Reserve University and spent two years as a Carnegie postdoctoral fellow at the University of Pennsylvania, where he assisted in the organization of the Annenberg School of Communications. Now chairman of the English Department of Beaver College, Patrick Hazard also films, edits, and writes cultural newsreels for Philadelphia television stations and is the American correspondent for *Contrast*, the television magazine of the British Film Institute.

The Dolphin Guide
to
HAWAII

PATRICK D. HAZARD

Dolphin Books
Doubleday & Company, Inc.
Garden City, New York

*Dedicated to the Asian and American grantees
of the East-West Center at the University of Hawaii
in the hope that they will fulfill the promise
of the best American idea since the
Declaration of Independence*

LIBRARY OF CONGRESS CATALOG CARD NUMBER 65–10608
COPYRIGHT © 1965 BY PATRICK D. HAZARD
ALL RIGHTS RESERVED
PRINTED IN THE UNITED STATES OF AMERICA

PREFACE

I am grateful to George Chaplin, editor of the Honolulu *Advertiser*, who patiently supplied me with a *second* copy of the Statehood Edition of his paper after some sneak (but intelligent) thief walked off with the first; Dr. James McCutcheon of the Institute of American Studies for mailing me the invaluable 1963 Progress edition of the Honolulu *Star-Bulletin* among many other favors, large and small; Dr. Carl Stroven, Librarian of the University, for his bibliography on the Literature of the Pacific, which, next to the course itself, is probably the best possible introduction to the subject; Mrs. Dee Prather of the Hawaii Visitors Bureau for many pictures and much information; Miss Louise Hinckley of the Library of Hawaii for patience and the picture of Popo Wong; Dr. Kenneth Slack of the Church College at Laie for the best luau my family ever had and background on his institution; Charles Tyng of the Ala Moana Shopping Center for keeping that place the handsomest man-made environment in all the Islands and letting other people know about it; Kenneth Asato of the high school at Kealakekua who showed me the real Kona; and Mrs. Ruth Rittmeister who, from booking last minute passage for us on the S.S. *Cleveland* to expediting my return trip to the Outer Islands, has made being a travel agent a satisfying art. Many transportation companies and island institutions have been helpful in supplying photographs which are duly acknowledged elsewhere in the text. My deepest hope is that someday soon I will be able to thank them and many others in person—there, preferably underwater at Hanauma Bay. And to typists Helen Moritz and Hazel Livergood, who deserve free trips to Hawaii for cracking the code, orchids.

Patrick D. Hazard

CONTENTS

Chapter I

INTRODUCTION

What Is So Great about Hawaii?

The question sounds like a simple one, until you discover that there are more Hawaiis than the one described by all the travel folders. Of course years and years of bad Kodachromes and kitschy hula music haven't been able to smother the real wallop to your senses that tourist Hawaii delivers on first encounter: that first breakfast next to the pool of the Edgewater Reef with sparrows buzzing your macadamia-nut pancakes; or, even earlier, jet-flown out of schedule, awaking to the predawn stirring of the trade winds on the lanai. The sheer sensual impact of these experiences is so completely new to most of us that it has to be felt to be believed. And when it is once felt, if you're not lucky enough to find a permanent place in the fiftieth state, you want to experience again this ever new freshness.

So there *is* an important physical side to Hawaii, and that is celebrated with gusto in these pages; but there is a further dimension to our newest state that I think even few of its *kamaainas* (Hawaiian for old-timers) are aware of. In fact, when a *malihini* (newcomer) like myself tries to explain this extra dimension, he is liable to be greeted by a painfully embarrassed silence or polite smiles. I think my fresh perspective came mainly from the job that brought me to Hawaii. For the first full year of its operation, I was the director of the Institute of American Studies at the East-West Center for Technical and Cultural Interchange, a long mouthful for the most exciting idea in the United States today: a federally supported scholarship and research program at the University of Hawaii in which Asians can learn how to modernize their countries and Americans can learn more about the languages

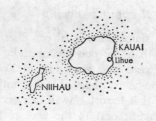

HAWAIIAN ISLANDS

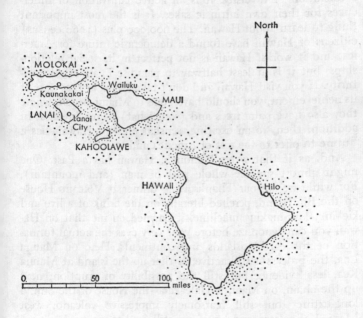

and cultures of the Asian countries we come into increasing contact with. The Institute of American Studies has the fascinating responsibility of explaining the nature of American civilization to the Asian grantees of the East-West Center.

The most challenging aspect of it for me, of course, was finding out in what ways Honolulu and Hawaii were like and unlike the rest of the United States. For this extraordinary mid-Pacific mixing (not melting) pot has kept alive several different ethnic strains (instead of grinding them down into a general American hamburger). This is much more than a toleration of diversity; it is an active cultivation of differences for their own intrinsic sakes. It is the most important thing to learn about Hawaii. The 600,000 plus (1960 census) citizens of Hawaii have found a democratic future for America, and it works! Hawaii is not perfect in its social relationships, but it is at least halfway to paradise in its ethnic maturity. If you visit Hawaii and don't take a look at that part of its achievement, you should have gone to Miami Beach, where they also have palm trees and (somewhat) balmy breezes. In addition, then, to an exciting, sensual present, Hawaii has a Future to offer to the rest of America and to Asia.

And, as if that weren't enough, Hawaii has a Past. One might almost say the whole past of man (and mountain). For while we ate our Thanksgiving dinner at Volcano House on the Big Island, perched literally on the brink of a live and kicking, lava-making machine, it dawned on me that on Hawaii you can synopsize before your very eyes the actual formation of the earth's islands and continents. Here on Mauna Loa, the process is still active; farther up the island at Mauna Kea, less evidence but still the possibility of eruption; next up the chain, on Maui, is Haleakala—the House of the Sun, a long-extinct but still fearsomely impressive volcano; west Maui, Kahoolawe, and Lanai are still further removed in time from the primeval upheavals; fly on to Honolulu and you have only the ancient craters of Punchbowl and Diamond Head to remind you of the terror that once rained on Oahu as its volcanoes gradually built up the island from undersea eruptions; still farther north is the Garden Isle of Kauai, where greenery thoroughly covers its oldest extinct volcanoes.

This historical record was expressed by the old Stone Age

Hawaiians by their myth of Pele, who first lived on Kauai, then went island-hopping in a southeasterly direction until she disappeared into the very volcano on the Big Island of Hawaii, where my geological daydream had begun. As in most myths, beneath the allegorical manner lay essential truths. But nowadays there is as much fun to be had savoring the manner as in understanding the matter. This mythic dimension is a heady bonus for the fact-fatigued American; every stone seems to be storied in Hawaii.

What *is* so great about Hawaii? Its fascinating Past, vigorous Present, and prophetic Future. It is the American dream of diversity in fullest embodiment.

How to Get There

If you're in a hurry, fly. Jets take four to five hours and the new economy fare is a hundred dollars one way from the mainland. Jet carriers let you choose, with no extra charge, your West Coast port of entry. For example, you can fly out on United Air Lines through San Francisco and fly back through Seattle/Portland on United or Northwest Orient. Pan American and United also offer a Los Angeles stop for no extra fare.

There are fine differences in service that seasoned air travelers select from the various airlines. United D-C 8's have a round lounge at the rear of the economy section which is ideal for families with slightly squirmy children. Pan Am's night flights out of Hawaii always dull the pain of leaving Alohaland with much free champagne, a particularly poignant removal if the prevailing trade winds give you the take-off pattern straight at downtown Honolulu, then veering down the Waikiki beachline, past a dark pit of Diamond Head, and then, reluctantly, seaward over the Pacific to one of the Big Three West Coast airports. For this splendid nightscape (it's not bad by day, either, since you get a great view of the coral formations in good weather) sit on the left-side windows. As you come in, the right side provides the best view, generally. If your airline won't reserve a seat, it's worth getting to the airport a little ahead of the last-minute crowd to select a prime seat. Since you must pass agricultural inspection (blame California, not Hawaii!) before leaving, it's good to get there ahead of time anyway. One final thing. If you plan to visit the Outer Islands, buy your tickets to them as part of your mainland-to-Hawaii ticket and you will save substantially.

There are two regular airlines, Hawaiian and Aloha, serving the Outer Islands. There is also a seventy-five-dollar all-day flight that circles the entire island chain, even featuring swoops over the Forbidden Island, Niihau, where 240 or so souls resist a jukebox-and-TV culture with dogged determination on the private estate of the Robinsons.

You can also fly *through* Hawaii, with stopover privileges, on certain foreign carriers: Japan Air Lines, if you're Tokyo bound; Qantas Airways, if your destination is Down Under; and you can fly to Honolulu via BOAC and Canadian Pacific Airlines, if you came from London or Vancouver, for example.

HONOLULU'S NEW INTERNATIONAL AIRPORT

In 1962 Honolulu opened its new jet terminal for international and overseas passengers. Its name—the John Rodgers Terminal—recalls an exciting episode in early aviation history. In August 1925, Commander John Rodgers, of the U. S. Navy, left San Francisco with a crew of four in the seaplane P-N-9-1 in an attempt to cover the 2100 nautical miles nonstop for the first time. All went well until the plane ran out of gas 350 miles short of its goal and it lost contact with the navigation ship *Aroostook*. That ship took a false bearing on the downed aeronautical pioneers, so that the Navy task force searched for them 300 miles south of where they actually were. For ten days they used their wits to evade fate. They rigged sails with fabric from the plane's wings, caught life-saving water with them during a half-hour rain squall, and rigged a keel from the plane's floor boards so that they could aim for shore. The currents and winds brought them to within one hundred miles of Oahu (they saw the lights of Schofield Barracks one frustrating night!), but they had to aim for Kauai, after they overshot Oahu. Ten miles off Kauai, a Navy submarine picked up the exhausted aviators. In honor of their heroism, the terminal is named for their leader.

Be sure either to arrive or leave during the day so that you can fully enjoy the exquisite gardens at the airport. The Japanese Garden there is particularly attractive, but there are Chinese and Hawaiian ones too. While the shops at the airport are extensive and well stocked, you must remember that should you buy many gifts on your way to the plane you can easily overshoot the forty-four pounds allowed economy passengers and sixty-six pound limit for first-class passage. Better to scout the shops as you wait for incoming baggage and get a fix on the prices. The agricultural inspection is another reason for spending a leisurely preflight nightcap or a daylight excursion around the terminal before your flight.

People with more money and time, however, sail to Hawaii. Well-heeled enough to own a sailboat and hire a crew, they compete in the San Pedro race, held every two years. With as little as $250 (mostly up, up, up) and four and one-half days and five nights, one can sail in style on the luxury liners that ply under the flags of Matson, American President, and P & O-Orient lines. I can speak personally of only the American President Lines, specifically the S. S. *Cleveland*. It was a wonder. Baby-sitting and separate meals for adults and children. Endless variation in a gourmet's menu. Games if you want to play; privacy if you don't. And, best of all, your arrival will be heralded at dockside by the Royal Hawaiian Band.

HONOLULU'S PORT

The sea has been crucial to Hawaii ever since its Polynesian settlers first pushed the prows of their outrigger canoes onto its shores. Today Honolulu (which means "Fair Haven") has a modern harbor with 51 wharves and 2 small ferry landings to service the ships that use its 4000-foot long, 500-foot-wide main channel. Seven miles to the west of Honolulu Harbor is Pearl Harbor, headquarters of the Fourteenth Naval District and the Hawaiian Sea Frontier, where as many as 528 ships have been berthed at one time. All told, over 1000 ships flying many flags dock somewhere in Hawaii each year. Shipping has come a long way since Captain Robert Dollar, dean of American shipping, started his Pacific fleet in 1901 with a tiny coastal schooner.

Where to Stay

By the end of 1963, Hawaii had twelve thousand rooms to offer her almost half-million annual overnight visitors. Oahu accounts for ten thousand of the total; the Outer Islands for the rest. Except for the peak tourist periods (summer, Aloha Week in October, Christmas vacation) it is always possible to find some accommodations at short notice, at least on Oahu. And the young at heart can always stop off in their rented car at Sears Ala Moana on their way in from the airport to buy sleeping bags for real exposure to tropical America on Hawaii's beaches and in the state parks. A free list of those is available from the Hawaii Visitors Bureau. But most tourists will prefer to write that most helpful agency for its annual list of hotels. (Since a thousand new rooms were projected on Oahu alone for the year 1964, it is wise to get the latest list.) And summer-school students consult the university's housing bureau.

Before commenting on a representative sample of hotels, one should indicate the major types of accommodations available. The most famous, of course, and (with one exception) the most expensive, are the oceanside "name" hotels on Waikiki on either side of Waikiki's main street, Kalakaua. The farther one goes inland from the beach itself, the lower the rentals—and the less elegant the room. But for the average tourist of limited income, the best bet, if one wants to stay at Waikiki, is to rent a hotel back from the beach toward the Ala Wai Canal. At the other extreme, the really wealthy flee the Miami Beachy quality in Waikiki altogether by putting up at the so-called "destination resort" areas, all but one of which are on the Outer Islands.

Downtown hotels are the next category to consider. Some cater mainly to Orientals, but in broad-minded Hawaii that is no impediment to an Occidental in search of unique styles of life. Downtown haole hotels are older and more reasonable than Waikiki counterparts, and for the beach-shunning, museum-seeking visitor they are the best buy. The final "ordinary" category is the unpretentious motel appearing with increasing frequency on the Outer Islands. These are no better or worse than the mainland prototypes they model themselves on, except that the trade winds and palm trees are bonuses that make their slightly higher prices worth while. There is still another class of accommodation in addition to the starry sky for those who would combine adventure with economy: rooming with local families by the week or month. By writing ahead for the Sunday edition of the Honolulu *Advertiser-Star-Bulletin*, a canny visitor can cut costs and see the nontourist side of Hawaiian life. Best, however, not to contract for such housing sight unseen. Check into a regular hotel for a day, and check the leads found in the newspaper's want ads. Visitors who qualify should also consider the Y.M.C.A., the Y.W.C.A., and the University of Hawaii Housing Bureau.

WAIKIKI HOTELS

(Beginning at the Diamond Head side and going toward Ala Moana.)

Between the War Memorial Natatorium in Kapiolani Park (which is one end of Waikiki Beach) and Diamond Head itself, there is an increasing number of co-op apartments. It is possible to rent these exclusive places by the month for upward of $200 furnished, much upward in most cases, and for fairly long leases. However, there is also a growing practice of apartment swapping, especially between Honolulu and the West Coast. This is an expensive way of combining nearness to the action of Waikiki Beach with relative isolation. And the seaside views in these high-rise apartments can be breathtaking. Do your mainland sleuthing in the Sunday papers. Some of these accommodations can be rented directly:

Center Apartments, 2987 Kalakaua Avenue, Honolulu. One bedroom and bath, fully equipped kitchen, private telephone, maid service, seaside view, $100 a week and up.

The Colony Surf, 2895 Kalakaua Avenue, Honolulu. Almost a hundred hotel apartments and penthouse suites, with complete maid, kitchen, laundry, and garage service. Daily rates between $10 and $30. Not the least attraction of this place is Michele's, offering some of the best French cuisine in the fiftieth state.

Coral Strand Hotel, 2979 Kalakaua Avenue, Honolulu. Ten studio apartments, singles from $12 daily, doubles from $18. One-bedroom apartments fully furnished from $28 a day. Breakfast included.

Luxury Hotels—Waikiki

Foster Tower, 2500 Kalakaua Avenue, Honolulu. Right across from Prince Kuhio Beach, the heart of the public swimming area in Waikiki, this hotel sparked an urban planning crisis because it wrecked the silhouette of Diamond Head (from the lanais of earlier luxury hotels). It's not the best modern architecture, but it has a great deal of well-integrated regional art, and the view is great *from* this 135-unit high-riser. Rates range from $16 to $45 daily and from $112 to $315 weekly.

Moana Hotel, 2365 Kalakaua Avenue, Honolulu. Its Banyan Court is world-famed as the site of the "Hawaii Calls" radio series. It is a pleasant place at any time, but a leisurely drink there watching lights on the ocean after dark is an indispensable bit of Hawaiiana. It has over 250 rooms on the European plan. Singles $10 to $15, doubles $14 to $19. This is one of the former Sheraton hotels just purchased by a Japanese syndicate in anticipation of more and more Oriental visitors. (One-fifth of Hawaii's tourists in 1963 came from the Far East.) This hotel adjoins the slightly higher and newer Surfrider Hotel, under the same management.

Princess Kaiulani Hotel, 120 Kaiulani Avenue, Honolulu. This is another of the former Sheraton hotels, across the street from the Moana. Almost half of its over 500 rooms are air-conditioned, making it a good bet during muggy Kona weather of December to February. It has penthouse suites for around $50 a day, but its regular rooms are competitive with the Moana and the Surfrider, under the same management. If you can't afford a penthouse, you can sip with the view on the roof-top Robert Louis Stevenson Room, one of the finest prospects in all Hawaii and my favorite at Waikiki. Also take a good look at the architectural ceramics outside its unique set of convention and conference rooms.

Royal Hawaiian Hotel, 2259 Kalakaua Avenue, Honolulu. Before the destination resort areas became the new status symbol, this was *the* hotel. There are still those whose one-upmanship keeps them loyal to the Royal, disdaining the jet-set's flight to the Outer Islands. Singles range from $16 to twice that; doubles from $21.50 to $37 a day. Take the Royal the easy way—through its handsome bars (the Kalakaua-side bistro has a fine Ben Norris mural) or by squatting for free in its cool, tree-shaded garden, or by splurging $10 or $15 for two for dinner and entertainment at the Monarch Room.

Halekulani Hotel, 2199 Kalia Road, Honolulu. "House of Heaven" is the English translation of this handsome hostelry. It has almost 200 accommodations in cottages in a five-acre tropical garden and is the best of the old Waikiki. Family cottages begin at about $30 a day. Don't fail to have lunch at its beachside restaurant. You can even walk up from swimming at Prince Kuhio Beach for a snack, except on the crowded weekends. Then I would advise walking in the opposite direction toward the equally casual Queen's Surf Bar for a breezy, tasty break.

Yacht Club–Waikiki

Hilton Hawaiian Village, Kalia Road and Dewey Court, Honolulu. As habitués of TV's *Hawaiian Eye* may have gathered, this is a small world of its own. While I don't like its beaches as well as the Queen's Surf, I do recommend the pool next to the Kona Koffee Shop where you are welcome if you have lunch there. Also be sure to find out what's showing at the Buckminster Fuller Dome while you're in Hawaii. And the complex of shops between the Dome and the Hotel Lobby is a must stop. Among the hotel's thousand plus accommodations are rooms for as low as $14 single.

The Waikikian, 1811 Ala Moana Boulevard at the Yacht

Basin, Honolulu. Across the lagoon from the Hilton Hawaiian Village and overlooking the Ala Wai Yacht Basin is one of the handsomest meldings of Polynesian motifs with modern architecture in Hawaii. It is the best work of architect George Wimberley and sculptor Edward Brownlee, in my judgment, far superior to the concrete pillboxes marching on Diamond Head. And its rates start at $12 for a single, $14 for a double, out of the high rent district as it is. It is midway between Ala Moana Shopping Center and Waikiki shops. It's my personal choice because of its architecture and location. At least treat yourself to breakfast there at its Tahitian Lanai restaurant.

Other Waikiki Hotels

Edgewater Hotel, Beachwalk at 2168 Kalia Road, Honolulu. For couples who want to cut corners on food, this is ideal with kitchen apartments starting at $12 a day. Yet it's just across Kalia Road from the beach. Across the street on the beach is The Reef run by the same people where a seaside room for two without kitchen starts at $18. In fact, the Roy Kelley hotels (he also runs the Reef Tower and Edgewater Lanais nearby) seems to me to combine good service, low cost, and nearness to the Beach. In general, the same goes for most of the smaller hotels and motels on Beachwalk (Hale Puanui, The Breakers, Hawaiian Hotel, Hotel Tropic Isle, and the Polynesian) and on Saratoga Road across from Fort De Russy (Malihini Hotel, Kai Aloha, Aloha Punawai), Honolulu. The minute differences in price and location can best be studied in the free directory and map called "Hawaii Hotel Guide," available from the Hawaii Visitors Bureau.

Edmund's Hotel Apartments, 2411 Ala Wai Boulevard, Honolulu. The other way to find bargains in housing is to go inland from the beach toward the Ala Wai Canal. Here, for example, are eight studio apartments at $6 a day, $35 a week, double occupancy. And you're only a brisk five-minute walk away from the heart of Waikiki.

The Surf Tide, 432 Namahana Street, Honolulu. Ten minutes from the heart of Waikiki you can find studio units complete with kitchens for as low as $8 a day. Also remember that in the off seasons you're able to get many hotels with low occupancy rates (between Kuhio Avenue and Ala Wai Boulevard) for considerably lower than prime season rates. A little dickering will save you cash for other sectors of the Hawaiian economy!

DOWNTOWN HOTELS

Alexander Young Hotel, 1077 Bishop Street, Honolulu. Has 200 rooms in the heart of downtown. Singles from $7; doubles from $11. Ideal for someone interested more in seeing a lot of the cosmopolitan side of Hawaii, as opposed to the touristry side. Near museums, Oriental district.

Blaisdell Hotel, 1154 Fort Street, Honolulu. Has 63 units starting as low as $4 single, $6 double.

Armed Services Y.M.C.A. Hotel, 250 South Street, Honolulu. Military personnel on shoestring budgets should consider this most attractive center.

Kobayashi Hotel, 250 North Beretania Street. Features a Japanese bathhouse, has 30 rooms with private baths, maid service, singles starting at $5, doubles from $8.

AIRPORT

Skylane Inn, 2628 Waiwai Loop, Honolulu. Next to the turn-off to the old airport, it is five minutes by car from the new Honolulu International Airport. Swimming pool, bar, and restaurant. Free transportation to airport. Singles $8, doubles $10. Ideal for travelers en route by air who want a place to freshen up after an all-day tour of Oahu or to use as a staging point for Outer Islands air visits.

DESTINATION RESORT SHOW PLACES

To save yourself long-distance toll charges, make reservations through Honolulu travel agencies; any on Kalakaua Avenue will do.

Oahu

Kahala Hilton, off Route 72 in Waialae-Kahala District of Oahu. This is Oahu's first luxury hotel built to disperse the flow of the most affluent visitors from overcrowded Waikiki. It's a tropical showplace fifteen minutes beyond Diamond Head.

Maui

Sheraton-Maui, Kaanapali Beach, Maui. Has 212 air-conditioned lanais (fresh-air porches). American-plan singles from $25 to $32.50, doubles from $39 to $46.50. Golf course by Robert Trent Jones. Superb dining facilities.

Royal Lahaina Beach Hotel, Kaanapali Beach, Maui. Adjacent to Sheraton-Maui. Ground-floor suite (two bedrooms, three baths, living room, kitchen, lanai), $75 to $80 a day. Less exalted surroundings as low as $17.50 for a single; $25 double.

Hotel Hana Maui, eastern tip of Maui. Has 50 rooms and suites with private lanais. Singles $34 and up, doubles $23 to $29 per person, suite for two, three, or four $25 per person. This is accessible by private airstrip and is one of the loveliest retreats in Hawaii.

Kauai

Coco Palms Resort Hotel, on Route 56 near Wailua. In the state's largest palm grove and next to a beautiful lagoon. Has 160 rooms and 2 swimming pools. American plan. Singles $24 to $38, doubles $36 to $50. European plan available at $6 less.

Kauai Surf, overlooking Nawiliwili Bay outside Lihue. Has 132 rooms: 28 standard, 104 de luxe. Standard single $16, double $20, de luxe $20 and $24. Add $8 for American plan. Spectacular open-air restaurant, especially grand at night.

Hanalei Plantation, on northern tip of island. Site of movie *South Pacific*. Has 50 individual guest cottages. Full American plan $38 to $43 for single, $50 to $55 double, and $68 to $75 triple. Unique circular bar, The House of Happy

Talk, is architecturally interesting. Have breakfast in the stately Chandelier Dining Room if you can't afford to stay there. If you leave Lihue at seven, you'll have a fine appetite by eight-thirty for breakfast.

The Big Island

Volcano House, Hawaii National Park. Has 37 rooms. American plan. Single $16 to $19, double $25 to $28. European plan $5 less. Children under eight, half fare. If you don't stay here, have dinner and watch the volcano movies. Come early enough to see twilight fall over the grotesque landscape from its dining-room picture window.

Hotel King Kamehameha, Kailua, Kona. Has 92 rooms, each with a sea view; on the white sand beach of Kamakahonu Bay. American plan. Single $20 to $38, double $30 to $50. European plan $6 less per person. Splintered Paddle Bar is a showplace.

Kona Inn, Kailua, Kona. Has 143 rooms: 76 standard, 67 de luxe. European-plan standard single $16, double $20, de luxe $20 and $24. American plan add $8 per day. Center of game-fishing sport. Congenial open-air bar dedicated to the cultivation of spirited fish stories.

Lanai

Lanai Inn, Lanai City. Has 8 twin bedrooms, 2 single rooms. American plan. One person in a room $14, two persons $26. There is no fancy hotel on Lanai yet; in fact there's only one!

Molokai

Seaside Inn, Kaunakakai. Has 33 rooms on the beach. European plan $6 and up. American plan $12 and up. Just a clean, friendly motel, really.

OTHER OUTER ISLANDS ACCOMMODATIONS

There are other less expensive motels and hotels on the Outer Islands of Maui (seventeen places), Hawaii (seventeen), and Kauai (twelve). And more are opening every month. To get an up-to-date listing, drop a postcard to the

Hawaii Visitors Bureau nearest you (Room 618, Wrigley Building, Chicago; Room 309, 609 Fifth Avenue, New York; Room 809, 3440 Wilshire Boulevard, Los Angeles). And if you have friends in Hawaii, rent through them, since frequently there are differential rates for *kamaainas* (old-timers) and *malihinis* (visitors).

Fido: Stay Home

One thing pet lovers planning to visit Hawaii should be forewarned about: this rabies-free island wants to stay that way. Therefore, your cats and dogs, should you decide in a burst of generosity to bring them, will not really enjoy their vacation with you. They will be promptly removed to the Animal Quarantine Section for four months at your expense (about sixty dollars for their isolated stay). Write the Hawaiian State Department of Agriculture in Honolulu for forms if you're determined to bring along the family's best friend.

How to Know What's Going On—Fast

Waikiki Beach Press (with neighboring island supplements) is the best tourist guide. Three times a week. Free.

"What to Do": Daily events guide put out by Hawaii Visitors Bureau (HVB) is more comprehensive. Call 92-211 for last-minute changes.

Outer Islands HVB phones: Hilo office: Tel. H 5-3205

Maui office: Tel. M 72-6225

Kauai office: Tel. LHU 2-2935

"Today on Oahu," Honolulu *Advertiser* (morning paper).

"Pulse of the City," Honolulu *Star-Bulletin* (afternoon paper).

"This Week on Oahu," joint Sunday edition. Note ethnic entertainments on TV and at movies.

To learn ahead of time what big events will occur during your stay, call or write HVB regional offices:

Los Angeles, Room 809, 3440 Wilshire Boulevard, Tel. 385-5301

Chicago, Room 618, Wrigley Building, 400 N. Michigan Avenue, Tel. WH 4-6694

New York, Room 309, 609 Fifth Avenue, Tel. PL 9-3655 or 9-3656

CULTURE BY QUARTERS

Summer (when most of the visitors come)

June: Fiesta Filipina is a two-week festival of music, folk dancing, games, and pageantry from the Philippine Islands.

June 11: Kamehameha Day. The parade down King Street and into Iolani Palace is outstanding. Get there an hour or so before the parade starts. I found the curbing just opposite the gates to Iolani Palace the happiest combination of comfort and visibility. The floats sponsored by each island are a marvelous popular art. Native flowers and grasses are used to spell out themes and identifying marks. The colorful horseback riders, the uniforms of the Hawaiian societies, and the gay holiday mood make this parade *sui generis*. Be dazzled by the abundance of leis on Kamehameha's statue. And plan to stay for the luau given at Kawaiahao Church. Between the parade and lunch explore the segregated burial grounds, the well-kept haoles behind the church on the way to the old mission houses and the depressed area where Hawaiians were laid to rest.

June: Outdoor Circle Home Tour and Victorian Fashion Show.

Every weekend practically (especially July and August): The Japanese Bon Dances. We went to an especially good one in July at the Shinto Temple between the Pali Expressway and Nuuanu Avenue. Come early so you can sit in the front row of folding chairs (and you can gradually discover and localize as we did the tantalizing odor of *teriyaki*-marinated steak strips served from outdoor bazaars by children of the temple parish). These affairs start slowly, so don't get restless. Notice the bewilderingly diverse brilliance of the kimonos. And surely don't leave before the band starts to perpetrate its magic. They will drift in and fill a gaily decorated box around which the dancers circle. The drums and (particularly) the flutes start a rhythm in the atmosphere that at the risk of a cliché I can only call intoxicating. The steps look too complex to try, but aren't. Start by imitating the foot movements of someone who is really good. Then, with the step memorized, start looking at the hands and body. And don't be bashful, even if you have no kimono. You are welcomed if you're brave enough to get on your feet. And you should be ashamed if you don't because of the ages of the Japanese children taking part in the dances. These dances honor the dead. What a civilized custom! The temple holding this weekend's dances will be listed in "This Week on Oahu," in your Sunday *Advertiser-Star-Bulletin*, or in the *Waikiki Beach Press*.

The 50th State Fair, held in Waikiki Shell, Kapiolani Park, in late June or early July, combines the standard American midway with interesting regional overtones, such as tropical-fish competitions and orchid displays and flower arrangements. A smaller fair with less midway and more local color is held in June on the McKinley High School playground off Kapiolani Avenue, toward the mountains and downtown from Ala Moana Shopping Center.

July 4: Naalehu Rodeo, Big Island.

August Sunday afternoons: Hula Festivals. In Kapiolani Park. Old-time hulas, modern hulas, kids' hulas, comic hulas.

Second two Sundays in August: The Oahu Hula Festival, culminating in a session with hundreds who have learned to dance in classes sponsored by the city of Honolulu. Thomas Square, Honolulu.

August or September: The Chinese Moon Festival. The Chinese Moon Festival commemorates the visit of the Emperor Ming Huan to paradise with moon-cake displays and pageants. Held on some roped-off streets in Chinatown, this is worth going to only if you love mobs or have the foresight to eat that night at Wo Fat's and get a table overlooking the platform where the Dragon Dance and other fascinating ethnic material are performed for the benefit of people in the front row or on stilts. If you come early enough, it is fun to wander around the Chinese stores for far-out foods and candies.

Labor Day Week: The Whaler's Spree. Lahaina, Maui, is overhauling its past for the delectation of tourists, and this is their first major attraction. Whale meat on sale all week!

First week in August: The Hawaii County Fair, in Hilo.

Early August: Hilo Bay, Big Island. Canoe-racing clubs from all over the island chain cart their *koas* here for the state championships. Torchlight parade begins it Friday night, and a luau ends it—officially.

Fall

October: Orchid Show.

October: Aloha Week. For eight (or more, each succeeding year) days each year this is the largest and best of the Hawaiian celebrations. Most of the biggest ceremonies are held at Waikiki or Ala Moana Park. To begin the celebration, the king of the festival sails in from Waikiki to the park in a catamaran. There he meets his queen and her attendants, each representing one of the Outer Islands. The week ends with a *holoku* ball. Don't miss the free entertainment in the Ala Moana Shopping Center. And if you took the efficient aeronautical way over from the mainland, please take time out to go to Aloha pier so you can see how ships make a splash when they enter in the middle of Aloha Week. An exhilirating spectacle.

November: Festival of the Pacific. Ethnic song and dance. Begun in 1963 to counteract the tourist doldrums between Aloha Week and Christmas.

Fall: Annual Hawaiian Art and Prints Show at the Honolulu Academy of Arts. The islands have a flourishing community of visual artists. Don't miss this exhibition. There is also the Contemporary Arts Center in the Newspaper Building Court for changing exhibits of individual artists.

Fall: Honolulu Academy of Arts. You can get a good idea of the catholicity of this museum by its commitment to an annual of best advertising. Look especially for the way old Hawaiian motifs are put to new uses in, for example, Tom Lee's fine directory covers for Hawaiian Telephone. Also includes some fashion design.

December 7: Pearl Harbor Anniversary.

Bodhi Day falls on the Sunday closest to December 7 and is the anniversary of the enlightenment of Buddha and his establishment of Buddhism.

December 19: Princess Bernice Pauahi Bishop's birthday anniversary. Hawaiian societies observe it with ceremonies at the Royal Mausoleum and at the Kamehameha Schools.

Winter

December 30: Rizal Day. It honors the memory of José Rizal, the George Washington of the Philippines, who helped his country win independence from Spain.

New Year's Eve: You have never known noise per se until your ears have survived a Chinese-firecrackered New Year's celebration. I suggest getting a vantage point on Mount Tantalus or at La Ronde Restaurant to maximize the sights while (impossible) minimizing the sounds.

Narcissus Festival: January or early February, depending on the new moon. There are Chinese beauty queens, dances, and a dragon parade in Chinatown. The Narcissus Festival is based on the Chinese lunar calendar. It is named for the white "spirit lilies," which stand for good fortune.

Ka Palapala Beauty Pageant is a spring multiracial beauty contest held among the coeds at the University of Hawaii. For a long time it was held at the end of February, but its dates vary.

March 3: Girl's Day. Japanese dolls are set up on special shelves in living rooms as well as publicly in store windows and parks. The Japanese Girl's Day, or Doll Festival, is held to honor the birth and happiness of daughters. It comes from a custom of giving dolls or some other remembrance to a baby girl on the first March 3 following her birth. On her thirteenth birthday the young lady puts away her dolls until her marriage.

Spring

March 26: Prince Kuhio Day. Jonah Kalanianaole (for whom the unpronounceable highway is named) was Hawaiian territorial delegate to Congress for a score of years. School is out and there is a ceremony at the Royal Mausoleum where he is buried.

April: Cherry Blossom Festival. The highlight is a week-long festival of folk dancing, tea ceremonies, and electing the Cherry Blossom Queen is a major event in the Japanese community. The Cherry Blossom Festival usually runs from mid-March to mid-April. It is in effect a Japanese spring festival with cultural shows (especially at the handsome Japanese Chamber of Commerce buildings in Moiliili near the University of Hawaii), pageants, sports, drama, and a stage show from Japan.

April: Wesak Day. This amounts to the Buddhist Easter, on which the temple halls are cleared and the image of Buddha is washed with jasmine tea. The Wesak Day Flower Festival, held in Kapiolani Park, commemorates Buddha's birthday.

May 1: Lei Day.

May 5: Boy's Day. Brightly colored carp kites fly outside homes on poles to urge boys to be brave.

May 30: Memorial Day. Services at Punchbowl, the National Military Cemetery.

May: Hibiscus Show is a one-day event at Ala Moana Park in May.

Last Week in May: Honokaa Rodeo, Big Island.

May: Annual Festival of Music and Art of This Century. University of Hawaii: Orvis Auditorium for music, George Hall for art. A must.

A Sunday late in May. Honolulu. The Hawaiian Song Festival: Features prizes and performances for original Hawaiian Songs. Climax of three months of competition.

Hawaii at Home

The best way to get ready to go to Hawaii is to dip into the voluminous literature on the subject. Here are ten books to begin with. To get a really thorough introduction to the life and culture of the mid-Pacific, take Professor Charles Hunter's highly popular course on Hawaiian history and Professor A. Grove Day's excellent course on the literature of the Pacific, both offered at the University of Hawaii's summer session.

A. Grove Day, *Hawaii and Its People* (New York: Duell, Sloan and Pearce, 1955). Designed "to stress social history even at the expense of politics and diplomacy," this volume will interest the literary reader who will savor the successful efforts of a literate English professor to establish a lively image of Hawaiian history through voyagers' narratives, biographies, visitors' accounts, and literary sketches by such writers as Robert Louis Stevenson, Jack London, Charles Warren Stoddard, Isabella Bird Bishop, and Mark Twain. Full of leads to further reading of that sort.

A. Grove Day, *Hawaii, Fiftieth Star* (New York: Duell, Sloan and Pearce, 1960). A children's book by the most productive historian of the islands. High-school age level.

A. Grove Day and Carl Stroven, eds., *A Hawaiian Reader* (New York: Popular Library, 1961). The prolific historian of Hawaii and the librarian of the University of Hawaii have pooled their incomparable knowledge of the literature of the South Pacific to present an inexpensive collection of pieces on the fiftieth state. Captain Cook, Hiram Bingham, James J. Jarves, Mark Twain, Charles Warren Stoddard, Isabella Bird Bishop, Robert Louis Stevenson, Jack London, and James Jones are among those included. A "best buy" bargain, as they say in *Consumer Reports*.

Lawrence H. Fuchs, *Hawaii Pono: A Social History* (New York: Harcourt, Brace, 1961). What started out as a study of ethnic block voting grew into a brilliant socioeconomic study of twentieth-century Hawaii. It caused howls among the *kamaainas* when it appeared, but its point of view agreed with everything I saw in the islands. In order to see beneath the aloha formalities, this is indispensable to the serious student of our laboratory of democracy.

J. C. Furnas, *Anatomy of Paradise; Hawaii and the Islands of the South Seas* (New York: William Sloane Associates, 1948). Very engaging philosophical essays on the meaning of the South Seas to us, punctuated by breezily written anecdotes loosely in support of observations. Debunks paradise, making it at the most a limbo, if not a purgatory.

Gerrit P. Judd IV, *Hawaii; An Informal History* (New York: Collier Original Paperback, 1961). Written by a descendant of a famous missionary doctor who wielded significant power in the kingdom period. While consciously counteracting what was felt to be the antimissionary bias of James Michener's novel, *Hawaii*, it is fair, succinct, and lively. Next to a fast panoramic introduction to the basic outlines of Hawaiian development to the twentieth century, available in the Michener novel, this is the busy adult's best briefing.

Ralph S. Kuykendall and A. Grove Day, *Hawaii: A History; From Polynesian Kingdom to American State* (Englewood Cliffs, N.J.: Prentice-Hall, rev. ed., 1961). Written by a historian and an English professor at the University of Hawaii. Good comprehensive survey. Probably best single volume for nonspecialist.

Kathleen Mellen has written a four-volume saga of the Hawaiian kingdom. The first is about Kamehameha the Great, *The Lonely Warrior*. The second is a biography of his favorite wife, Queen Kaahumanu, and is called *The Magnificent Matriarch*. *The Gods Depart* chronicles the disintegration of the old Hawaii, and *An Island Kingdom Passes* brings the story up to the turn of the twentieth century, when Hawaii became a U.S. territory. Mrs. Mellen is a highly revered figure who has done a great deal to revive amateur and semiprofessional interest in Hawaiiana.

Douglas L. Oliver, *The Pacific Islands* (New York: Doubleday Natural History Library, rev. ed., 1961). A contentious, antiprogress summary of what was there when the white man found the Pacific islands, and what the white men have done to and for them. A fascinating combination of economics and anthropology in the context of the changing Pacific. Highly recommended.

Stanley D. Porteus, *A Century of Social Thinking in Hawaii* (Pacific Books, Palo Alto, California, 1962). Since 1881 the twoscore members of the select Honolulu Social Science Association have been meeting religiously eight times a year to exchange their ideas about Hawaii as a social phenomenon. Porteus, an internationally known professor emeritus of psychology from the University of Hawaii and a member of the H.S.S.A. for twenty-eight years, has edited, from the more than six hundred essays of the association, the highlights to "show the trends of thinking and many changes that have occurred" since the association first met.

How to Speak Hawaiian

Hawaiian is a fascinating language to study and melodious to hear. At first it looks very difficult to pronounce, but it is really amazingly easy if you follow a few rules.

1. Pronounce every letter. (There are only twelve, so every one counts.)

2. The consonants H, K, L, M, N, P, W are pronounced as in English, except that W inside a word is pronounced like V. Hence Hawaii is HAH-VA-EE. And the small island off the coast of Maui, Kahoolawe is said KAH-HO-OH-LAH-VEH. And *ewa*, the direction opposite from Diamond Head, is EH-VAH.

3. Every consonant is followed or preceded by at least one vowel. Kaaawa has three A's (and you say them all), KAH-AH-AH-VAH, even though saying it fast sometimes makes it hard to hear all the A's distinctly.

4. The vowels have the values based on those in Italian: A is like AH; E is like the long A in Fame; I is like EE; O is like OH; U is like OO.

5. The trickiest looking word, say, Kalanianaole, is simple as licking poi if you break it into syllables and pronounce

everything: KAH-LAH-NEE-AN-NAY-OH-LAY. This gives you a heady feeling once you get the swing of it!

If you get hooked on this aspect of Polynesia (as I am), I suggest that you pick up Henry P. Judd's and Mary Kawena Pukui's *Introduction to the Hawaiian Language* (Tongg, publishers) and Dr. Samuel Elbert's LP on pronouncing the language at the University of Hawaii bookstore in Manoa Valley. The former contains a more detailed guide to pronunciation and a dictionary of five thousand common English words with their Hawaiian equivalents and a similar word list in Hawaiian-English.

Carol Roes has composed songs and lyrics, *Eight Children's Songs from Hawaii,* that are fun for lower elementary grades. The record that comes with the text tells a child how to pronounce Hawaiian names and how to do a hula sign language with songs like "The Counting Song" and "The Streets of Waikiki" and "Eight Islands," which is instant geography for the pre-Twist set. Most book and novelty stores stock this and you can write to the author for it at 988 Kealaolu Avenue, Honolulu, Hawaii 96815, if you'd like to get the children ready for the visit painlessly.

There are intriguing etymologies described. For example, when the white man came, the Hawaiians had the word *moku,* which meant "severed" or "cut off," and by extension "district" or "island." Because of the great size of Western ships, when the Hawaiian first saw them he called them *moku* because he thought they were floating islands. From that first misapprehension came later words: steamers were *mokuahi,* or fire ships; airplanes were *mokulele,* or flying ships; and Pearl Harbor submarines were *mokulu'u,* or diving ships. By a similar process, *ka'a,* which means "to roll" or "revolve," was adapted to signify railroad trains, *ka'aahi,* or fire cars; and streetcars, *ka'auwila,* or lightning cars!

Another way the Hawaiians adjusted their vocabularies was simply to filter the new Western terms through the sieve of their own limited set of seven consonants and five vowels. Telephone became *kekepona,* telegraph came out *kelekalapa,* and wire was heard as *uwea.* If you're in the Islands over the Christmas season, you may wonder where they got the expression *Mele Kalikamaka*. Simple. That's the only way they could pronounce Merry Christmas with the phonemes in their language. (Since they had no written language until the missionaries gave them an alphabet, it's not accurate to say they had twelve of our letters: that's the way it sounded to the Greek- and Latin-trained New Englanders who transcribed the Hawaiian language for the first time.)

In recent times, too, Polynesian scholars have insisted on an eighth consonant, the glottal closure, an almost inaudible click in the throat which slows down the pronunciation of contiguous syllables. It is represented by an inverted comma in writing and printing. A fine point unless you should be using the three "simple" words *'a'i*, which means "the neck"; 'ai, "food"; and *ai*, "sexual intercourse." Two little letters, instead of three little words, but you'd better keep one ear on your glottal stops if you use them! Diphthongs are too complicated to go into here, so look in Judd-Pukui for the details.

Grammatically, nouns generally come before their adjectives. And verbs precede their subjects. The same word is very often used as a noun, adjective, adverb, or verb with no change in pronunciation. But for the most part, you will meet only Hawaiian words, not sentences, mixed in as well with the pidgin of the beach boy as with the cultivated American of the professors at the university.

A Malihini's Dictionary

alii: a chief or noble.

aloha: a greeting that means hello, farewell, fond greetings, or (in its subtler psychological ramifications, I've found) whatever a *kamaaina* wants it to mean.

hala: a tree, the leaves of which (*lauhala*) are used in making roofs, mats, and very many other things.

haole: originally, foreigner, but now mainly white person.

heiau: temple.

holoku: a long, brightly colored dress with a train used at formal dances and other high occasions. The loose-fitting garment, (which the missionaries contrived in order to get the naked Hawaiians used to clothing) felt so good, in its looseness, to Kamehameha the Great's queen that she exclaimed, *"Holoku!"* (We can run in it). And they still do, but most have forgotten where the name came from.

hukilau: a community fishing party.

hula: an ancient dance that tells a story.

imu: the cooking pit in which the *luau* is prepared.

kahili: a symbol of royal office, a long pole with red and yellow feathers on top.

kahuna: a name for a specially trained person in the old kingdom, from a man who caught the special red and yellow feathers for cloaks, helmets, and *kahilis,* for priests and witch doctors.

kamaaina: old-timer, but the original meaning is "child of the land."

Kamuela: the Parker Ranch "capital," the way the Hawaiians said "Samuel," one of the early Parkers.

kapa: the inner bark of the mulberry tree or the special cloth made from it.

kaukau: food.

koa: a tree of fine-grained wood that used to be used in the construction of canoes. Because it is scarce, it now appears mostly in bowls and souvenirs. But you can see handsome large objects made of it in the Bishop Museum.

kona: the side of an island away from the prevailing winds. Look at a map of Hawaii (the island, not the state) and try to figure out what would be the Kona coast if the prevailing winds were blowing in a southwesterly direction from Alaska to Hawaii.

kona weather: the hot, muggy kind that generally inflicts Oahu from the direction of the Kona coast of Hawaii.

lanai: porch.

lehua: the fluffy red flower from the ohia tree.

lei: a garland of flowers.

luau: a Hawaiian feast.

makahiki: a Hawaiian Olympics or sports tournament held in the harvest season; literally "year."

malo: a loincloth.

opu: stomach.

paniolo: Hawaiian cowboy, so called because the Mexicans who taught the natives the skills of cowpunching spoke *español*.

pau ka hana: work is done.

pilikia: trouble.

ukulele: the small, four-stringed instrument shaped like a guitar, introduced to Hawaii by the Portuguese. In Hawaiian the word means "jumping flea," a metaphor for the swiftly flying fingers needed to play the uke.

ti: a palm plant, the leaves of which are used to make hula skirts.

Authentic Hawaiiana

A BRIEF LAYMAN'S GUIDE TO LEIS

Although Hawaiians have used flowers for centuries in ceremonies of friendship, it was not until tourism began to expand in the 1920's that the lei became almost synonymous with Aloha hospitality. In 1928, one spring day, Don Blanding, of the *Star-Bulletin*'s advertising department, had a bright idea. Why not set aside a day each year when every island inhabitant would wear a flower lei? Grace Tower Warren, that paper's society editor, suggested that May Day be Lei Day. And it has been ever since. The *Star-Bulletin* promoted the idea in its pages, and the Bank of Hawaii offered the lobby of its new building as a display for the leis. A contest for the best leis was started, and a Lei Day Queen selected. Not until you've been through a Lei Day can you really appreciate the profusion of Hawaii's flowers and plants. Today it is the occasion for a kind of horticultural one-upmanship. "To wear a lei on Lei Day means you are a lover of Hawaii" became the motto for the event. And so a lovely tradition began expanding the already attractive one of giving leis throughout the year as a gesture of aloha and love.

The spirit of the lei is infectious, and we were delighted to see our eight-year-old daughter start threading her own leis with a sewing needle and thread (there are special lei needles and string) from plumeria trees in the front yard. The announcement of a forthcoming visit to the airport to pick up a visitor or news that a friend of hers was about to go to the mainland would send her packing with a plastic bag to the nearest plumeria tree. I won't say that these were the handsomest leis I saw on the islands, but, crude as they sometimes were, they were great fun to make for the feeling of participation they gave in the unique life of the islands. Don't let your small children send a visitor away without trying their hands at lei making. You can interest them in this custom by relating some of its history and pointing out the astonishing range of materials available for lei making, of which the plumeria is simply the easiest to start with.

(Hotel flower shops charge about twice what street and wharf-stall owners do.)

Carnation: A nonindigenous flower frequently used. Seventy for a single garland! Tend to be expensive.

Gardenia: Enduringly beautiful and fragrant. About thirty-five to a lei.

Ginger: Probably the commonest lei flower in all its many colors and varieties. White and pale yellow are most popular colors. Their Latinate scientific names mean, poetically, "sweet snow." You can count on two or three days of powerful fragrance from one lei hung in a room.

Ilima: This is an orange to yellow flower that is the official bloom of Oahu. Almost extinct, which explains the ugly, glow-in-the-dark orange paper leis.

Lehua: This red flower grows on the ohia tree almost in the bowels of the volcanoes on the Big Island. Given its location and color, it is understandable that it is Pele's flower. The color is much like that of the iiwi bird, now practically extinct, from which red plumage for feather cloaks was plucked in the old kingdom.

Lokelani (also roselani): This is the flower of Maui. Related to the rose, it is pink to red in color. Beetles have been giving it a hard time lately.

Maile: This is a glossy leaf, not a true flower. It is regarded as symbolic of the poetic spirit.

Mauna Loa: This is the purple flower of a lowly bean. They resemble pairs of wings and are sewn in a tight row on a narrow tape.

Mokihana: This purple berry is used on Kauai to make leis.

Orchids: It confounds mainland economics to get a leiful of these for a dollar. Everyone is orchid-rich in Hawaii.

Pikake: This is a species of white jasmine from which an island perfume is also made. Because it is fragile and hard to grow, leis made of it are rare. It is a considerable honor to receive one. If you aren't that lucky, you can see Pikake Gardens, east of Diamond Head, at 4192 Huanui Street.

Plumeria: This is everyman's lei material. There are other names for the flower honoring the French botanist Charles Plumier: frangipani, temple flower, *pua melia* (which is how it sounded to the Hawaiian's ear). It has five petals, white on the rim to yellow in the center in the most common variety, and rose and cherry in other kinds. It is the easiest kind to learn lei making with.

Loraine E. Kuck's *Hawaiian Leis and How to Make Them* is an illustrated booklet recommended for those who would like to do-it-themselves in the art of lei making. While it isn't recommended to *save* money (where can you buy on the mainland for a dollar the thirty-five or so gardenias, seventy or more carnations, and over fifty orchids that go into their respective varieties of leis?), it is fun.

THE HULA

The revival of the authentic hula is an impressive achievement in "applied ethnology." It reminds mainland Americans that history and culture don't have to be cheapened to become economically useful. The Bishop Museum and the state's Department of Education deserve special commendation here.

The hula has almost become a trademark of Hawaii, but miles of Hollywood celluloid have perhaps distorted the true picture of the dance and its meaning. Take the grass skirt, for example. Strictly speaking, such gear is for Samoan and Tahitian shake dances. The more mellifluous-looking hula should be danced with large ti leaves making the skirt. In the beginning the hula was a sacred dance to honor gods and praise chiefs. It was performed by trained dancers. Women wore the short skirt or pa'u; men wore a tapa-cloth malo. Especially impressive was the ceremonial, pure-white pa'u. Whale-tooth or bone necklaces and bracelets added to the décor of the professional dancers. The hula school was called the *halau*. While they were being trained, the dancers lived in, under strict rules. Since the hula repertoire included about two hundred separate dances, learning was no easy task. The hula teacher, called the *kumu hula*, taught chants and prayers as well as dances. Chants were sung on two notes only, to the accompaniment of rattles and drums. Songs (*meles*) had two or three notes and were delivered mainly by poets. *Meles* were handed down from father to son through the generations. Some songs were prayers; others were love songs. Through them family history was kept alive. A bard might have a hundred *meles* on the tip of his tongue. Dancing usually accompanied the singing of *meles*. Due to missionary disapproval of those scantily clad, gently undulating hips, the hula went underground until King Kalakaua, the Merry Monarch, revived it. When he crowned himself Kalakaua Rex, some two hundred *hulas* were danced, a testimonial to the endurance of this submerged art form.

There are several instruments generally used in hula dancing. The *pu ili* is made of split bamboo and makes a rattling sound when one of a dancing pair strikes the other's *pu ilis*. *Ili ili* are small, smooth stones clicked together, two by two, by each dancer holding a pair in his hands. A hollow gourd that makes an eerie set of sounds when hit in syncopation against various parts of the body is called the *ipu*. Seed-filled gourds that make sounds much like those of Latin American maracas, are called *uli uli*. Nowadays feathers in the royal yellow and red are added to enhance the color of *uli uli*.

For understanding the storytelling part of hula, it is necessary to master its basic "vocabulary." Hand positions and gestures for waves, clouds, stars, flowers, and water are easy for even the newcomer to decipher. Others are not much harder: a rainbow is suggested by arching finger tips; rolling one hand over another brings to mind an image of the rolling surf. To close a story, a hula dancer brings both hands forward palms down. To dance the hula correctly, you must learn to bend your knees and keep your feet flat on the floor as the body shifts back and forth in a pattern resembling a figure eight. If you really want to see some fancy hulaing, go to Kapiolani Park during the summer hula festival.

The old hula survived in two environments despite the displeasure of the missionaries. In remote districts the old people tried to keep their customs alive; that is why most of the surviving hulas come from Kauai, which has always been the most isolated island. Mrs. Pukui's collection of eight hundred ninety-three hulas was mostly from the Garden Island. Every time there was a royal progress through a village, it was customary to create a hula for the event. This was as *de rigueur* as making a feast for the great visitors. Mrs. Pukui believes that thirty or forty of these dignified and serious hulas still survive. The other environment where the hula led a kind of underground existence was in the brothels, where it was souped up to the sailor's sense of the bawdy.

In the most finished type of hula, gestures were very slight: a lifted eyebrow meant assent; a wriggle of the nose, refusal. What Westerners would regard as lewd hulas were danced for a serious purpose: sexual excitation to bring children to the childless. Only married people took part in this dance, in which the *kumu* hula would touch a man and a woman who would then retire to the dark. They might remain together for several days or until it seemed likely that conception had taken place. Issue from such liaisons was ascribed to the husband's genealogy. This particular dance was called the *ume*, which means "attraction" or "coming together."

SURFING: THE SPORT AND ITS LORE

Between 1860 and 1910 surfing almost died out in Hawaii. Then Alexander Hume Ford, a journalist and the precocious playwright of *The Little Confederate*, came to the islands in 1910 looking for dramatic material. Instead he found a culture to trumpet to the world. He was particularly struck with the possibilities of reviving surf riding, which by then was practiced only occasionally at Lahaina. He soon learned how to surf and started to teach others the old sport. He begged the site for the Outrigger Canoe Club from the Queen Emma estate, and before long he had made the surfer the image of Hawaii. Ford also helped found the Pan-Pacific Institute to make Honolulu the cultural and intellectual center of the Pacific.

Nathaniel B. Emerson contends that the sport was not restricted to nobility in the old days, as so often is heard. In ancient times the boards were ridden in a reclining position. The ancient *olo* (long) board was comparatively narrow and thick—about six inches—and convex on top and bottom, which made it too unstable for a standing ride. Some of the surfboards of koa wood used by the old Hawaiian chiefs have been found to weigh as much as two hundred twenty pounds, compared with the twenty-five to forty pounds of today's plastic boards.

The *wiliwili* boards were sometimes eighteen feet long and weighed one hundred fifty pounds. They were stained black, dried in the sun after use, rubbed with coconut oil, and put under a roof until needed again. Only chiefs used these big boards, which were thicker, tapering and convex on both sides, in contrast with the six-foot boards, made of koa or breadfruit wood, which were thin and nearly flat. Modern boards are six inches wider than the ancient eighteen-inch boards, flat on the top with a slightly convex bottom.

Back in the 1930's, when the hollow surfboard was not yet wholly accepted, Tom Blake and Olympic swimmer Duke Kahanamoku conducted a lifesaving test with a sailor "drowning" one hundred yards behind his ship. The surfers had the man back aboard before a lifeboat manned by six men was free from the ship. That is why the American Red Cross considers the hollow surfboard the most efficient kind of lifesaving equipment ever invented. A Hawaiian rescue squad always has one.

One of the early surfing authorities, Tom Blake, pointed out that the average ride on a surfboard at Waikiki is not over two hundred yards, and the surf must be running *blow-hole-break* to make this ride. When the surf gets a little larger it is called *first-break*, and a rider can cover a maximum of three hundred yards. Only about three times a year does the great *kalahuewehe*, or Castle-break, run. With it you can ride the maximum distance all the way to shore.

Surfing has its mythmakers as well as its humorists. Umi was perhaps the world's grumpiest surfer in history. He was the high-living son of a king of Hawaii who insisted for his son's safety that Umi travel incognito on his pleasure and adventure trips. Once Umi got wind of a surfing carnival at Laupahoehoe on the Big Island and sent a challenge. He raced against one of the local petty chiefs, named Paeia, for the high stakes of four large outrigger canoes (two-thousand-dollar value). Umi won after a most exhilarating contest. But several years later, when he became king at his father's death, he went to Hilo to have Paeia sacrificed at the local *heiau* for allegedly bumping his board slightly during their contest.

THE KAAHUMANU SOCIETY

The black *holoku* and yellow feather lei are the official garb of one of Hawaii's prominent women's groups, the Ahahui (or Society) Kaahumanu. You will easily recognize this society by its distinctive costume at the Kamehameha Day parade and other patriotic Hawaiian celebrations. It was founded in 1905 by a group of public-spirited women of Hawaiian blood who were distressed that no attention was being paid to the graves of the *aliis* at the Royal Mausoleum. They assumed the duties of supplying leis and flowers on significant Hawaiian feast days. Later they began to take care of funerals of their own members. In 1962 there were four hundred fifty members in chapters on Kauai, Maui, Molokai, and Oahu. All part- or full-blooded Hawaiian women between eighteen and sixty are eligible for membership.

Hawaii can be just tropical relaxation, which is value

enough for the nerve-frazzled mainland American. But, to get more subtle values out of a visit, you should dig more deeply into this unique culture—as I have tried to lure you to do—with these vignettes on its language and customs. There is much more, all of it endlessly fascinating.

Chapter II

AMERICA DISCOVERS PARADISE

A Tourist's History of Hawaii

Two or three million years ago, a great convulsion on the floor of the Pacific began the formation of a two-thousand-mile chain of islands, the last four hundred miles of which are visible as the Hawaiian Islands. The ocean was three miles deep before submarine volcanoes started to push land up toward the surface. The successive layers of lava along a two-thousand-mile fissure in the floor of the Pacific had to displace 6435 square miles of ocean to form the eight larger islands in the Hawaiian group. Ages later, the hard lava had been weathered into soil by the rains brought by unceasing trade winds. The trades that come from a prevailing north-easterly direction gather moisture clouds in their long trek across the ocean from Alaska. When they hit the barrier of the mountains, they are pushed up into cooler atmosphere; this condenses much of the moisture into rain that falls on the windward side, leaving the lee side relatively dry, so that irrigation is needed for most agriculture there. What kept the soil from washing away at sea? The millions of coral animals whose skeletons over the ages built protective barriers around many of the islands.

How Hawaii got its flora is a fascinating problem in speculative botany. Eighty-three per cent of the plants growing in the Hawaiian Islands are endemic—more than anywhere else in the world. It is generally agreed that the postvolcanic land lay completely bereft of vegetation for many thousands of years. Although the Hawaiian Islands look like tropical islands, they are really only semitropical, a zone of moderate climate between steamy equatorial jungles and arctic coolness. The first plants to take root in the first soil that gathered in rain pockets were probably ferns and mosses. They grow from spores, tiny organisms smaller than seeds, so small that they can fly high in the air like dust. Seeds had a harder transit. It is guessed that birds caught seeds in their feathers or in dirt on their feet; given a long enough time, the odds were that one would catch on, and then reproduction took over. Other seeds may have been eaten by birds and survived when they were excreted in a kind of ready-made fertilizer package. Still other plants came by ocean currents. The hala, or pandanus, tree, from the leaves (*laus*) of which *lauhala* mats and sundry other things are made, probably came this way. Notice when you circle the islands how hala can be seen near the beach. Plants with large seeds, say, the coconut, could have traversed the long voyage from the Southwest Pacific safely alive. Smaller ones might have gotten a ride on a log or branches that resembled a raft.

Insects like flies and beetles were probably blown to the islands. Birds may have become lost in their transoceanic rendezvous. Slowly, all these flora and fauna adapted to the varied conditions of the islands: seashore salinity, lowlands, dry places, wet and shady valleys, rain forests, and forbidding mountain peaks. Aeons later the Hawaiians came and found a lush, verdant paradise to which they brought pigs, chickens, and a variety of domesticated vegetables. Captain Cook added goats and some melons, pumpkins, and onions. Captain Vancouver did his bit with sheep and cows. From India came the contributions of plumeria and mango. Africa donated the beautiful shower trees of many shades. Japan gave the plum. The missionaries brought still more fruits and vegetables. That is why Hawaii today is a kind of garden place of the world, the very pleasing result of several centuries of international horticultural exchange.

The original Hawaiians lived here for fourteen centuries before the coming of the *haole* (which literally means "foreigner" but has come to mean "white"). They are part of the Polynesian family that had discovered and peopled the central and southern islands of the Pacific long before Europe entered its Age of Discovery. It still staggers the imagination to try to understand how these intrepid explorers even managed to *find* the islands they populated. When our European forebears scarcely dared to venture beyond the Mediterranean, Polynesian sailors crossed thousands of miles of the uncharted Pacific.

How did they do it? By using sun, clouds, currents, waves, stars, and birds as navigational devices. By watching the patterns of waves, the navigator with a really experienced eye could sense the presence of land ahead by turbulence. Cloud masses might also reveal a far-off mountain. The Polynesian sailor could identify one hundred fifty stars by name, could place them by latitude, and knew how they changed position throughout the year. (Visit the Bishop Museum's planetarium if you can when they are giving their popular program on the skies as the Polynesian saw them.) Not all of the sailors made it, but enough followed to ensure the success of these migrations.

There are many theories of Polynesian migration. You may even have read about Thor Heyerdahl's voyage on the Kon-Tiki to prove one theory. The most widely held theory now is that the ancestors of the Polynesians left Southeast Asia for the western islands of Indonesia before the Christian era began. Gradually, they either moved or were pushed farther and farther east until about A.D. 100 or 200 they had reached Hawaii and the central islands of the Polynesian triangle (Hawaii, New Zealand, and Easter Island are its three points).

Anthropologists used to believe that the migration ran eastward through Indonesia, along the New Guinea coast, through Melanesia to Central Polynesia, whence the race spread to outlying islands. There is now strong evidence, however, to support an alternative theory. This route is more northerly; it goes through Micronesia, with one group leaving the eastern Carolines northeastward to Hawaii, and a larger one going in a southeasterly direction into Central Polynesia. However this prehistory is extremely speculative. Some believe that the discoverers and earliest inhabitants of Hawaii arrived directly from Central Polynesia.

The eighteenth-century European discoverers of Oceania were astonished at the speed of the Polynesian canoes: some of them achieved the unbelievable speed of twenty knots. A great voyaging canoe could make a hundred miles a day with a good wind and was able to stay at sea for as much as a month if necessary. When fresh food was exhausted, the rowers lived on dried foods, such as pandanus flour, cooked breadfruit, and sweet potato. Double canoes of sixty to eighty feet in length could hold as many as sixty people on a deck between the two boats. Religion hallowed canoe making, as it did every important activity in Hawaiian life. For example, when two men made canoes, one working on the outside, one inside, they offered prayers and chants to Tane, the god of forests and crafts. "Awake to work for Tane, great god of the artisans!" they chanted as their stone tools smoked from continued friction with the wood they hewed. They made such objects well to please the god Tane. When a canoe was finished, they celebrated and covered it with flowers as it slid into the waters for a shakedown float.

When an outrigger is first launched, a young pig is put into the boat. If it lies still, the canoe will be a slow one. If it runs back and forth and tries to get out, you're lucky: you have a fast racing canoe. The first day the canoe is in the water it belongs to everybody, and anyone who wants can take a spin in it. The kahuna has a prayer to bless a new canoe with:

> Uplifter of the heavens, Uplifter of the earth,
> Uplifter of the mountains, Uplifter of the ocean,
> Grant a canoe that shall be swift as a fish,
> To sail in stormy seas,
> When the storm tosses on all sides.

It takes three years for a log of Hawaiian mahogany or koa to dry out enough to be worked into a canoe. Sometimes the birds get at the trunk and wreck it. In olden days, hot stones were used to burn out the center of the canoe. This had the effect of searing the pores of the wood shut, making it watertight. The koa is very hard wood and takes a high polish; outriggers are made of hau. Finishing is done with coconut and *kukui*-nut oil. Wiliwili used to be used for surfboards and canoes, but it is rare now; it and large haus have been destroyed by lava.

However they got here, the first Hawaiians lived isolated from the rest of Polynesia for several hundred years. Radiocarbon dating puts the first level of debris on the earliest site yet uncovered on the island of Hawaii as 957, plus or minus two hundred years. These first settlers were transformed by later legend into the mythical *menehunes*, indefatigable dwarfs who performed extraordinarily rapid engineering feats in constructing temples, fishponds, and watercourses.

Sometime between the beginning of the eleventh century and the end of the fourteenth, the Polynesian area underwent another great period of migration, lasting about two centuries. Central Polynesian mariners visited Hawaii, and Hawaiian navigators repaid the visits by voyaging south. It was the Polynesians from the south at this time who brought all the cultivated plants as well as dogs, pigs, chickens, and the paper mulberry tree. Their culture was more highly developed than that of the *menehunes*, and the invading chiefs (*aliis*) soon took over control of the island chain. The new priests took over the temples and introduced new observances and some new divinities.

When the long voyages ended, Hawaii once again enjoyed several centuries of isolation. As the population increased, *alii* struggled to enlarge their small landholdings until finally there emerged four kingdoms dominated by the families of the chiefs on the larger islands—Hawaii, Maui, Oahu, and Kauai. Once in a while a smaller island became independent, but generally it was held as a prize of war by a dominant neighbor. These political conditions were very volatile, since they depended on the rise and fall of individual leaders. Every so often a particularly ambitious chief would set out to conquer the entire chain, but no one did so until Kamehameha, and he succeeded probably because of the shrewd advantage he took of the white man's tools of war.

In many ways Hawaii before the white man resembled feudal Europe of the Middle Ages. Chiefs at the top ruled without cavil the common people, who did the dirty work at the bottom. There was a class of kahunas (doctors, priests, navigators, and other skilled technicians of the primitive Hawaiian arts and sciences), but they were beholden to their chief, who stayed in power partly through their talents. The political volatility of the islands made wars frequent and bloody. Each top chief owned the land and divided it among his retainers, but he could and did repossess. The common people were attached to the soil, where they worked not only their own taro patches but also the lands of the chief to whom they owed fealty. Their chief also got part of their own produce and part of their fishing catches.

Most of the Hawaiians lived next to the sea or within sight of it. They fished for a good part of their food and for recreation. Be sure to look closely in the Bishop Museum at the marvelous facility of the Hawaiian fisherman; his hooks and lines and lures and sinkers are a triumph of imagination over limited resources. And notice the fantastic husbandry in the Polynesian exploitation of the coconut.

It was a man's responsibility to provide food. The two biggest staples in the diet were poi and fish. You can see poi made at Ulu Mau Village—in Honolulu's Ala Moana Park— from its growth in a taro patch to the intricate pounding and wetting with a mortar-and-pestle-like affair that produces the sticky stuff that I still think tastes like library paste, with or without raw salt! (One of the nicest natural patterns in Hawaii is the quilt work of taro patches seen from a great height. Two spots especially good for this purpose are near Hanalei, on Kauai, and at the Wailua Overlook, on the way to Hana, on Maui.)

The taro from which poi is made is one of the most concentrated plants man has found. According to G. W. Bates, one square mile of "wet land" taro could support over fifteen thousand Hawaiians a year. Because taro has to have a lot of water like rice, taro patches have raised ridges like those of rice paddies. To get the large amount of water needed, the Hawaiians devised irrigation systems. The taro farmer had to work up to his waist in mud. Foreigners often thought that the Hawaiians were lazy because they rested all day; they didn't realize that the shrewd native used the cool moonlight hours to wrestle his taro patch in the mud.

Fresh water has always been a problem in the middle of the Pacific. The importance of irrigation in ancient Hawaiian times may be inferred from the linguistic fact that *kanawais* (or "water rules") became the generic term for all laws. A further indication of the importance of water can be seen in the word for wealth, *waiwai*, the word for "water" duplicated.

Preparing the daily poi was an arduous task. First the root had to be steamed for hours in an underground oven, or *imu*, to break up the tiny, sharp crystals that cut the tongue if not cooked enough. Poi dough could be dried and kept for weeks, at which time water turned the "instant" paste into poi. (The best place to see this process at work today is the Saturday *hukilau*, or fishing party, at the Church College in Laie on the windward side of Oahu.) Just getting the oven fire started was no mean trick. It had to be made with a Polynesian invention called the "fire plow." This was a pointed stick that was rubbed fast and hard along a groove in a plank until wood dust smoked enough to set flame to tinder.

Starchy poi led to obesity, but it was a sign of status to be fat—I mean *really* fat. Women often weighed three hundred pounds; ruling chiefs and their wives hit the four-hundred-pound mark. Along with poi there were less extensively used vegetables, such as sweet potatoes, yams, coconuts, breadfruit, sugar cane, arrowroot, and seaweed. Pigs, chickens, and dogs were also raised to be eaten. The Hawaiians did not know the "three squares a day" tradition of the American. When food was plentiful, he might eat five or six times a day and get up for a midnight snack. In times of scarcity, he could go for two or three days without a meal.

The Golden Rule of Hawaiian life was hospitality. It was a cardinal belief of their "world view" that the gods would look after those who shared what they had with a stranger or visitor. This hospitality ethos of old Hawaii is fascinating. An ancient Hawaiian who permitted a stranger to depart from his door hungry was subject to public shame. Houses were left unlocked so a visitor could use what was there when he dropped in. There was usually a common taro field in each village just to provide for visitors. When a visitor came, neighbors dropped in to question him so they might capitalize on his next move by giving the next hospitality. An entire village rallied to make the entertainment of the guest as generous as possible. These are the historical roots of the aloha tradition.

While the men ensured the food supply, the women tended the children, wove mats, and made bark cloth from the mulberry tree. This kapa, or tapa, was extremely difficult to make, and one of the cultural cliff-hangers of Ulu Mau Village is whether or not Mrs. Solomon will recover the art of tapa making. She has even been given research grants to visit South Pacific islands in her efforts to recover this lost craft of her forebears. Some of the handsomest indigenous fashions by the way are patterned after the almost modernistically geometric abstractions of tapa decoration. Dyes made from natural materials in shades of gray, blue, brown, yellow, and red were used in printing tapa cloth.

Little clothing was used before the white sailor brought venereal diseases; and the missionaries, Western notions of sexual propriety. Women wore short skirts. Men wore the malo, or loincloth. More for magnificence than modesty, long robes of tapa were worn by those who could afford them. In rainy seasons (today called "kona weather" by a grim chamber of commerce) matting was worn. You can see examples of clothing and jewelry at the Bishop Museum.

The name of the *holoku*, or long dress, has many explanations. One interesting but possibly apocryphal story says that, when the natives watched the missionaries use the sewing machine to make the long-sleeved, loose-fitting dresses, they named them after the machine, which stopped and then started, after the Hawaiian words for go (*holo*) and stop (*ku*). Male Hawaiians at first didn't like the notion that as soldiers they had to keep their uniforms on. When the Englishman George Beckley was put in command of the fort at Honolulu, he introduced the tradition of uniforms for the garrison. When he insisted that the soldiers wear them, he earned the sobriquet Humehume (Cover Up).

Most splendid of all, of course, are the Hawaiian feather cloaks and helmets woven from the plumage of thousands of small birds. It is copies of these that greet you as you disembark from plane or boat. Don't fail to see the real thing at Bishop Museum. There was a special cadre of feather gatherers who had to snare the precious mamo and o-o birds to get the rare feathers that made the royal cloaks. Only two yellow feathers could be taken per bird; therefore, the kahunas who specialized in bird gathering contrived a snare that would catch the birds with the unique feathers and allow them to be released to grow more for another *alii* another day. Stalking birds for feather capes was thus an exacting task. Certain birds were mostly in the mountains, so hunting expeditions of several days had to be organized. Red feathers from the *iwi*, green feathers from the *u*, orange from the mamo, and white from the *ku ula* extended the palette, whose basic color was the yellow of the o-o, the bird that supplied yellow and black feathers. No dyes of any kind were used in these cloaks, which explains their continuing brilliance of color over these many years. Some of the birds were killed with a sling made of a pointed stone tied to a coconut string fiber. After lying in wait, a stalker would whirl the stone around and launch it with consummate accuracy at the frequently small birds. Nets and snares were preferred for reasons of conservation, however.

The *kahili*, now a stylized emblem of royalty, once had a very functional purpose: it was a high-class fly swatter. While the chief slept, attendants waved the *kahili* over him to discourage insects. Only an *alii* could have such equipment, some of which (but not most) were thirty feet high.

Fighting was a staple of this Stone Age culture, as of many others. A great deal of time went into the making of weapons: hardwood spears with polished points, daggers and clubs carved from wood, swords fashioned from bones or shark's teeth. Hau fibers were braided to form slings for the casting of smooth round stones.

Mark Twain may have sneered that the coco palm looked like a feather duster struck by lightning, but you can't look in the Bishop Museum or Ulu Mau Village for long without being amazed at the versatile ways the Polynesians used the coconut. On some islands that have no drinkable water or only that caught in rain showers, the milk is prized as the only beverage. The meat is eaten plain or mixed into taro, yam, and sago puddings. Oil squeezed from the meat becomes food, an unguent, or cosmetic. A hollowed shell serves admirably as a flask; a clean, scraped shell becomes a cup or spoon; it can also be the raw material for carved ornaments. The fibrous husk that separates the nut from the hard outer shell can be used to make cord. The tough trunk of the tree can be turned into furniture, building timbers, utensils. Huts are thatched and baskets woven from the coconut's leaves.

And when a palm is felled its pith is eaten. On islands nearer to Asia, the sap's sugar is drawn off by tapping the flower bud and fermented into an intoxicating drink.

Since the coco palm requires warm temperature the year round, a lot of sunlight and moisture, and well-drained soil to grow, these trees do best in low altitudes near the coast. The seed is the mature, fallen nut—a hollow kernel of oily white meat a half inch in thickness, encased, as any *malihini* knows who has tried to shuck one, in a hard woody shell. A palm begins to bear in eight to ten years and lives for almost eighty years. One tree produces about fifty nuts a year, a horticultural fact that keeps a good many tree-trimming parties at work anticipating the trees' inhospitality to unsuspecting tourists.

The "little grass shack" of the kitschy tourist ditty snubs an edifice that took great skill to erect. Take a look at the structures in Ulu Mau Village at Ala Moana Park, to get some respect for the Polynesian as architect before the Westerner brought him saws and other metal tools. The old Hawaiians spent a great deal of time erecting these buildings, since each family required several of them. The *kapu* (or taboo) system was the cause of this decentralization of Hawaiian domestic architecture. Because a woman couldn't eat or work under the same roof as a man, there had to be a separate female hut. There was also a separate house for the family idols. Some Hawaiians stored their food in separate houses; some made their canoes in still another. So it was not uncommon for one family to have as many as six houses. It was a tough job to build even one, because the Hawaiians had neither beast of burden nor the wheel. They carried both framing logs and pili grass for thatching on their backs. House-raising, not surprisingly, under this primitive technology became a communal affair followed by prayers and feasting when the house was completed. A thatched roof of grass, sugar cane, or ti leaves would last five to ten years. The 'ie vine, or sennit, that held the roof on was actually superior to the nails the Hawaiians later became so fond of, because the "give" of the vines was better suited to the high winds than were rigid nails.

Robert C. Suggs has pointed out in *The Island Civiliza-*

tions of Polynesia (Mentor, 1960) that one of the chief difficulties facing the ethnologist and archaeologist who wants to re-create what early Hawaiian art styles were like is the perishability of the materials they used. The wood and vegetable fibers they relied on so much in their material culture simply don't last under these climatic conditions. The Bishop Museum collections show what an able craftsman the Hawaiian was technically. There you can see mats of intricately woven fine strands, the exquisite feather cloaks and helmets, the grand *kahilis*, glossy wooden bowls, drinking gourds with geometric designs and whale-tooth neck amulets.

The notable exception, of course, is the petroglyph, literally "rock writing." These drawings, which are found all over the islands, represent, sometimes with a striking economy of style, men, gods, lizards, canoes, turtles, and other images. It appears that these images were chipped or incised into the rock surfaces as doodles while two natives passed the time of day. Some of the glyphs probably had a more formal origin, to indicate important locations or to memorialize significant events. These designs are used in striking ways in contemporary Hawaiian art. The mailing wrapper of *The Conch Shell* (the Bishop Museum quarterly members' bulletin) uses a petroglyph, as do aloha shirts and some Christmas cards. They are Stone Age images that appeal strongly to jet-age sensibility.

Of ancient Hawaiian sports the most prestigious was ti-leaf sliding. Chiefs used to coast down the steep hills on narrow sleds; children imitate them today with the same muddy results. There were also Hawaiian forms of bowling, darts, throwing and guessing games, and a kind of checkers called *konane*. Spectator sports included military exercises, fake battles, and hula contests. Hula itself was valuable, not only as a form of entertainment, but also because it was both a system of physical training and a religious exercise. Remember *that* as you focus your ground glass at Kodak's weekly shutterbug session behind the beach at Queen's Surf off Kalakaua in Waikiki!

Religion was crucial to Hawaiian life. The proper ceremony had to sanctify every significant activity, whether making a house or canoe or starting a battle. The purpose of the ceremonies was to set up and maintain the proper relations between the community and the unseen power the Hawaiian sensed in the grand nature around him. Their gods personified natural objects and forces of nature. The Big Three of Hawaiian divinity were Kane, Lono, and Ku; Kane was the god of life and light; Lono (whom the Hawaiians thought they saw in Captain Cook, to his immediate benefit but ultimate disaster) was the god of the harvest; Ku was the deity of war. All Polynesia honored these three; it is believed that Ku was accorded the greatest worship in Hawaii.

A stone-paved platform or terrace, called a *heiau,* surrounded by stone walls was where the Hawaiians worshiped. One of the eeriest feelings I've ever had on the islands was standing on the *heiau* across Kealakekua Bay from where Captain Cook is memorialized. Like few other things in the now placid islands, these crude and savage stone heaps seem to symbolize for me that savage life before the white man. Human sacrifices were offered there.

The religious order was enforced by a *kapu* system. "*Kapu*" is a curt imperative you will soon notice on signs around the islands. It means that you are being warned or told not to do something "forbidden." It is also a kind of shorthand "no trespass" sign. In the old days, there were many things *kapu** that made you *kaput* if you tried. The idea originated in the distinction between what was sacred or divine and what was common or earthly, and between what was male and female. From this distinction derived many, many prohibitions for which the penalties were stunningly severe. A common person, for example, might not stand in the presence of the chief, who was sacred, or even touch his clothing, consciously or not. Women were not allowed to eat with men; in fact they couldn't eat such things as pork, bananas, coconut, and certain kinds of fish. The lesser chiefs shared the top chief's divinity to smaller degrees. Obviously great injustice could develop from an arbitrary system of this kind. The power of the kahunas, or priests, was great and the people understandably feared it. One ironic instance of self-fulfilling prophecy

---

* Think of *kapu* as *taboo,* since *k* and *t, p* and *b* are nearly interchangeable in Polynesian languages.

is that of a native stopping eating when he knew that a kahuna was praying him to death, thereby starving himself. The *kapu* system was enormously complex. Sometimes a *kapu* was very brief; other times it could last as long as thirty years. During a period of strict *kapu*, a village had to put all its lights and fires out; bathing and canoeing were forbidden; even animals were muzzled to insure quiet. (Chickens were put under calabashes!)

Like most primitive peoples, the old Hawaiians held the belief that you could control a man or do him harm if you got hold of anything directly connected with his body. The Hawaiian historian William Patterson Alexander, for example, noted: "It was absolutely necessary that the kahuna secure something connected with the person of the intended victim, as the parings of the nails, a lock of hair, the saliva from the mouth, etc., which was termed the mauna, or bait. For this reason the chiefs always kept their most faithful servants around them, who carefully buried or burned everything of the kind, or sunk it out at sea." Hence developed too the custom of spittle boxes, which every well-protected *alii* had carted around after him. One way the chiefs had of rubbing it in on a conquered opponent was to stud a slop basin with the teeth of the dead enemy.

The ancient chiefs were buried in the almost inaccessible niches that pock the steep cliffs above Kealakekua Bay. An *alii's* corpse was lowered from the top of the cliff by fiber ropes, then put into a cavity that was then sealed to discourage sacrilegious attempts at robbery. The dead man's personal possessions were entombed with him—costly materials such as kapa, calabashes, fishing nets, battle garments, even a canoe. To this very day, landslides and earthquakes keep revealing these well-covered sacred places.

Into the idyllic "paradise" of *kapu* and periodic wars came new complexities for the Hawaiians. At dawn on January 18, 1778, Captain Cook's two ships, the *Resolution* and the *Discovery*, en route from Tahiti sighted an island to their northeast and then soon another to the west of the first. They were thus the first white men to see Oahu and Kauai.

It is surprising in a way that it took the West so long to discover the group that Cook called the Sandwich Islands in honor of his patron and friend, the Earl of Sandwich. After all, men like Magellan and Drake had long ranged the Pacific. For over two hundred years the Manila galleons had risked scurvy in the long voyages between Mexico and the Philippines. Their routes, however, ran north and south of Hawaii. Ironically it was not a Spanish, Dutch, or Portuguese navigator but an Englishman who found the islands while looking for something that didn't exist—the Strait of Anian, which was to shorten the trip from Europe to Asia by going through North America.

Cook had surveyed the coast of Newfoundland from 1763 to 1767 after serving in the French and Indian War in America. In 1768 he went to Tahiti in command of an expedition to observe the planet Venus cross the sun and to explore the surrounding South Pacific. In this voyage he explored the Australian and New Zealand coasts and circled the globe in the *Endeavour*. Three voyages in ten years were to make him the most celebrated figure in his era in Pacific discovery.

On his third voyage he was supposed to go first to the Society Islands and from there to the American coast at about 45 degrees north latitude to search northward for the Northwest Passage. He had left Borabora in the Society Islands in December 1777. There is still no better way to read about his discovery than through his own vigorous prose:

The next morning [he wrote with James King in the posthumously published *A Voyage to the Pacific*, 1784] we stood in for the land, and were met with several canoes filled with people, some of whom took courage and ventured on board. In the course of my several voyages, I never before met with the natives of any place so much astonished as these people were upon entering a ship. Their eyes were continually flying from object to object; the wildness of their looks and gestures fully expressing their entire ignorance about everything they saw. . . .*

* The most convenient source for firsthand accounts is the admirable paperback edited by Day and Stroven, *A Hawaiian Reader* (Popular Library).

He marked their passion for bits of iron and later got a great feather cloak for a few pieces of the metal. But he had the usual attitude of the Western trader/explorer confronting the native. "They were," he noted, too, "in some respects naturally well bred, or at least fearful of giving offense, asking where they should sit down, whether they might spit upon the deck, and the like." They also "stole" everything in sight, or, to be more precise, took openly whatever they took a fancy to. This would lead inevitably to his own personal tragedy. Cook also reported that when he went ashore "the very instant I leaped on shore, the collected body of the natives fell flat upon their faces and remained in that very humble posture till by expressive signs I prevailed upon them to rise." He saw another aspect of their system of authority when a high chief came out to meet him aboard ship:

> He came off in a double canoe and, like the King of the Friendly Islands, paid no regard to the small canoes that happened to lie in his way, but ran against or over them, without endeavoring in the least to avoid them. And it was not possible for these poor people to avoid him, for they could not manage their canoes, it being a necessary mark of their submission that they should lie down till he had passed.

His eye for aesthetic detail and apt ethnological observation is remarkable. Take, for example, his description of the feather cloak:

> Amongst the articles which they brought to barter this day, we could not help taking notice of a particular sort of cloak and cap, which, even in countries where dress is more particularly attended to, might be reckoned elegant. The first are near of the size and shape of the short cloaks worn by the women of England and by the men in Spain, reaching to the middle of the back and tied loosely before. The ground of them is a network upon which the most beautiful red and yellow feathers are so closely fixed that the surface might be compared to the thickest and richest velvet, which they resemble, both as to the feel and the glossy appearance. The man-

ner of varying the mixture is very different; some having triangular space of red and yellow alternately; others, a kind of crescent; and some that were entirely red had a broad yellow border which made them appear, at some distance, exactly like a scarlet cloak edged with gold lace. The brilliant colors of the feathers, in those that happened to be new, added not a little to their fine appearance. . . .

The most interesting aspect of this meeting of the East and West (which continues to this day in Hawaii) is the freshness of the way the different parties greeted the discovery of each other: Consider, by contrast, the way a native reported how Cook's appearance looked to them:

It is at Waimea, on Kauai, that Lono first arrived . . . and when daylight came the natives ashore perceived this wonderful thing that had arrived, and they expressed their astonishment with great exclamations. One said to another, "What is that great thing with branches?" Others said, "It is a forest that has slid down into the sea," and the gabble and noise was great.

Cook remained for two weeks in the northern islands without discovering those members of the chain to the southeast of Oahu. He sailed on to the northwestern American coast to continue his explorations.

It was eight months before Cook returned. By then word of him had reached the windward islands of the chain. The natives decided that when he returned he should be worshiped as the god Lono, god of the *makahiki* (harvest) season. It has been suggested that to the natives' eyes the sails of Cook's squadron may have seemed to be the kapa banners of Lono in his *makahiki* procession. Late in November 1778, Cook raised the north coast of Maui and saw Molokai from afar. Maui's king, Kahekili, visited the *Discovery* and gave Cook's colleague a red feather cloak. Three days later the Big Island king, Kalaniopuu, who was at war with the Maui chief, spent the night aboard the *Resolution* with his retinue of chiefs. These visitors included Kamehameha, who was soon to parlay his close observation of white men's ways into a kingdom that lasted more than a century.

Cook toured the eastern end of Maui and the eastern and southern sides of Hawaii at his leisure until January 17, 1779, when the *Discovery* and the *Resolution* dropped anchor in Kealakekua Bay on the Kona coast of Hawaii. Ten thousand overjoyed natives greeted him. Ashore he was taken to the *heiau* of Hikiau. There he was acknowledged as the god Lono in a priestly ceremony. While the whites probably didn't comprehend the religious meaning of the ceremony, Cook was treated with adoring respect until the last day of his life.

The ships then refitted and provisioned for two and a half weeks to get ready for an arctic trip. King Kalaniopuu visited Cook once more on January 25 and they exchanged names and gifts. Cook received several feather cloaks, and gave the Hawaiian chief a linen shirt, a sword, and a complete chest of tools. On February 4 farewells were exchanged and the two ships started north along the Kona coast. A storm off Kohala forced them to return to Kealakekua Bay to repair the foremast of the *Resolution*. On the afternoon of February 13 there were several run-ins with the natives. The following morning they found that the *Discovery's* large cutter had been stolen in the night. Because Captain Clerke was sick, Cook went ashore to bring back King Kalaniopuu, intending to hold him hostage until the missing cutter was returned. But the tables were turned, and Cook was wounded and captured by the natives. Their chief, who had intended to hold but not kill Cook, heard the captain groan. At this the people shouted that because Cook felt pain he therefore was no god and they immediately slew him. Cook's bones were divided among the high chiefs and priests. After a week of more violence, most of Cook's bones were returned and buried in the waters of the bay on February 21.

The stage was now set for changes that were to bring this Stone Age culture into a world of jets and mass production in fewer than two hundred years.

KAMEHAMEHA I

The Hawaiian most revered for setting his people on the road to modernity is Kamehameha I, the first ruler of a united Hawaii. In 1796 began a period of peace during which "The Lonely One" used the power of his strong personality to establish the Hawaiian kingdom securely.

Kamehameha's birth has mythic overtones. When he was born on a stormy winter's night about 1758 in Halawa on the northern Kohala section of the Big Island, a kahuna told his mother, the High Chiefess Kekuipowa, that the infant would grow up to become a powerful ruler who would slay all rival chiefs. An uncle who then ruled the island got wind of the prophecy and decreed that the child be killed. Friends of the mother stole him away and hid him in a secret cave. The king's warriors found the cave but not the basket in which the baby was hidden. When the crisis seemed over, the friends took the young Kamehameha to live in a secluded valley until he was five, when another uncle, Kalaniopuu, high chief of Kau district, brought him to his court. His early isolation made him a lonely, secretive lad who became known as "The Lonely One," Ka Mehameha. His parents were nobles, and he grew up in the court on Hawaii, but he was not in line to succeed to the kingship. At the time the islands had four kingdoms, each under the control of an *alii-aimoku*, or leading chief. Kahekili, of Maui, and Kalaniopuu, of the Big Island, an uncle of Kamehameha, were the most important of the four.

Shortly after Captain Cook's visit, the old chief Kalaniopuu relinquished his power to his son, Kiwalao. He also made Kamehameha guardian of the war god. He was then given the magic conch shell of Kau. If you blew on this shell, the gods would help you. Should you be at sea without food, a blast on it would bring many fish; if you were without water, it would bring rain. Its powerful sound would vanquish the enemy in battle. In performing his role as defender of the war god, Kamehameha angered the new chief by sacrificing a captured rebel leader while Kiwalao was getting ready to do the same ritual, so Kamehameha withdrew from public life to his Kohala estate until after Kalaniopuu died in 1782. Then, responding to the inherent instability of the feudal land system, five Kona chiefs conspired with Kamehameha to be their leader for fear they would lose their lands in a reshuffling. In the battle that followed, Kiwalao died, and after the victory at Mokuohai the young chief divided the Big Island into three regions and he himself retained control of Kona, Kohala, and (the northeast) Hamakua. For a decade civil war flared as Kamehameha fought Keawemauhili of the Puna (southeastern) district, and Keoua of Kau (southwestern) district, as well as Maui's king, Kahekili.

An incident fondly recalled today by Hawaiians, one that reveals the magnanimity and stature of the emerging national leader, centers around the so-called Law of the Splintered Paddle (*Mamalahoe Kanawai*). While raiding the Puna coast, the chief leaped ashore alone to attack some fishermen. As he chased them, his foot caught in a lava crack; a particularly intrepid fisherman returned and splintered a canoe paddle over the trapped leader's skull. Later, when the attacker was brought to judgment, Kamehameha publicly admitted his own guilt for attacking innocent parties. To set a higher example, he gave the aggrieved parties gifts of lands. Some years later, remembering this incident, he called one of his decrees the Law of the Splintered Paddle: "Let the aged men and women and little children lie down in safety in the road."

In 1790 there occurred an incident that seemed incontestable proof that the fire goddess Pele was on the side of Kamehameha. He was now allied with Keawemauhili, chief of the Puna district, and was waging war against Oahu and Maui chiefs. Kiwalao's brother Keoua, chief of the Kau district, took advantage of Kamehameha's absence and invaded the Hilo district and killed his ally Keawemauhili. Keoua also inflicted severe damage on Waipio, in Hamakua, and Waimea, in Kohala. Kamehameha returned and began to push the invaders back into their home district of Kau. As Keoua's army passed by the Kilauea volcano, it erupted; the ash and smoke killed a third of his forces along with their families. How could one fight the favorite of Pele?

Keoua and Kamehameha soon reached a stalemate, each

mastering half of the island. Kamehameha consulted a famous oracle on Kauai that advised him to build a large *heiau*, or temple of worship, in honor of the war god at Puukohola, Kawaihae, on the northwest coast of his Kohala district. When the temple was finished, Kamehameha invited his archenemy Keoua to come to the holy place for a reconciliation. Instead, Keeaumoku, one of Kamehameha's chiefs, slew the leader of Kau as he came ashore. A rather startling contrast to the Law of the Splintered Paddle! Kamehameha then consolidated his power on the Big Island by slaying Keoua's companions. Thus in 1791, the king of the island of Hawaii was ready to begin forging a Kingdom of Hawaii.

The next big conflict was between him and Kahekili, who by now had added Molokai, Kauai, and Oahu to his control of Maui. Kamehameha had nearly destroyed Kahekili's army in 1790 in the famous battle of Iao Valley, where the stream beneath the Iao Needle landmark ran red with the blood of Kahekili's army. But at that point Kamehameha had to return to the Big Island to stop Keoua. And while Kamehameha was in the Puna district punishing Keoua, Maui's Kahekili and his brother Kaeo took this opportunity to avenge their defeat at Iao Valley by pillaging northern Hawaii. Clearly the sooner one chief could get (and keep) the upper hand the better for the people of all the islands. It seems probable that the factor that turned the tide in Kamehameha's favor was his use of foreign arms and recruits. The chiefs who were visited less by foreign traders thus suffered an insuperable disadvantage.

For example, when Kamehameha's canoes defeated the invading fleet of Maui's Kahekili off the northern coast of Hawaii, although both sides had small cannon obtained from fur traders, the Hawaiian weapons were better aimed because of the counsel of two seamen he had detained from passing American ships, Isaac Davis, of the *Fair American*, and John Young, boatswain of the *Eleanora*. Both had been made chiefs by Kamehameha and were a great help in the furtherance of his kingdom. Until 1795 the foes lived in a precarious truce, trying all the time to gain the crucial advantage by building up their own forces with the help of the foreign traders who gradually increased the frequency of their island visits.

When the old chief Kahekili died in the summer of 1794, he split his kingdom between his son Kalanikupule and his brother Kaeo. These two immediately began to squabble. Kalanikupule managed to kill Kaeo with the help of two trading vessels, the *Prince Lee Boo* and the *Jackal*, under Captain William Brown. After the battle Brown was murdered and his ships put in Kalanikupule's Oahu fleet. The British sailors who had been forced to run the ships under guard fled to Kamehameha's island and informed him of these events. Kamehameha thought that his time had come, so he assembled the greatest fleet of war canoes ever seen to that time and started his campaign: first Maui, then Molokai, then Oahu. After landing at Waikiki he marched to the Nuuanu Valley; there Kalanikupule waited with his army for a last-ditch stand. It was then that in a bitter losing battle, a great many of Kalanikupule's warriors were forced over the Nuuanu Pali (*pali* means "cliff") to be mangled on the rocks below.

Only Kauai and Niihau remained for the Alexander of the Pacific to conquer. An attempted invasion of Kauai in the spring of 1796 was a failure because a storm smashed his fleet. In the fall of 1796 he had to make a quick return to the Big Island to put down a last revolt. Since Kauai and Niihau were eventually to submit to his domain without a fight, his fighting days were over. He could now concentrate on organizing his kingdom. As a conquerer, according to Hawaiian practice, he owned everything, in feudal fashion. He rewarded his loyal chiefs with lands but also kept a number of valuable districts as a great private estate. His chiefs in turn subdivided their rewards among their loyal retainers. The four chiefs of Kona were rewarded for their loyalty by receiving the largest areas and by being appointed to a council of advisers with the right of succession to their sons. Kalanimoku, an able younger chieftain, was made prime minister and treasurer of the kingdom, the highest post next to that of the king. The separate islands were put under control of governors: John Young on the Big Island and Keeaumoku, a Kona chief, on Maui. Kamehameha's shrewd use of the white man's culture to consolidate his hold over a Stone Age people can be seen in part from the arsenal he had accumulated with the help of advisers like John Young by 1804: six hundred muskets, fourteen small cannon, and a score of armed sailing vessels.

The civil-war period had taken a fearsome toll on the islands. Famine was a common problem. For example, Kamehameha had tried to forestall possible rebellion on Oahu when he left there for Kauai by killing all the hogs on the island. Thousands were dying of starvation. The new king made an inspiring example by laboring to raise food with his own hands. He suppressed crime and disorder, and the country soon recovered from the demoralization of the civil-war years. Kamehameha's policy of fairness with foreign traders further aided the growth of prosperity. Sandalwood became an important commodity for export in the last decade of his life.

Kamehameha set up his court at Kailua when he returned to the Big Island. He spent considerable time speculating on how he would capture Kauai and for several years built a huge fleet of more than eight hundred large double canoes with sails and platforms, the fabled *peleleu* fleet. He first sailed this fleet to Maui; after a year there he sailed on to Oahu. His plans to move on to Kauai were interrupted by a great plague that broke out on Oahu. This *mai okuu* was probably cholera or bubonic plague and it killed a great many people, including all the other great chiefs besides Kamehameha, who nearly died himself.

Still he persisted in his ambition to conquer Kauai. By 1809 his fleet had almost fifty sailing vessels built at Waikiki, with the advice of the growing number of haoles now serving him. Kaumualii, Kauai's young king, sensed that the time had come for him to go to Honolulu and swear fealty to Kamehameha. He was permitted to rule Kauai in exchange for an annual tribute. The kingdom was formally complete.

One thing the new king could not understand was the distance between British royalty and its subjects. A Scottish sailor, Archibald Campbell, who was made a chief by the Hawaiian king when he was recovering from Alaskan frostbite in the islands, reported an interesting conversation.

Campbell was ready to leave for England in 1810 on the sealer *Duke of Portland*. Kamehameha asked him to give his compliments to King George. "I told him that, though born in his dominions, I had never seen King George; and that, even in the city where he lived, there were thousands who had never seen him. He expressed much surprise at this, and asked if he did not go amongst his people, to learn their wants, as he did? I answered that he did not do it himself, but that he had men who did it for him. Kamehameha shook his head at this, and said that other people could never do it as well as he could himself."

King Kamehameha enforced a strict adherence to the ancient Hawaiian religion. Since the war god had rewarded him with martial victories, he saw to it that as official guardian of this god these rites were performed. Other priests placated other deities. *Heiaus* were kept in good repair and new ones were erected. The *kapu* system was enforced. Executions for violating bans are recorded as late as 1817. Since the missionaries did not arrive until 1820, and since the white men who landed before his death did little to inspire confidence in Christian theology and ethics, Kamehameha's faithfulness to the gods that had allowed him to establish a kingdom was unchallenged.

When Captain George Vancouver visited Kamehameha in the spring of 1794 on his third voyage to the islands, the king and his leading chiefs went aboard the *Discovery* and ceded the Big Island to Great Britain, the beginning of a long era of English ascendancy in Hawaii, perhaps symbolized by the flag the Hawaiians eventually adopted, an obvious cross between the Stars and Stripes and the Union Jack. Vancouver also brought California cattle into the island, on which animals the king put a ten-year *kapu* that allowed the now flourishing ranching industry to start. Cattle came as gifts in 1793; horses a decade later. Kamehameha put a tabu on killing them until John Parker, a sailor who arrived in 1815, received lands from the king around Mauna Kea and tamed the by then wild cattle and horses. On his last trip Vancouver gave the king three young bulls, two cows, five rams, and five ewes. When he asked how the "big hogs," or cattle, he had brought on his second trip had weathered their first year on the islands, he was told that when the first calf was born the king was at Hilo. Keeaumoku was so eager to have him see the firstborn bovine that runners carried it on their backs, feeding it fish, on the three-day journey.

Russia made its move for control in Hawaii late in Kamehameha's reign. Early in the nineteenth century, when the Russian American Company had created a monopoly in the Alaskan fur trade, they sought to establish trading posts in California and Hawaii as sources of supply, and in 1812 did establish Fort Ross on the California coast above San Francisco. When a Russian ship, the *Bering*, was wrecked off the coast of Kauai in 1814, Governor Baranoff, of the Fort Ross Company, sent a German physician, Georg Scheffer, ostensibly to try to recover the cargo the natives of Kauai had salvaged from the wrecked ship *Bering*, but actually to establish the kind of trading post already maintained in California. Scheffer won the support of Kaumualii on Kauai through his medical skill, and Kamehameha allowed him safe-conduct in his travels around the islands. In the spring of 1816 Scheffer received the support of two ships and landed his men in Honolulu to found a fort there. Kamehameha's adviser John Young warned the king to send the Russians away, and he completed the fort for Kamehameha. (This is the battlement for which Fort Street in downtown Honolulu is named.) Rebuffed on Oahu, Scheffer returned to Kauai, where he tried to convince Kaumualii to secede from the Hawaiian kingdom and grant monopolies to Russia. The Russians constructed breastworks at Hanalei with the help of native labor and put up a formidable fort at Waimea on the southwestern coast of Kauai in 1817. When the Russian flag was raised over the fort, American traders were able to convince the King of Kauai that the Russians were in fact his enemies, who should be—and finally were—expelled to California. Scheffer went to St. Petersburg eventually to present his concept of Hawaiian annexation to the czar, but the Russian Government would not support his ambitions.

In 1824 a German naval officer, Captain Otto von Kotzebue, in the service of the Russian Navy, visited the islands for the third time and left us in *A New Voyage Round the World* one of the most vivid series of impressions of life in the islands. The innocent wonder with which the Hawaiians accepted and adapted Western ways is fascinating to read about. For example, Von Kotzebue describes "Chinau Kinau the governor of Wahu [Oahu] in a curious dishabille. He could hardly walk from the confinement his feet suffered in a pair of fisherman's shoes, and his red cloth waistcoat would not submit to be buttoned, because it had never been intended for so collosal a frame." Queen Dowager Namahana, one of the widows of King Kamehameha, who had died in May 1819, a huge woman, six feet two in height and "rather more than two ells in circumference," is described as dressing by putting on "a white calico hat decorated with Chinese flowers . . . a large Chinese fan in her hand, and . . . completed her toilette by drawing on a pair of clumsy sailor's boots. . . ."

Another craft that was completely new to the Hawaiians was the art of portraiture. When one of Von Kotzebue's officers secured permission from the queen to do her portrait, he recorded her surprise:

The limner's art is still almost a novelty here; and many persons of rank solicited permission to witness the operation. With the greatest attention, they watched every stroke of the outline, and loudly expressed their admiration as each feature appeared upon the paper. The nose was no sooner traced than they exclaimed—"Now Nomahanna can smell!" When the eyes were finished—"Now she can see!" They expressed especial satisfaction at the sight of the mouth, because it would enable her to eat; and they seemed to have some apprehension that she might suffer from hunger. At this point, Nomahanna became so much interested that she requested to see the picture also: she thought the mouth much too small, and begged that it might be enlarged.

Well might the queen dowager worry about the size of her mouth, to judge from Von Kotzebue's description of her marathon eating feats. Here surely is the original form of conspicuous consumption! She possessed, according to the world-traveled German officer, "certainly the greatest appetite that ever came under my observation."

How much had passed the royal mouth before my entrance, I will not undertake to affirm; but it took in enough in my presence to have satisfied six men! Great as was my admiration at the quantity of food thus consumed, the scene which followed was calculated to increase it. Her appetite appearing satisfied at length, the queen drew her breath with difficulty two or three times, then exclaimed, "I have eaten famously" . . . By the assistance of her attendants, she then turned upon her back and made a sign with her hand to a tall, strong fellow, who seemed well practised in his office; he immediately sprang upon her body, and kneaded her as unmercifully with his knees and fists as if she had been a trough of bread. This was done to favor digestion; and her majesty, after groaning a little at this ungentle treatment and taking a short time to recover herself, ordered her royal person to be again turned on the stomach, and recommenced her meal.

That the old ways were sure to change had been foreshadowed by the nobility of Kamehameha's death. Reminding one of his splintered-paddle magnanimity, the old king forbade the kahunas from offering a human sacrifice as a desperate measure to keep the failing king from dying. He is said to have ordered, "The men are *kapu* for the king," enjoining his successor, his son Liholiho, to thereby raise the ethics of the community to a new level of civilization. Also contrary to custom, no human sacrifice was offered at Kamehameha's funeral. His remains were secreted in a cave so that it was said in his kingdom, "Only the stars of the heavens know the resting place of Kamehameha."

The mourning for the beloved Kamehameha went to cruel lengths of self-mutilation. Kotzebue noted that it was "a still more striking proof of the universal grief for his loss that on the anniversary of his death all his subjects struck out one of their front teeth; and the whole nation have in consequence acquired a sort of whistle in speaking." Kinau, a daughter of Kamehameha I, did something even more self-effacing: she had the words "Our good King Tameamea [Kamehameha] died on the 8th of May 1819" tattooed on her tongue, "of which she gave me ocular demonstration . . . it is surprising that an operation so painful, and which occasions a considerable swelling, should not be attended with worse consequences."

KAMEHAMEHA II

Liholiho was twenty-two when he took over the throne his father had held for twenty-four years. The young prince, who did not have his predecessor's strength of character, faced many grave problems: what to do about the ancestral religion, which seemed to be eroding fast; how best to see to it that commerce and the sandalwood trade benefited the Hawaiians. To complicate further the short, five-year reign of the young monarch, in 1819 a financial crisis made specie very scarce and so New England traders stepped up efforts to get sandalwood, which was acceptable as a substitute for money in China. In the fall of that same year a whale was killed by New England ships off Kealakekua Bay, presaging the impact of a new industry. The following year the first missionaries arrived.

Kamehameha I had appointed his favorite queen, Kaahumanu, as *kuhina nui*, which made her practically as powerful as the inexperienced young king. Added to the circle of prudent counselors who made up for his inexperience and lack of character were Prime Minister Kalanimoku, from his father's cabinet, and Keopuolani, his own mother. Despite this a strong chief, Kekuaokalani, whom Kamehameha I had made guardian of the war god, began to plan an open revolt as leader of a conservative faction. Liholiho assuaged the nobles temporarily by cutting them in on the sandalwood monopoly.

When his prestige soared after a visiting French warship acknowledged his authority, Liholiho and his counselors took a fateful step: they abolished the venerable *kapu* system. In actual fact many Hawaiians had already begun to break the *kapus* against men and women eating together, and women eating such foods as pork, bananas, coconuts, and certain fish. The fact that foreigners broke the rules with impunity and that the Tahitians were reported to have abolished idolatry and taboos gave them courage to do these "monstrous" things in private. Liholiho, with the explicit support of the high priest Hewahewa, decided to flout the *kapu* against eating with a woman. During a feast at Kailua, on the Big Island, early in November, he practiced *ai noa* (free eating) in public with a woman. When finished, he gave the more startling directive to destroy all the *heiaus* and their idols.

Understandably, many Hawaiians refused to give up the old ways and the old gods. The war-god protector, Kekuaokalani, was outraged and wouldn't even listen to a peace delegation sent to him. Kalanimoku led the king's army against the protector of the war god and of the old ways and defeated the conservatives at Kuamoo in December 1819.

Some of Liholiho's chiefs were less successful in adjusting to the new affluence of the sandalwood trade. When he let them share the proceeds with him, a status-symbol splurge ensued. The chiefs deliriously ordered the finest silks, liquors, foreign clothing, and furniture. Price was no object—one chief paid eight hundred dollars for a mirror. American traders shipped whole boatloads designed to relieve these *nouveaux riches* of the commodity so valuable in the China trade. Liholiho and his chiefs bought some sailing vessels, not all of which were seaworthy, for outrageous prices—over a quarter of a million dollars in all. When the buyer's avarice outgrew the immediate supply of sandalwood available, foreign traders extended credit, further burdening the common people with oppressive taxes. It was a shameful spectacle, most depressing of all because the common people were sweated mercilessly to slake the thirst of their chiefs for Western baubles. Hundreds died from working in the wet, cold mountain regions where the trees flourished.

Kamehameha I had put a *kapu* on young trees as a conservation measure. But the craze got out of control as men, women, and children chopped down the trees, cut them into three-foot lengths, two to eight inches or so in diameter. Food supplies were neglected, and the famine that ensued took away many people who were weak from overwork. The traders sold the wood in China at almost a 50-per-cent markup, and since they paid the gullible Hawaiian chiefs in merchandise rather than in cash, they profited at both ends of their transactions. About 1830 they had worked out the forests except in all but a few inaccessible places. By then, however, provisioning the whalers replaced the sandalwood industry as a source of income.

Sandalwood came from the original name of the tree, *santalum*. The story has it that a sailor discovered its aromatic qualities by accident when burning some in his ship's galley before Kamehameha had consolidated his empire. When Captain Vancouver arrived in 1792, a primitive trade in the stuff was already going. It brought $125 a ton in Canton, where the Chinese craved it for sacred incense, images, and furniture. And when the naïve chiefs were paid in cash instead of in overpriced trinkets, they were likely to prefer the pretty moon dollars of silver to the ugly yellow sun dollars made of gold. Sandalwood was also used for fuel on funeral pyres, and medicine, perfumes, and cosmetics were made from its distilled oil. About the only trace of the once thriving trade today is that the name for Hawaii in Canton is Sandalwood Mountain.

In 1822 young Liholiho renewed the ancient tradition of making royal progresses through his kingdom. A court retinue of over a thousand individuals accompanied him on these ceremonial visits. In the summer of 1821, he had decided to test the allegiance of Kauai's king, Kaumualii. He set out from Waialua, on Oahu, with over thirty people crammed into a small boat that almost didn't make it across the treacherous channel that separates Kauai from Oahu. He brought the king back to Oahu, where he was wedded to the *kuhina nui*, Kaahumanu, adding thereby to the stability of his throne.

But the king and his consort, Kamamalu, desired to see the larger world. He believed that a trip to England would also consolidate the relationship of protection his father had assumed with that sovereign power. He left for England with his wife on the British whaling vessel *L'Aigle* on November 27, 1823. Oahu's Governor Boki and his wife joined the small party. Kamehameha II decreed, before departing, that his nine-year-old brother, Kauikeaouli, was the heir apparent, and that Kaahumanu would be regent in his absence. Almost six months later the party arrived in Portsmouth. The British

Government put the entourage of royal Hawaiians up at a luxurious hotel and entertained them regally. Tragically, Kamamalu was stricken with measles and died on July 8. Liholiho was heartbroken and he too succumbed less than a week later.

THE MISSIONARIES

There is a smart-alecky wisecrack current in Hawaii to the effect that the missionaries came to the islands to do good and really did well for themselves. Don't believe it. Their record here is an inspiring one, whatever one may finally think about the superiority of Western Christianity to Eastern Buddhism or Polynesian polytheism. Courage, dedication, and hard work are admirable qualities whatever a person's world view.

The missionaries have been referred to as the "Pilgrims of Hawaii" inasmuch as they arrived in Hawaii precisely two hundred years after their ancestors landed at Plymouth Rock in 1620. Behind the decision of the American Board of Commissioners for Foreign Missions to support a mission in the Sandwich Islands lies a touching story. One Captain Brintnall brought a young Hawaiian named Opukahaia (pronounced Obookiah in New England) to his home in New Haven, Connecticut. One day the boy was found sobbing on the steps of Yale College because of his ignorance. Several students felt compassion for the youngster and offered to teach him. Having become a devoted Protestant, he resolved to repay their kindness by going back to the islands as a missionary to convert his heathen people. When the American Board discovered several other Hawaiian youths in the country who seemed promising scholars, it enrolled Opukahaia and the other three in a school it established in 1816 to train native Hawaiians for teaching or the ministry. Opukahaia never did get a chance to convert his fellows, for he died in 1818 and the Sandwich Islands Mission was not organized in Boston until the fall of 1819.

The first ship to carry missionaries to Hawaii, the brig *Thaddeus*, sailed from Boston. Included on its manifest were names that were to become prominent in Hawaiian history: two ministers, Hiram Bingham and Asa Thurston; a farmer, Daniel Chamberlain, who brought his family of five children; a physician, Dr. Thomas Holman; Elisha Loomis, to become Hawaii's first printer; two schoolteachers, Samuel Ruggles and Samuel Whitney; their wives; and four young islanders: John Honolii, Thomas Hopus, William Kanui, and George P. Kaumualii. The last young man was a son of the King of Kauai and had been in the United States getting an education. He was to give the establishment a lot of trouble in later years.

The missionaries sighted land, the Big Island, on March 30, 1820. They were heartened by the news that Liholiho had abolished the *kapu* system after the death of his father. It seemed a good omen for the start of their assignment. The missionary band paid their respects to the young king at his court in Kailua a few days later. They explained their desire to found two missions, one in Kona and one in Honolulu. Liholiho finally agreed to the proposal.

By ballot Thurston was assigned to Kailua. Additional missions were set up in Honolulu, at Waimea on Kauai, and at Kawaihae on the Big Island. The chiefs were greatly interested in the work of the preachers; by the end of the year almost a hundred persons of every age and both sexes were under instruction. Wisely, the missioners concentrated at first on the "influentials" among the noble families. As soon as they had devised an alphabet for the Hawaiian language, school attendance for the elite boomed. The first printing in the language was accomplished early in 1822—a pamphlet containing the Hawaiian alphabet and spelling and reading lessons such as those which Von Kotzebue described in use in 1824 in the apartment of Queen Namahana. The New England zeal for the printed word soon produced an unending torrent of tracts, texts, and Bible translations. The first sermon in the native tongue was preached by the Reverend William Ellis, a London-based missionary whose six years in Tahiti enabled him to master the related Polynesian language in a few weeks.

The great invention of writing, which the missionaries introduced upon their arrival in 1820, astonished the Hawaiians. Indeed we can recover a sense of the miracle of this everyday skill by seeing it freshly through their eyes:

Nomahanna spoke with enthusiasm on the subject of writing. Formerly, she said, she could only converse with persons who were present; now, let them be ever so far distant, she could whisper her thoughts softly to them alone. She promised to write me a letter, in order, she said, that I might prove to every one in Russia that Nomahanna was able to write.

The royal court became a kind of vast schoolroom in the first flush of enthusiasm over becoming literate.

The stairs were occupied from the bottom to the door of the queen's apartments on the second floor, by children, adults, and even old people, of both sexes, who, under her majesty's own superintendence, were reading from spelling books, and writing on slates—a spectacle very honorable to her philanthropy. The governor himself, Kinau, had a spelling book in one hand, and in the other a very ornamental little instrument made of bone, which he used for pointing the letters. Some of the old people appeared to have joined the assembly rather for example's sake than from a desire to learn, as they were studying, with an affectation of extreme diligence, books held upside down.

Von Kotzebue may have maligned those elderly students, for anthropologists have found that it is an artificially acquired convention to hold the book right side up! For example, with more ethnological insight missionary wife Laura Fish Judd noted: "It is astonishing how so many have learned to read with so few books. They teach each other, making use of banana leaves, smooth stones, and the wet sand on the sea beach, as tablets. Some read equally well with the book upside down or sidewise, as four or five of them learn from the same book with one teacher, crowding around him as closely as possible." As for the elders dominating the student population, Mrs. Judd understood that situation, too, better than Von Kotzebue: "The children are considered bright," she wrote, "but too wild to be brought into the schools. We intend, however, to try them very soon."

When the second band of American missionaries arrived in 1823, a station was established at Lahaina, Maui. There the passions of shore-leave sailors and the convictions of stubborn religious zealots were soon to come into explosive conflict. Hiram Bingham described a riot in 1826 in Honolulu directed against him in his classic autobiography, *A Residence of Twenty-one Years in the Sandwich Islands* (1847): "Mad Jack" Percival, a lieutenant in command of the U.S.S. *Dolphin*, the first American warship to enter the port, was enraged that the newly Christianized Queen Regent Kaahumanu had forbidden Hawaiian girls to prostitute themselves with visiting sailors. Percival demanded an audience with the queen regent at which the missionary Bingham was to be excluded on purpose.

He said to me [Kaahumanu reported later to Bingham], "Why tabu the women? Take heed. My people will come: if the women are not forthcoming they will not obey my word. Take care of your men, and I will take care of mine. By and by they will come to get women, and if they do not obtain them, they will fight, and my vessel is just like fire." I said, "Why make war upon us without a fault of ours as to restraining our women? We love the Word of God, and therefore held back our women. Why then would you fight us without cause?" He said, "You formerly attended properly with Kamehameha to the ships, both American and English." I said, "In former time, before the Word of God had arrived here, we were dark-minded, lewd, and murderous; at the present time we are seeking a better way."

The dignified queen regent then touched a nerve that must have infuriated the captain, who was twisting the truth and his own conscience to appease the frustrated hopes of his crew, whose dreams of South Sea romance had run aground on the reefs of conversion: "But why are you angry with us for laying a tabu on the women of our own country? Had you brought American women with you, and we had tabued them, you might then justly be displeased with us." Percival went in a fury then to Governor Boki of Oahu, bullying him to release the women, to no avail. He came back to Kaahumanu and vilified the missionaries ("a company of liars; the women are *not* tabu in America") and threatened to give his men rum and then send them ashore. "Declare to me the man that told you the women must be tabu, and my people will pull down his house. If the women are not released from the tabu tomorrow, my people will come and pull down the houses of the missionaries." That was Saturday. On Sunday, February 26, 1826, Percival let double the usual number of men take shore leave. What ensued could have been predicted.

One hundred fifty sailors rioted at the time and place usually reserved for the royal family's Sunday service. They broke seventy panes of glass in the windows of Prime Minister Kalanimoku's hall. Then they made for Bingham's house. There they seized the missionary and threatened him until the natives resorted to violence to suppress the riot. Finally, Governor Boki acceded to the requests for women, and the *Dolphin* earned the sobriquet of "the mischief-making man-of-war." Bingham concluded glumly: "With that term was associated the shout of the vile which was heard in the harbor as the first boatload of vile women was seen to pass under its flag. Never did the advocacy of licentiousness or opposition to the tabu appear more odious. While some exulted for a time in the partial triumph, those citizens and subjects of other countries and leading natives, who had been looking for something not less friendly, wise, and honorable in a naval 'chief' from the United States than had appeared in Lord Byron, a recent English visitor, were disappointed. But he that makes the wrath of man to praise him overruled this temporary triumph to the increase of the confidence of some in the Gospel and its propagators." The Reverend William Richards, in Lahaina, wasn't as lucky as Bingham was. His house was sacked by a passel of concupiscent tars.

The Hawaiian language had no words for chastity and prostitution. It did have a custom called *punalua*, which the sailors found congenial. By this custom a Hawaiian man could have more than one wife and a Hawaiian woman could have more than one husband. A single standard. If there had been no such custom the Hawaiian men would have frothed with rage in jealousy every time a whaler put into port. There were exceptions, especially among the higher chiefs. Jealousy in a sense was a royal luxury. Kamehameha, for example, threatened to kill anyone who persuaded his favorite Kaahumanu to be unfaithful. That the missionaries had their work cut out for them is clear from a J. Edgar Hoover-like report in their magazine.

The missionary organ, *The Friend*, published an interesting list of cases punished in the year 1846, when whaling was still a big thing in Hawaii:

Adultery, fornication, et cetera	126
Theft	43
Gambling	35
Reviling language	12
Working on the Sabbath Day	30
Slander	1
Passing false coin	1
Heathenish practices	3
Rape	2
Furious riding [Polynesian hot-rodding?]	6
Interference with police	3
Drunk and disorderly	6
Assault and battery	7
Total	275

Almost half of the punishable offenses were sins of the flesh—or at least the et cetera! The trouble was, of course, that you couldn't put *all* the Hawaiian women in jail. And the Hawaiian jailers at the fort had a way of letting their charges slip into the ocean behind the fort to swim out to the ships—for money to pay fines with, if you can be charitable about such things. The missionaries were confused but not willing to give up. Finally, in 1843 they had a law enacted that said that you could jail a girl only if her crime were "committed in the open streets or public thoroughfare." What started out as a moral struggle ended ignominiously as an antilitter campaign.

And the next time you swat a mosquito in Hawaii, swear

The Polynesian war canoe was a triumph of Stone Age technology, an incredibly sophisticated use of local materials. (BISHOP MUSEUM)

Hanauma Bay, thirty minutes from Waikiki by car.
(PAN AMERICAN AIRWAYS)

Above, Kamehameha I, The Lonely One, first unified the island kingdoms. (BISHOP MUSEUM) *Below,* Kamehameha School student keeps alive the old traditions with new tools. (KAMEHAMEHA SCHOOLS)

[3]

Makiki Christian Church in Honolulu is the kind of architectural surprise in store for those who admire blendings of East and West. (PATRICK D. HAZARD)

[4]

Age-old skills like those of this net-mending fisherman coexist . . .

. . . with the most modern agricultural techniques of the pineapple industry. (Both, UNITED AIR LINES)

[5]

Popo Wong is the Grandma Moses of Hawaii; her tropical still-lifes make as much magic with the sun as those of her mainland counterpart do with the snow.
(LIBRARY OF HAWAII)

[6]

Ceramics Hawaii enhances many new buildings with striking murals.
(FIRST INSURANCE COMPANY OF HAWAII)

Alfred Preis's Memorial for the U.S.S. Arizona at Pearl Harbor is the most creative monument in contemporary America. (PAN AMERICAN AIRWAYS)

[7]

The John F. Kennedy Theatre at the East-West Center is the first in history planned specifically to accommodate oriental and occidental dramas equally well. (EAST-WEST CENTER)

[8]

quietly at the Reverend William Richards of Lahaina—and shiploads of frustrated lechers. The story goes that one sea captain became so infuriated at the missionary's embargo on female favors that he brought ashore a tub of stagnant water full of mosquitoes, until then unknown in the islands. "That'll show the damned, meddling missionaries," grumbled the vengeful captain, who apparently was after blood.

The "Third Company" of New England missionaries arrived on the *Parthian* in 1828. Aboard were an able physician who was destined to hold significant power in Hawaii as a governmental adviser, Dr. Gerrit P. Judd, and his new bride, Laura Fish Judd. Her lively memoirs have already been excerpted in these pages. Her description of her first view of Honolulu is charming in its nostalgic comparison with New England:

> Sunday morning, March 30 [1828]. The island of Oahu, our Ultima Thule, looms up in the distance, displaying gray and red rocky hills, unrelieved by a single shade of green, forbidding enough in aspect. Now we pass the old crater, Diamond Head, and we can see a line of coconut trees stretching gracefully along the sea beach for a mile or more. "Please give me the spy glass for a moment. There! I see the town of Honolulu, a mass of brown huts, looking precisely like so many haystacks in the country; not one white cottage, no church spire, not a garden nor a tree to be seen save the grove of coconuts. The background of green hills and mountains is picturesque. A host of living, moving beings are coming out of that long, brown building; it must be Mr. Bingham's congregation just dismissed from morning service; they pour out like bees from a hive. I can see their draperies of brown, black, white, pink and yellow native tapa."

She quoted one of her companions: "'Here we are to live and labor until the land is filled with churches, schoolhouses, fruitful fields, and pleasant dwellings.'" After they anchored in the peaceful harbor, she couldn't sleep because she missed the incessant rocking of the boat. Ashore, they were offered transportation in a yellow horse wagon and two blue carts, all of which were drawn by natives, at the request of the

Queen Regent Kaahumanu. The exotic, half-assimilated Western dress of the natives attracted her notice.

> She [Kaahumanu] was dressed in striped satin, blue and pink, with a white muslin shawl and Leghorn bonnet, the latter worn doubtless in compliment to us, as the common headress is a wreath of feathers or flowers. . . . a crowd of natives, men, women, and children, dressed and undressed [followed us]. Many of them wore a sheet of native cloth, tied on one shoulder, not unlike the Roman toga; one had a shirt minus pantaloons, another had a pair of pantaloons minus a shirt; while a large number were destitute of either. One man looked very grand with an umbrella and shoes, the only foreign articles he could command. The women were clad in native costume, the *pa-u*, which consists of folds of native cloth about the hips, leaving the shoulders and waist quite exposed; a small number donned in addition a very feminine garment made of unbleached cotton, drawn close around the neck, which was quite becoming. Their hair was uncombed and their faces unwashed, but all of them were good-natured. Our appearance furnished them much amusement; they laughed and jabbered, ran on in advance, and turned back to peer into our faces. I laughed and cried too, and hid my face for very shame.

Her reticence in the presence of nudity reached a high point one morning when, arising early to fix the mission's breakfast, she found a nude and filthy native man squatting, frying taro before her fire. "I suppose travelers in southern Italy," she observed demurely, "become accustomed to this statuesque style, but I am verdant enough to be shocked, and shall use all my influence to increase the sales and use of American cottons." The observations and ruminations of this young woman, not yet twenty-four when she arrived in Honolulu, are still among the most personal and lively documents we have for recapturing the feel of those early missionary days.

Another first-rate reporter of those confusing times when Hawaii was "in a transition state between heathenism and missionaryism" was James J. Jarves. Son of the Boston manufacturer of Sandwich glass, Jarves came to the islands at age nineteen in 1847. For almost nine years he worked as planter, merchant, and editor of a weekly newspaper, the *Polynesian*. This was the period when French, British, and Americans jockeyed fiercely for the ultimate control of the place. In these skirmishes, Jarves took the side of the American missionary element. This precarious era of journalism netted him a French challenge to a duel and a British horsewhipping. His descriptions of the "extraordinary intermixture of civilization and barbarism" in *Why and What Am I? The Confessions of an Enquirer* (1857) still make fascinating reading. "Within sound of one of Watts' hymns, as sung by a native choir," he noted, "the curious visitor would be cautiously conducted into the premises of a high chief, who was surreptitiously indulging himself in witnessing wanton dances by young, half-clad maidens, followed by scenes not to be described. . . ."

> "Nearer by, the monotonous tones of natives, earnestly praying to Jehovah, would strike his ear, interrupted, perhaps, by the profane and vulgar mirth of groggy sailors ashore on a spree, but kept like wild animals chafing within the limits of some white man's enclosure, from which they and their female companions could sally forth only at the risk of being arrested by native constables, greedy to collect the fines imposed upon drunkenness or debauchery. Should he wander into one of those huts so recently the scene of a devotion, its owner—a church member, perhaps a deacon—would not unlikely welcome him in the spirit of the former hospitality of his race, and inquire if it would be agreeable to him to have a female to share his couch. Possibly the next day he would meet the same woman at hard labor on the public highways, betrayed by a spy, and condemned to an infamous punishment for indulging in what in her early youth she had been taught to consider a virtue, but which now was very properly denounced as a vice. . . ."

The pathos of these Stone Age men and women living in a world where the old faith had died and the new one was waiting fully to be born is best expressed in the saying the Hawaiians had: "Me mikonaree here," pointing to the head;

"*aole* mikonaree," no missionary here, designating the rest of the body. "Brass joined to clay they indeed were," concluded Jarves.

One most dramatic incident in the Christianization of the Hawaiian natives, comparable in impact to Liholiho's breaking the *kapus* over eating in public, was Queen Kapiolani's public baiting of the goddess Pele. She showed how much faith her Christian belief gave her by descending into the volcano of Kilauea in December 1824.

When people talk about the missionary influence in Hawaii, they tend to overlook the relatively small number of New Englanders involved in Protestant missionary work. Between 1820 and 1854 they totaled only one hundred forty-five, and only forty-two of these were ordained ministers, the others being doctors, teachers, women, and other "lay helpers." In 1854, when the mission was turned over to Hawaiian control as a Christianized area, there were but twenty-six ministers in the field, three physicians, eight lay helpers, and forty-one women. About one-third of these returned to America at the completion of their service, the rest remaining as the nucleus of a permanent American settlement. Another way of looking at this, of course, is that it was a testament to the zeal and energy of this small band who made so great an impact on the quality of life in the islands.

For one thing, the missionaries helped the Hawaiians modernize their agricultural practices. For example, the Reverend Richard Armstrong wrote from his station at Wailuku, Maui, July 7, 1840: "I have assisted the natives to break in some twelve yoke of oxen, which have done a great deal towards relieving the people of their burdens. Three years ago everything, food, timber, potatoes, pigs, stones, lime, sand, etc., were carried on the backs of natives, or dragged on the ground by their hands . . . but almost all this drudgery is now done by carts and oxen, and the head men say they cannot get the men of their lands to submit to such work as they once could. This is clear gain." Armstrong also showed them how to use plows and raised some ten acres of sugar cane to help support the mission school.

Because the Hawaiians had destroyed their own gods just a year before the missionaries arrived, they were very reluctant to listen to messages about the new god. Kaahumanu insisted firmly, "No, we are through with gods. We will have no new ones! We want no *pulepule* [praying] only *palapala* [paper, i.e., literacy]." That is why it was much easier at first to get Hawaiians into school, where they could study the "designs" of the "magic machine," the printing press, than to get them into church.

Obookiah (Opukahaia), Hawaii's first Christian convert, was zealous about his new faith. He heaped scorn on the old religion of Hawaii. "Hawaii gods, they wood—they burn. Me go home, put 'em in a fire, burn 'em up. They no see, no hear, no anything. We make 'em." Looking to the heavens, he would conclude: "*Our* God, He make us." But the attitude of most Hawaiian royalty to the new religion was a rather sophisticated one: "If the *palapala*—the written word—is good, we wish to possess it first ourselves; if it is bad, we do not intend our subjects to know the evil of it." And so the wives of one of the missionaries reported in a letter home: "The king forbids our teaching any but the blood royal." Kaumualii, the King of Kauai, on the other hand, wrote a letter to Boston thanking the missionaries for sending their religion to him:

> I wish to write a few lines to you to thank you for the good book, you was so kind as to send by my son. I think it is a good book; one that God gave for us to read. I hope my people will soon read this and all other good books. . . . My gods I have hove away; they are no good, they fool me; they do me no good. I take good care of them. I give them cocoa-nuts, plaintains, hogs, and good many things and they fool me at last. Now I throw them all away. I have none now. When your good people learn me, I worship your God . . . I thank all American people. I feel glad to see you good folks here. . . .

The extremely personal way the king took his theological and ethical problems is a good indication of how much work the missionaries had cut out for them.

Some Hawaiians went to church to wear their squeaky shoes up the center aisle, much to the consternation of Bingham. To complicate the status panic, they sometimes took off those shoes and dropped them out the window to a waiting friend who wanted to make an equally elegant entrance. The Hawaiians were so fascinated with squeaky shoes that an ex-con named Crispin, who escaped from Botany Bay, developed a system of watering silent shoes to turn them into the squeaky kind the natives favored. The bigger the squeak the higher the fee. When the Hawaiians first saw the missionary ladies, they were amused by their queer long dresses and by the hats "that look like a spout" (sunbonnets or poke bonnets). "Their faces are so far in; their necks look so long," the Hawaiians observed, dubbing the new visitors "Longnecks."

At first the missionaries permitted the converted heathens to hula *if* they wore long dresses under their grass skirts. But this finally didn't satisfy the missionaries. Once Hiram Bingham tried to catechize some hula dancers whom he caught throwing their leis into an enclosure considered sacred to the god of the hula-hula. His questions and their answers poignantly underscore the gulf between the two cultures:

"Does the god of the hula-hula know anything?" Bingham asked.

"No."

"Can he see?"

"No."

"Can he hear?"

"No."

"Can he speak?"

"No."

"Can he do anything?"

"No."

"What is he good for? And why do you have such a god?"

"For play," they answered.

Hawaiians weren't always such slow learners. The missionaries' *ho-iki*, or examination day, was a unique combination of New England educational zeal and Hawaiian love of pageantry. As many as two thousand or more students of all ages and ranks gathered in Honolulu from windward Oahu and the Outer Islands. Hiram Bingham stressed the democracy of learning by having commoner and chief face examinations together. He would face the group and command it to sit up straight. At the next order, they stood at attention.

Next, they presented slates as in military drill. Then the missionary dictated the sentence to be written, at which all the examinees scratched noisily against their slates. Then teachers examined the slates. On April 18, 1824, Queen Dowager Kaahumanu was in the front line of a group of five hundred students taking examinations in reading, spelling, and writing. The audience of thousands held their collective breath as she correctly spelled the first word. Then she dramatically held up her slate, wrote a sentence, and signed her name boldly. The crowd cheered enthusiastically.

At least some of the resentment that missionary families felt surely derived from the sanctimoniousness of a few who fancied that the Lord was very much on their side. Amos Starr Cooke, a Connecticut bookkeeper who resigned his mission teaching job to start a retail and wholesaling business that became one of the Big Five, noted on his first day of business in 1851: "The foreigners are creeping in among the natives, getting their largest and best lands, water privileges, building lots, etc. The Lord seems to be allowing such things to take place that the Islands may gradually pass into other hands. This is trying but we cannot help it. It is what we have been contending against for years, but the Lord is showing us that His thoughts are not our thoughts, neither are His ways our ways. . . . Our large plain of sand is now covered with vegetation and is laid out in lots. I am proposing, ere long, to purchase some of them. . . ." Thus did one New England idealist slowly learn to conform his own ways to those of His more knowing Creator!

And the missionaries' fear of contamination could never endear them to others. Sereno Bishop recalled in *Reminiscences of Old Hawaii* (1916) that white children were forbidden to learn Hawaiian to keep them from what he called "mental contamination": "There was no reserve whatever upon any subject in the presence of children in the social and domestic conversation of the native people. The vilest topics were freely discussed in their presence and the children grew up in the atmosphere of the grossest impurity. The same strict tabu was enforced in nearly all the mission families." Later on in life, of course, if one were to become a missionary he had to learn Hawaiian—to teach them.

If the sailors resented the missionaries for keeping the girls off the streets and boats of Lahaina, businessmen fumed when their larcenous markups of the baubles the chiefs loved were exposed. A chief might take a recently purchased mirror to the missionary for appraisal. When the Hawaiian learned that he had paid four hundred dollars for a forty-dollar mirror, he wasn't often again such a sucker for New England-type wooden nutmeg peddlers. One American merchant in Honolulu, John Coffin Jones, Jr., developed a violent hatred against the missionaries. In 1826 he wrote: "Trade never will again flourish at these Islands until these missionaries from the Andover mill, the Theological Seminary, are recalled. They are continually telling the King and Chiefs that the white people traders are cheating and imposing on them, consequently have depreciated the value of most articles. I believe it is a fact generally acknowledged by all here, that the natives are fifty per cent worse in every vice since the missionaries began their hypocritical labor here: these blood suckers of the community had much better be in their native country gaining their living by the sweat of their brow, than living like lords in this luxurious land, distracting the minds of these children of Nature with the idea that they are to be eternally damned unless they think and act as they do; and that Providence would put a whip in every honest hand to lash such rascals naked through the world."

As Hawaii made its painful transition from paganism to Christianity, it was often extremely rough going for those who decided to hold firm to the old ways. Consider, for example, how Lucy Goodale Thurston described the fate of a pagan priest who would not abjure the old idols: "In the presence of the king he was brought to the test of renouncing the system of idolatry by being required to eat some poi from the women's calabash. He *would not* do it. As a consequence, the king required him to drink a whole quart bottle of whisky. The natives then placed him perpendicularly by the body of a tree, and lashed him to it with a rope, in such a snug manner that in a short time it squeezed the very life out of him."

In 1830 there were two fresh offshoots from the abandoned old religion on the island of Hawaii. One group worshiped the late king and prophesied that he would return. Another claimed that the hand of a dead child had divine power. A few years later Sheldon Dibble (1843) in *A History of the Sandwich Islands* described the emergence of a nativistic cult that weirdly combined the old paganism with the new Christianity.

In Puna, a district at that time under my missionary superintendence, and about thirty miles from my place of residence, some young men took advantage of the state of things to bring themselves into notice. They devised a system of religion half Christian and half heathen. They promulgated that there were three gods—Jehovah, Jesus Christ, and Hapu (a young woman who had pretended to be a prophetess and had lately deceased). They dug up the bones of Hapu, adorned them with kapas, flowers, and birds' feathers; deposited them in a prominent spot, and marked about this spot a definite enclosure. This they called *the place of refuge*. They went from house to house and from village to village, and exhorted the people with much earnestness and eloquence, to go to the place of refuge, saying, that the heavens and earth were about to meet and all who were not found in the place of refuge would be destroyed.

Many took the advice, built a *heiau* that Dibble later got them to burn in repentance, and they stayed until hunger and no disaster persuaded them to leave. Another imaginative local theologian turned the first three Hawaiian gods (Kane, Ku, Lono) into a Christian-like trinity and the fourth, Kanaloa, as a fallen angel, the spirit of evil and death in the world.

The weird fetish worship of the old Hawaiian religion had its moments of magical terror. Mrs. Laura Fish Judd, on a visit to the Kona coast of the Big Island, met the man at Kealakekua who ate the heart of Captain Cook after his body had been dismembered as trophies. "He stole it from a tree, supposing it to be a swine's heart hung there to dry, and was horrified when he discovered the truth. The Sandwich Islanders never were cannibals. This made him famous, and he is always spoken of as the man who ate Lono's heart."

Finally, however, most Hawaiians got the Word. Hilo's

Reverend Titus Coan had to devise a kind of mass-production baptism at the height of his Great Revival, when he baptized 1705 Hawaiians lined up in rows. He used a whisk broom dipped in a bucket he carried to inundate a handful of converts at one swoosh.

KAMEHAMEHA III

When Kauikeaouli ascended the throne at the age of eleven as Kamehameha III, he began the longest reign in the history of the throne. The older chiefs had called a meeting to establish sound policies, just after Liholiho left for England and within the year the regent Kaahumanu had promulgated a succinct civil code obviously based on the major ethical concepts of the missionaries. It outlawed stealing, fighting, murder, and Sabbath breaking. We have seen in the accounts of Bingham and Jarves how ambiguous was the support to these tenets in the early years of Christianization.

When Kauai's king, Kaumualii, died in 1824, civil war threatened. The king's son, George Kaumualii, attacked the fort in Waimea in August. It took several months before the island was secured, with a chief of high rank appointed as governor. However, when Liholiho's death in London was reported, there was great public mourning, but not the civil disorder one might have expected in the Hawaiian society just a generation before.

The ship that brought back the royal remains was skippered by a remarkable man, George Anson, Lord Byron, who was a cousin of the poet. He made some suggestions to a national council of chiefs which met to approve the accession of Kauikeaouli; one of those accepted was trial by jury. He tried to convince the chiefs that the Hawaiians would have to make their own laws. Byron then sailed to Hilo, where he surveyed the body of water that became known then as "Byron's Bay." His party also scientifically observed Kilauea volcano and erected a memorial to Captain Cook at Kealakekua Bay.

The excesses of the chiefs' passion for the fineries that sandalwood financed led to increased American concern about the islands. The Americans had a near monopoly of the trade, and the tendency of the chiefs to buy more than they could pay for eventually made it necessary to bring governmental persuasion to bear. The earliest written tax law in Hawaii exacted from every able-bodied man in the kingdom a picul of sandalwood or four Spanish dollars, but this didn't really solve the arrears; it all but devastated the sandalwood stands.

Another source of trouble was the deserting or carousing sailor. It is significant that the first laws printed in the kingdom, in 1822, were designed to punish the deserter and the rioter. Gradually, however, the chiefs tried to replace the outmoded *kapu* system with constitutional government.

When Queen Regent Kaahumanu died in 1832, her successor as *kuhina nui* was Kinau, a daughter of the first Kamehameha and hence considerably older than the eighteen-year-old Kamehameha III. After enduring joint rule for a year, he went on a two-year rampage. In March 1833 a crier proclaimed that henceforth only the laws pertaining to murder and theft still obtained. The hula and other ancient sports were re-established, and many subjects overcompensated for what they regarded as the severity of the preceding years. It was kind of a breather between paganism and Christianity. Two years of dissipation and unruliness convinced Kamehameha III that his kingdom needed more stability.

He gave the control of the government largely over to Kinau, and early in 1835 a new penal code was proclaimed. It dealt with matters such as homicide, adultery, and divorce, drunkenness, fraud, and theft. Penalties for theft included a fine twice the amount of the theft, imprisonment, or lashes. One of the chief difficulties in law enforcement was the resistance of foreigners to inclusion in the system. This convinced the chiefs not only that they had better write treaties with each of the major powers, but also that they had better learn more about how civilized countries ran their affairs. For two years they looked for an American who could teach them government and economics. In the summer of 1838 they found their man: the Reverend William Richards, who had a personal motive for seeing more law and order in the islands—frustrated sailors had shot up the missionary's house in Lahaina in 1827 with cannon fire for not letting them consort with Hawaiian girls. He lectured an eager group of chiefs and they quickly put what they learned into a series of constitutional changes. An early result was the proclamation in 1839 of the so-called Hawaiian Magna Carta, whose preamble had a stately ring: "God hath made of one blood all nations of men, to dwell on the face of the earth in unity and blessedness. God has also bestowed certain rights alike on all men, and all chiefs, and all people of all lands. These are some of the rights which he has given alike to every man and every chief: life, limb, liberty, the labor of his hands, and productions of his mind." But it was not until 1840 that the first constitution made provision for a popular assembly giving ordinary people a say in their own government.

Another problem arose when French Catholic missionaries opened a chapel in Honolulu in 1828. Because Protestant Christianity had become almost a state religion, the chiefs considered conversion of natives to Catholicism a kind of insubordination. Thus in August 1829 they forbade their subjects to attend Catholic worship. Some continued to attend and a few were actually punished for the act in the following decade. Two French priests were exiled to California in 1831. A British priest arrived in 1836, to be rejoined by the California exiles in 1837. A tug of war between the chiefs and British, American, and French authorities ensued. Finally the French priests were banished again, and Kamehameha III forbade Catholic teaching in an edict of 1837.

The French Government regarded itself as the protector of all Catholic missionaries in the Pacific. For example, in the fall of 1838 Captain du Petit-Thouars had exacted reparations from the Queen of Tahiti for having expelled Catholic clergy. In July 1839, Captain C. P. T. Laplace, in charge of the French frigate _Artémise_ on a world cruise to develop French commerce, put in at Honolulu. He had orders to use force if necessary to demand reparations. Laplace sent a manifesto to the king demanding that a twenty-thousand-dollar bond be deposited with him to ensure that the Catholic religion would be allowed and that land be given for a church in Honolulu. He further stipulated that the French flag be given a twenty-one-gun salute. A few days later still more arbitrary articles were successfully demanded: that Frenchmen in the islands be tried by a foreign jury chosen by the

French consul and that French merchandise, especially liquors, be given preferential treatment. Again, looking down the barrels of the French gunboat, the king had little he could do but sign.

It became increasingly necessary to settle the relations between Hawaiian and foreign countries because the foreign investors who wanted to develop agriculture in the islands were reluctant to do so until there was greater stability. The first formal recognition of the kingdom's independence was received in July 1842. From President John Tyler, Secretary of State Daniel Webster gave the Hawaiian envoys—William Richards and Timothy Haalilio—a document from the United States. The state paper noted that the U.S. had a greater interest in Hawaii than had any other country, and that no country should try to possess it or exert undue control. However, in February 1843 the British ship *Carysfort* threatened to fire its guns on the town of Honolulu if the demands of the British consul, Alexander Simpson, were not met. Kamehameha III, trusting to the ultimate fairness of the British throne, provisionally seceded his kingdom to Great Britain. The British flag replaced the Hawaiian; a twenty-one-gun salute was followed by the ship's band playing "God Save the Queen." Captain Lord George Paulet even took three Hawaiian ships and renamed them the *Albert*, the *Victoria*, and the *Adelaide*. The islands were under the British flag until the end of July. American Commodore Lawrence Kearney protested the cession from his squadron's flagship, *Constellation*, on July 11. When Admiral Thomas arrived two weeks later aboard the frigate *Dublin*, conditions had almost reached the ignition point. He assured the king that Britain respected his independence as long as her subjects' rights were respected. In the re-enthronement ceremony of July 31, 1843, Kamehameha used the words that have since become the motto of Hawaii: *Ua mau ke ea o ka aina i ka pono* (The life of the land is preserved by righteousness). Admiral Thomas resided in Honolulu for six months and became a great favorite, a fact symbolized by Thomas Square in Honolulu, the site of the restoration ceremony, named for him in affection and gratitude. In November 1843 the Queen of Great Britain and the King of France jointly declared the independence of the Sandwich Islands; they invited the U.S. to join the statement, but it refused on the grounds of avoiding entangling alliances.

Kamehameha pushed forward with the constitutional developments that were to make him one of the wisest and most admired of the Hawaiian monarchs. In 1846 a most important part of the Second Organic Act was that pertaining to landholdings. A land commission supervised The Great Mahele (Division). To begin with, all land in the kingdom was divided between the king and the chiefs. Next the king gave the larger half of his land to the public domain, keeping the rest as crown lands. Chiefs gave part of their lands to the government and got clear title to the rest. Common people occupying and cultivating land were given outright grants. These *kuleanas* ranged in size from one to forty acres. The land hunger of Hawaii today stems from the division established at the time, added to the natural scarcity of the commodity in an island territory.

Though the three great powers had acknowledged Hawaiian independence in 1843, it took a decade of diplomatic struggle to secure treaties to uphold these theoretical rights. Incidentally, the twenty thousand dollars extorted by Captain Laplace in 1839 was returned, unopened, in the original boxes, in 1846. In 1849, however, a contentious French consul, Guillaume Dillon, precipitated another crisis when he persuaded Rear Admiral de Tromelin to use force to protest the king's request for the consul's recall and secure his demands. Tromelin seized several government buildings and ships, but the American and British consuls protested, and an embassy was sent to France to obtain justice. On this voyage Alexander Liholiho, the heir apparent, and his younger brother, Lot Kamehameha, got a valuable exposure to the larger world when they visited Great Britain and the United States. In 1851 the French again resorted to gunboat diplomacy. In desperation the king signed a secret proclamation putting the islands under the protection of the U.S. The French then retreated and never again resorted to force.

The California gold rush, however, had greatly increased the numbers of American residents in the islands, and in the fall of 1851 there was consternation lest filibusters from the

Pacific coast overthrow established authority. A great small-pox epidemic in 1853 badly affected the native Hawaiian population, and the missionary advisers of the king were blamed for the epidemic. Kamehameha III shook up his cabinet to meet the opposition, and throughout the agitation it was considered that annexation to the U.S. might make a good emergency move if things finally got out of hand. The king wanted to insist that Hawaii be admitted as a state and that his family and chiefs receive $300,000 a year compensation. But he died before the treaty could be signed and it would be many years before annexation became a reality. Toward the close of his reign, the constitution of 1852, strongly influenced by the ideas of his American advisers, such as Dr. Gerrit Judd, appeared as another step in the gradual Westernization of Hawaii.

The almost thirty years of his reign also marked the high point of missionary enterprise. In all some thirteen companies of preachers and their helpers were sent from New England. Conversion was no trivial matter to the Protestant evangelists, and it is worth noting, for example, that only thirteen hundred persons were given church membership in the first seventeen years of the mission. As a result of the Great Revival a great boom in conversions took place between 1838 and 1840, some twenty thousand. Although the king never joined the Christian church, the Sandwich Islands were regarded as a Christian nation by 1840, for the constitution of that year said that no law could be enacted that conflicted with the word of God. The percentage of the native population adhering to the Protestant church increased from 18 per cent in 1840 to about 30 per cent in 1853. Many more attended church, if you include children and nondeclared believers. Finally, in 1849, James Kekela became the first pastor of Hawaiian ancestry ordained. Indeed Hawaiians began to go to the Marquesas and Micronesia to convert other heathens. At first the American Board had discouraged the missionaries from owning land or becoming citizens. But as more and more missionaries began to worry about the education of their children, a "homeward current" began. To counter this, the board reversed itself. It divided most of its holdings among the missionaries and allowed them to become citizens.

In 1853, it regarded the Sandwich Islands as Christianized, and Hawaii became a home rather than a foreign mission under the newly organized Hawaiian Evangelical Association. It was as a result of these changes that the descendants of missionary families came to have such an influential part in the later development of the islands.

About 1840 the Protestants lost their monopoly with the entry of Catholic missionaries. In 1850 ten Mormons from the California gold rush settled in Honolulu. They made a point of quickly appointing Hawaiian converts to church offices. Against Catholic and Protestant opposition the Mormons were in all parts of the Islands by 1854. When the Mormons proposed a general gathering of their coreligionists in 1853, they chose Lanai as a headquarters for Hawaiian Mormons where a City of Joseph was founded.

It was during Kamehameha III's reign that the trading companies that were to exert so much economic power first developed. It bears mentioning here that facile judgments about the missionaries coming to Hawaii to do good and indeed doing very well don't fit very well with history. Even the Big Five corporations, so influential in Hawaii's economy, were not, as popular interpretations would have it, missionary enterprises plain and simple. True, Castle and Cooke and Alexander and Baldwin were founded by men of missionary extraction. But C. Brewer grew out of trader interests. American Factors was run by a family of Hamburg industrialists until expropriated as alien property during World War I. Theo. H. Davies, fifth of the Big Five, has always been owned by British interests. The degree to which the Big Five controls the island economy is harder to assess. In 1948 the Hawaiian Economic Foundation published a report which showed that 34,000 families out of Hawaii's 105,000 total owned the stock of the islands' 831 corporations with assets approaching one billion dollars. The largest of the Big Five, American Factors, owned only one twentieth of these assets; the Big Five together owned only one fifth. Since World War II the growing economic stake of the Japanese and Chinese and the entry of mainland capitalists like Henry J. Kaiser have further diluted Big Five power. A further source of countervailing power followed the unionization of docks, sugar, and pineapple by Harry Bridges' I.L.W.U.

After sandalwood disappeared because of overexploitation, the whaling industry was the chief economic support of the islands. Before kerosene lamps and electric lights, whale oil was the principal artificial illuminant in the form of candles and lamps. Other by-products included whalebone for corsets and sperm oil for machinery lubrication. When whales were discovered off Japan about 1820, American ships found Hawaii a convenient supply depot, since Japan itself was still closed to foreigners. The two decades before the discovery of petroleum, 1840-60, were the high point of the whaling industry. About a hundred whaleships a year stopped at Honolulu or Lahaina in the first two decades of the industry. When new whaling grounds were found in the northern Pacific, business boomed even more. Whalers came to provision twice a year, in spring and fall. At the peak of the industry one could walk from one end of Honolulu's harbor without having to get off a ship, they were so jammed together in the port.

Since Honolulu was the only good harbor within a radius of two thousand miles at the heart of the whaling grounds, it profited most from the new industry. It benefited even more from the development of two-year (or longer) cruises, summers toward the arctic, winters near the equator, because ships stored oil and bone at the port or sent it home ahead on merchant ships that came to port to pick up such cargoes. As in the sandalwood era, however, the economy depended almost too completely on the single industry. Port charges and customs duties swelled the government exchequer, it is true, and Big Island cattle were good business in Lahaina. But the ships' demand for firewood began to denude the forests, and easy money in provisioning discouraged plantation development, a process that involved a great deal of capital and arduous labor, both subject to a heavy risk of failure.

We have already seen what a shoreful of whaler sailors could do to the missionaries. In the famous riot of November 1852 the seamen burned down the police station; but for a lucky shift in the wind, that fire threatened to ignite the entire fleet as the enraged sailors terrorized the city of Honolulu for twenty-four hours. Ships also discharged sick and disabled seamen who then became the charges of the consuls. Many native Hawaiians, about two thousand between 1845–47, went down to the sea in ships of every registry. This exodus to the world's forecastles was one of the reasons for the alarming decline in the population of native Hawaiians. In the 1840's and '50's Honolulu was the chief advanced base for whaling, since over 80 per cent of the whaling fleet worked the Pacific. One of the great classics of world literature was also in the gestation stage in these parts. Herman Melville spent four months in the islands in 1843, narrowly escaping confrontation with the ship he had jumped in the South Pacific when he shipped for New York on the frigate *United States* on August 17.

Whaling can be said to have ended officially in the great crush of the winter of 1871.

It was also in Kamehameha III's reign that significant strides were made toward wide-scale agriculture. Sugar cane grew wild on the islands, and Captain Cook had reported seeing natives chewing and sucking the sweet stalks. Manoa Valley, at the head of which the University of Hawaii now stands, was the scene of an early attempt by John Wilkinson, encouraged by Governor Boki, to raise cane commercially. He was stymied by high labor costs (twenty-five cents a day) and primitive tools such as the digging stick. Even though he put over a hundred acres under cultivation, the experiment never paid, and it was abandoned three years after his death in 1826.

In 1835 an American company took a fifty-year lease on land at Koloa, Kauai. You can see the site of that first sugar mill today on the Garden Island. Natives broke ground, drawing the plows themselves due to a shortage of draft animals. Wages were twelve and a half cents a day plus food. At that date being paid for work was so new that local chiefs complained about how the wage was draining off their workers. First they used a rude wooden press to squeeze the sugar from the cane, then an iron one in 1837, and finally one driven by water power in 1841. But not until a year later did they produce sugar of even reasonable quality. By 1850 three quarters of a million pounds of sugar was exported a year.

The gold rush in California caused a boom in the sugar production in Hawaii, but a drought and depression shook the industry severely in succeeding years. Nevertheless growing settlement of Oregon and California helped the sugar industry overall. The biggest problems were a high tariff in the U.S. and low-cost competition in China and the Philippines. Unsuccessful attempts were made in 1848 and 1852 to secure a treaty with the U.S. to circumvent the tariff.

Attempts were also made then to raise coffee on a large scale. In 1828 missionaries in Kona had set out plants that were to lead to that section's thriving specialty. For about a decade, too, there were silk-raising experiments at Koloa and Hanalei, Kauai. Insects, droughts, and high winds ended that industry about 1845.

Cotton growing was tried a little longer. The missionaries wanted to start a weaving industry, and in 1835 Miss Lydia Brown began lessons at Wailuku, Maui, to teach the natives spinning and weaving. About a year and a half after the American Board sent over this instructress, she watched her first class graduate in garments they had made themselves. The government co-operated with a factory building at Kailua, and for years it looked like a promising industry. But cotton never caught on as a major business. There was a boom in the Irish potato in the Kula district of Maui during the gold rush. Wheat farming followed for a while. Ranching prospered on the Big Island.

A declining native population—decimated by disease—impeded schemes to develop agriculture more fully. During the reign of Kamehameha III, Hawaiians diminished in number by 50 per cent. In 1850 the legislature had approved the contract labor system, which prevailed for the next half century. The Royal Hawaiian Agricultural Society brought three hundred Chinese coolies into the islands in 1851 and 1852 under five-year indentures.

TRANSITION INTO THE TWENTIETH CENTURY

During the middle period of the Hawaiian kingdom (1854–72), which is marked by the reigns of Kamehameha IV (Alexander Liholiho) and V (Lot Kamehameha), the role of the American missionary declined in favor of an Anglophilia best symbolized by the establishment of the Anglican Church. The constitution of 1852 represented a reversion to more autocratic and less democratic ideals. This was due in part to the visit the two brothers made to England, where they admired the government and the church, and to America, where they resented prejudiced treatment they received and learned to abhor the institution of slavery.

Kamehameha IV ruled for only nine years, dying at twenty-nine, his health destroyed by continuing bouts of asthma and grief at the death of the four-year-old Prince Albert. Kamehameha V was not as intellectually brilliant as his brother and predecessor, but he had a better practical sense. He was a strong-willed and benevolent despot. When, for example, it was proposed that the law forbidding the sale of liquor be repealed, he refused to sign the death warrant of his people. He died a bachelor after nine years, with no successor, the last monarch in the Kamehameha line.

Sugar production developed steadily in the middle period, with improved mills, machinery, and methods. Kauai had the first irrigation ditch in 1856. The vacuum pan, which allows syrup to be boiled without scorching, was developed in the 1860's. Steam power became widely used. In 1861 rice planting was a craze on Oahu. For a long time thereafter rice was second only to sugar as a cash crop in the Hawaiian economy. In the '60's and '70's a lively trade grew up in pulu, the silky fiber at the base of tree-fern fronds, used in filling mattresses and pillows in America.

In an attempt to attract tourists in 1871 and 1872 the government almost doubled its national debt by constructing the Royal Hawaiian Hotel at its first site, Richards and Hotel streets, for $110,000. Two unlucky cabinet ministers lost their jobs for getting behind this unpopular project. Additional new construction included what is now the state judiciary building, then the legislative and office building for the government, Aliiolani Hale, which was finished in 1874.

When Kamehameha V died, the only person left alive in the dynasty was Princess Bernice Pauahi. Had she married a prince, she could have inherited the throne. Instead she chose to wed Charles Bishop, a customs collector who became a banker. As a result, the Kamehameha lands came to private hands, where they were put in trust to support the school for native Hawaiians named after the first king of all Hawaii.

After Kamehameha V died without naming a successor, Lunalilo became the first king to be elected by the people. Lunalilo means literally "lost to view" from *luna* (above) and *lilo* (lost), or so far above as to be out of sight. He was chosen by popular vote on New Year's Day 1873. He went to the Big Island with Queen Emma and Princess Bernice Pauahi to regain his health, but died after having been "The King of the People" for not more than a year. He left his property and money to found the Lunalilo home for the aged and poor Hawaiians out near Koko Head.

The next king elected, David Kalakaua, the Merry Monarch, took his wife Kapiolani with him as the first king to visit the United States. His good-will trip in 1874 made such a good impression on President Grant and the Congress that he secured a reciprocity treaty allowing Hawaii to ship tax-free rice and sugar to the United States beginning in 1876, the most significant achievement of his administration. During the seven years of the treaty America was to have the right to use Pearl Harbor for a coaling station. As sugar production boomed, a grateful legislature authorized the construction of Iolani Palace for the Merry Monarch. His insouciant approach to affairs prompted his people to say of him that "he wore his troubles as lightly as a feather cape."

When Kalakaua went on his round-the-world tour to see what other kings were doing to express their power and dignity, he left his sister Princess Liliuokalani in charge. One of the gravest crises she had to cope with was a devastating volcanic eruption on the Big Island, reactions to which showed that the pagan religion was not wholly dead. Mauna Loa was shooting hundred-foot-high fountains of lava into the sky, and Hilo was threatened. A chieftainess who had been rocked on the knee of Kamehameha the Great offered to confront Pele. She went to the edge of the crater and threw in ohelo berries that quickly burned. Next she tried lehua blossoms because they were Pele's flowers. They disappeared. Then she took a gourd of *awa* water, which is Pele's drink, and threw it into the fire. In the smoke that resulted, Pele's shape was descried. The chieftainess pleaded: "Do not be angry with us. If we die, who will sing for you? Who will tell of your wonderful power?" That night the volcano stopped its destruction! A later tradition of interpretation, taken by E. G. Burrows, asserts that when Princess Ruth tried to stop the lava flow near Hilo in 1881, it is interesting to note that she threw haole substitutes into the lava as propitiatory offerings to Pele: brandy instead of the old *awa* and red silk in lieu of red ohelo berries. New kinds of wine for the same old bottles.

When King Kalakaua returned from his royalty-inspection tour, he announced to his subjects that every decent king had to be crowned properly. No matter that no other Hawaiian king had had a coronation ceremony. No other king, after all, had seen as much of how things were supposed to be done royally as Kalakaua had. So preparations were made.

The king ordered two crowns of gold and precious stones from England. Outside the recently finished Iolani Palace he had constructed a coronation gazebo decorated with royal crests. Dresses were ordered from Europe. The queen's eight ladies in waiting were dressed in black velvet and white satin. The queen was resplendent in a gown of red velvet trimmed in white fur. Kalakaua saved for himself the most glamorous costume of all: a white German uniform heavily becrusted with a generous assortment of medals and ribbons. His helmet had a red, white, and blue plume! To top things off, he crowned himself and then his queen. For a week he proved himself indeed the Merry Monarch with a round of festivities.

A major reason Kalakaua founded Hale Naua, the Temple of Science, when he returned from his world tour in 1881, was that he found Christianity had become "a waning cause" in the Western world. "Shall we Hawaiians take up the worship of a god whom foreigners are discarding? The old gods of Hawaii are good enough for us." The *hoomanamana*, or idolatry, he revived is quaint in the extreme. While in haole chronology it was founded on September 24, 1886, according to its own constitution it was forty quadrillions of years after the foundation of the world and 24,750 years after the birth of Lailai, the first woman. It was a travesty of Masonry mingled with pagan rites.

Carried away by his delusions of grandeur, Kalakaua fancied himself "King of the Pacific." Since he was fifty the same year Queen Victoria celebrated her fiftieth year as monarch, he decided that the coincidence ought to be widely noticed. After a huge birthday celebration in Honolulu, he, Queen Kapiolani, and Princess Liliuokalani went to England to help Victoria celebrate. He came home in haste to put down spreading disaffection. When his health failed, he went to California to regain it, never to return. Before he died on January 20, 1891, (probably of Bright's disease) he made a record on one of the earliest phonographs: "Tell my people aloha!" he said sorrowfully. "Tell them that I tried." The recording is still kept in the Bernice P. Bishop Museum.

Kalakaua had chosen his successor, Princess Liliuokalani, and she was known and respected throughout the islands and the world. The talented and accomplished woman was well educated. She composed music competently enough to create the beautiful Hawaiian song *Aloha Oe*. Her main problem was her strong will. She told her cabinet that the queen had a right to change the constitution whenever she wanted to. The cabinet met with a newly formed Committee of Safety to discuss a paper signed by eighty of the most influential people on the island, warning the queen that if she declared a new constitution they would fight her. Faced with this ultimatum, she backed down and went to the palace balcony to tell the people that she had relented. The Committee of Safety had gone too far, however, to retreat. Flushed with their first success against the strong-willed queen, they pushed their advantage to call for annexation to the United States. The impasse seemed a battle between old and new. On the one side the queen with her troops and most of the native Hawaiians; on the other, many businessmen and island leaders. In 1893 the Committee of Safety set up a provisional government with Sanford B. Dole as president. The American flag was raised at all government buildings, next to the Hawaiian one. The queen stepped down, confident that she would be vindicated by Washington when her story was heard. Grover Cleveland sent James Blount to study the question, and he reported in favor of the queen. But the Provisional Government would not give up the power it had assumed. It went ahead with its work to create a constitution for the republic. On the Fourth of July, 1894, President Dole announced from the steps of Iolani Palace that Hawaii was henceforth to be a republic. Dole was to be the first president for a term of six years. The flag of Hawaii was raised and *Hawaii Pono*, the national anthem, was played.

Queen Liliuokalani's supporters made one last effort to regain control, but the rebellion fizzled. The queen was tried and found guilty. Her sentence of five years' labor and a fine of five thousand dollars was never carried out, but she was banished from the palace, forbidden ever to hold political meetings, and was sent to her own house, Washington Place, which is now the Governor's Mansion in Hawaii. Lydia Liliuokalani, plain citizen, then made a trip to America, where she was shown great attention. She died in the great affection of her people after returning to the Republic of Hawaii.

The late John H. Wilson, the part-Hawaiian who was a long-time Democratic mayor of Honolulu, used to make a bitter quip about the McKinley Tariff of 1890, expressing the resentment of many non-haoles against the overthrow of Queen Liliuokalani by the sugar interests: "For two cents a pound in the price of sugar a queen beloved by her people was overthrown." And Aunt Jenny Wilson, his equally beloved widow, who died in 1962, echoed his sentiments: "They didn't take the country in a good way. They took it by force. They stole it from a queen who refused to sign away the rights of her people. They made her a prisoner." In the early days of territorial government there was an attempt among the Hawaiians to establish ethnic block voting. The slogan was *Nana ka hili* ("Look at the skin"). In those days the great majority of the electorate was dark-skinned. This terrified the haole politicians, who immediately saw to it that there would be racial representation on both parties.

The Spanish-American War finally precipitated the long-crystallizing process of annexation. American soldiers and sailors on their way to Manila were given a royal aloha. Then on July 13, 1898, an American warship was sighted coming around Diamond Head. Its signal flags spelled out an announcement: "ANNEXATION" that triggered a great celebration. Shortly thereafter President Dole read the paper signed by President McKinley making this Pacific outpost part of American territory.

In order to understand twentieth-century Hawaii one must also look at its economy. The four "legs" of this economy are the military, sugar, tourism, and pineapple—in that order. Its most intriguing aspect has been its rapid modernization. The story of the mechanization and industrialization of Hawaii's agriculture is epic in proportions, as we have indicated. Fuels, minerals, and electric power are in short supply because of the volcanic nature of the islands. (The construction industry, by the way, is slowly catching on to the good sense of concrete construction in an economy that has to import lumber and steel used in building; look for the handsome lava rocks and coral aggregates that are being used to give this kind of construction a decidedly regional cast.)

The present billion-dollar economy was first drawn from its primitive origins when sandalwood and whale-oil trading involved Hawaii in other national economies. The sugar plantations boomed when the reciprocity treaty of 1876 gave them entry to the U.S. market. The trading firms in Honolulu which factored for the plantations became the Big Five, which, until the emergence of economically articulate Orientals after World War II, virtually dominated the economy. You can see their handsome offices downtown: Theo. H. Davies, Alexander and Baldwin, Castle and Cooke, C. Brewer, and American Factors (the latter a name assumed like "liberty cabbage" for sauerkraut during World War I for a German firm, Hackfeld). In the beginning, population was more evenly distributed among the islands, and each depended on Honolulu, with a well-sheltered port and leeward protection from the elements, for its commerce with the outside world. As industrial agriculture became more mechanized, total acreage and the number of plantations both dropped, and Honolulu tended to become an employment center, too. This dependence on agricultural commodities continued through the mid-1930's.

Since World War II, however, the Hawaiian economy has been moving away from overdependence on sugar and pineapple, to more construction activity, retail trade, and service businesses, which depended in turn on expanding military and tourist expenditures. In the 1930's, for example, the military spent thirty-one million dollars a year. In 1963 it spent over ten times that amount. The Bank of Hawaii estimates that one-quarter of all business is dependent on military spending. The Hawaiian economy thus leans more and more heavily on federal spending and on the maintenance of prosperity on the mainland to keep tourists willing to come. The roughly one million tons of sugar produced a year is fairly constant and underpinned by a quota system. Pineapple, of which Hawaii supplied 90 per cent of the world's supply as recently as the late 1940's, is losing its share of the world market rapidly. It can try to keep part of the U.S. market by legislation (getting the fruit included in the federal lunch program, for example) or by new packaging (flash-frozen methods and increased communication with mainland home economists with recipes that *include* pineapple instead of making it the only ingredient).

What are the advantages and disadvantages that face the Hawaiian economy in the future? Its disadvantages include relatively few natural resources, high labor cost compared with competitive tourist areas, high taxes and high transportation costs discouraging to new industries, high land prices, relatively small local markets for which mainland production is cheaper, which also discourage industrial development. Hawaii's advantages, on the other hand, are considerable. Its incomparable climate and landscape top the list. Its geographical location gives the island chain strategic and political significance. And of course its multiethnic population living in peaceful productivity is an example to the rest of the world. A tourist economy can use these advantages, but such an industry is extremely sensitive to prosperity. Building stabilizing factors into the economy is thus extremely urgent. Surprisingly, education has seemed to the most thoughtful in Hawaii as the complementary factor that will stabilize the tourist economy. The East-West Center for Technical and Cultural Interchange at the University of Hawaii, for example, is supported by several millions in federal dollars each year, bringing Asians on government scholarships to acquire skills that will modernize their countries. Americans come to study Asian languages and cultures so that the United States can get along more humanely with its Asian "neighbors" in our shrinking globe. With the founding of the East-West Center, America has found a way superior to colonization in the Pacific. It says, in effect, that the Pacific will remain a paradise for Americans and others only as long as we help one another endure the promise and peril of modernization.

Chapter III

OAHU

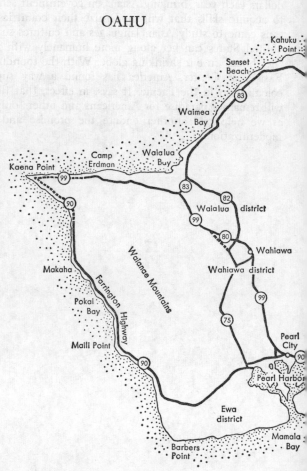

OAHU

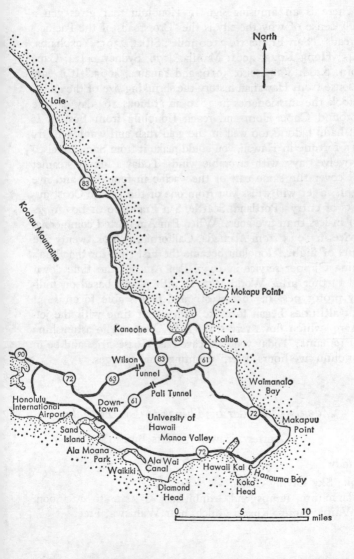

Honolulu in a Shrinking World

There is an amusing sign in Honolulu that gives you a lively sense of why the city is the "Crossroads of the Pacific." It reads: "San Francisco, 2100 miles; Sitka, 2395; Yokohama, 3445; Hong Kong, 4961; Manila, 4778; Sydney, 4424; Cape Horn, 6488; Valparaiso, 5916; and Panama, 4665." It is easy to sense from Hawaiian history the shrinking size of the globe. It took the missionaries in 1819 an arduous 164-day passage to round Cape Horn and reach Honolulu from Boston. If you hadn't done too well in the gold rush and wanted to try for a fortune in Hawaii, you could make it from San Francisco in twelve days, with favorable winds. Today a luxury steamer will cover the same part of the Pacific in four days and five nights; a jet will whisk you from one of the Pacific Coast airports of entry (Portland, Seattle, San Francisco or Los Angeles) in less than five hours. When Pan Am started commercial service in 1935 from Alameda, California, it took twenty-one hours of flight. Honolulu became the first stop for that line's China Clipper service in 1937. Pan Am cut the time down still further after World War II with planes based on military prototypes. In 1952 westbound flights able to cruise at high altitudes began to make even better time with the jetstream, which flows very strongly in winter. The astonishing fact remains: Today you can leave East Coast cities and be in Honolulu five hours "later," counting time changes.

Weekly Calendar of Things to Do on Oahu

(Courtesy, Hawaii Visitors Bureau)

Sunday

Aloha Sky Diving Club
   Parachute jumps and exhibitions, 8 A.M. to 12 noon, Waipio Acres, Kipapa Gulch, near Wahiawa. Free.

Church Services
All denominations (with special bus service, leaving from major Waikiki hotels, provided by the Honolulu Council of Churches). Consult newspaper or hotel desk.

Honolulu Skeet Club Shoot
9 A.M., Kaneohe Marine Air Station, Kailua, Windward Oahu. Guns and ammunition available. Contact Mr. W. K. Thom at 586-764 or 566-456.

Royal Hawaiian Band Concert
2 P.M., Kapiolani Park Band Stand (except August). Free.

Tennent Art Foundation Gallery
3 P.M. to 6 P.M., call 506-952 for further information. Free.

Luaus (Hawaiian feasts)
Hilton Hawaiian Village Hotel, 6 P.M., call 994-321; Royal Hawaiian Hotel, 6:30 P.M., call 937-311; Queen's Surf, 6:30 P.M., call 937-387 and the Duke Kahanamoku's, 7 P.M., call 937-377. Includes Polynesian entertainment, food, and refreshments. Reservations required.

Concert by the Sea
7:30 P.M., Moana Hotel Banyan Court. Island artists in program of light classics. Free.

Hike with Hawaiian Trail and Mountain Club
Meet 8 A.M., Hotel Street side of Iolani Palace. Bring water and lunch. For information call 92-211.

Monday

Clubs
East Honolulu Rotary, noon, M's Ranch House, Aina Haina; Pearl Harbor Rotary, 12 noon, Pearl City Tavern.

"Night in the Philippines"
7 P.M., Filipino dinner and program of songs and dances of the Philippines, Reef Hotel. For reservations call 938-436.

Ale Ale Kai V
Catamaran sunset supper sail, 5:30 P.M., Kewalo Basin. Two-hour sail with dinner, entertainment, and refreshments. For reservations call 576-355.

Tuesday

Chinatown Shopping and Temple Tour
9:30 A.M., Chinese Chamber of Commerce, 42 North King St. For reservations call 503-181.

Kodak Hula Show
10 A.M., on the lawn in front of Waikiki Natatorium. Free.

Flower Arrangements (seasonal)
Demonstration by Frances Thompson. 11 A.M., Hilton Hawaiian Village Hotel; 1:30 P.M., Princess Kaiulani Hotel or Moana Hotel. Free.

Clubs
Honolulu Lions, noon, Armed Services YMCA; Honolulu Rotary, noon, Royal Hawaiian Hotel; Honolulu Kiwanis, noon, Reef Hotel.

"An Evening in Japan"
6:30 P.M., dinner with geisha-Korean entertainment at a Japanese teahouse. For reservations call 933-861 or 938-436.

Malihini Night Party
7 P.M., Pikake Terrace, Princess Kaiulani Hotel. Buffet supper, fashion show, Polynesian entertainment. For reservations call 938-411.

Wednesday

Honolulu Senior Citizens Club
Recreation for islanders and visitors over fifty years of age; 10 A.M., Kapiolani Beach Center next to Queen's Surf. Bridge, checkers, croquet. Free.

Clubs
Wahiawa-Waialua Kiwanis, noon, Kemoo Farm, Wahiawa; Ala Moana Kiwanis, noon, Banquet Room, Ala Moana Center; Waikiki Rotary, noon, Reef Hotel. Visitors welcome at all clubs.

Fashion Show Luncheon
12 noon, Monarch Room, Royal Hawaiian Hotel. Fashions by Carol & Mary. For reservations call 937-311.

Ale Ale Kai V
   Catamaran sunset supper sail, 5:30 P.M., Kewalo Basin. Two-hour sail with dinner, entertainment and refreshments. For reservations call 576-355.

"Na Kupuna Night"
   6:30 P.M., old-timer Hawaiian party at Moana Hotel Banyan Court. Call 939-811 for reservations.

Luau (Hawaiian feast)
   6:00 P.M., Hilton Hawaiian Village Hotel, call 994-321, Special Events Desk.

Thursday

Kodak Hula Show
   10 A.M., on the lawn near Waikiki Natatorium. Free.

Flower Arrangements
   Demonstration by Frances Thompson. 10 A.M., Coconut Grove Lanai, Royal Hawaiian Hotel. Free.

Clubs
   Wahiawa-Waialua Rotary, noon, Kemoo Farm; Windward Rotary, noon, Mid-Pacific Country Club, Kailua; Waikiki Lions, noon, Moana Hotel; Waikiki Kiwanis, noon, Reef Hotel; Kaneohe Kiwanis, noon, Haiku Gardens, Kaneohe.

"A Night in Cathay"
   6:30 P.M., Lau Yee Chai Restaurant, nine-course Chinese dinner, fashion show, entertainment. For reservations call 992-487 or 998-753.

Slide Presentation on Hawaii
   8 P.M., Hilton Hawaiian Village Hotel in the Tree Fern Room. Free.

Friday

Fashion Show Luncheon
   12 noon, Makahiki Room, Hilton Hawaiian Village Hotel. For reservations call 994-321.

Clubs
   West Honolulu Rotary, noon, Hilton Hawaiian Village Hotel.

Ale Ale Kai V
Catamaran sunset supper sail, 5:30 P.M., Kewalo Basin. Two-hour sail with dinner, entertainment. For reservations call 576-355.

Luau Starlight Cruise
5:30 P.M., native feast, Hawaiian chants, lore, music and dances on board the *Kaimanu*, eighty-five-foot yacht. For reservations call 501-202.

"Polynesian Water Spectacular"
7 P.M., Reef Hotel. Buffet supper and beautiful water show. For reservations call 938-436.

Saturday

50th State Sport Parachute Club
Exhibitions and jumps, 8:30 A.M. to 1 P.M., Waipio Acres, Wahiawa. For information call 811-112. Free.

Saturday Art Mart
10 A.M. to 4 P.M., Honolulu Zoo Fence, Kalakaua-Monsarrat avenues. Display and sale of paintings by island artists.

Cricket
1:30 P.M., Kapiolani Park. Free.

Hawaii Calls
2 to 2:30 P.M., national network radio broadcast from Waikiki. Luncheon served from 12 noon. Reservations advised for luncheon; program is free. Location changes every Saturday; call 92-211.

DAILY ACTIVITIES

Academy of Arts
35 galleries of Oriental and Western art. Open 10 A.M to 4:30 P.M., Tuesday, Wednesday, Friday, Saturday; 10 A.M. to 9:30 P.M., Thursday; 3 to 6 P.M., Sunday. At 900 South Beretania Street, opposite Thomas Square. Free.

Aloha Tower
Famous landmark of Hawaii located at the foot of Fort Street. Open 8 A.M. to 5 P.M. daily. Free.

Aquarium
World's finest tropical fish collection plus other marine displays. Open Tuesday to Saturday 10 A.M. to 5 P.M.; Sunday 1 P.M. to 5 P.M. Admission 25 cents. Children under 16 free.

Bishop Museum
Houses world's greatest Hawaiian collection. Open 9 A.M. to 4:30 P.M., Monday to Saturday, admission charged. Sunday from 2 to 5 P.M. Free.

Foster Gardens
Public botanical park with fine orchid collection, plus rare tropical trees and vines. Open from 9 A.M. to 5 P.M. daily. Free. 1520 Nuuanu Avenue.

International Market Place
Authentic dancing, music, drumming, costumes of Hawaii, Tahiti, Samoa, and New Zealand, 7 P.M. Free.

Iolani Palace
Built as a residence for Hawaiian rulers during the monarchy. The only royal palace in the United States. King and Richards streets. Open Monday to Friday, 8 A.M. to 12 noon and 1 to 4 P.M. Saturday from 8 A.M. to noon. Free.

Kilolani Planetarium
On Bishop Museum grounds. Open daily except Monday. Programs at 10:30 A.M. and 3 P.M., Tuesday to Friday; 8 P.M., Wednesday, Friday, and Saturday; 2 P.M. and 3 P.M. Saturday and Sunday. Adults 75 cents; children 25 cents.

National Cemetery
Located in Punchbowl Crater. Panoramic view of half the island from parklike setting. Open daily 8 A.M. to 5 P.M.

Perfume Factory Tours
Browny's, call 583-861; Liana's, call 59-229. Monday to Friday. Free.

Pineapple Cannery Tour
Seasonal (January to October), weather permitting, conducted by Dole Corporation, call 563-411 for day's tour schedule. Monday to Friday. 50 cents per person.

Queen Emma Museum
Former summer palace of King Kamehameha IV and Queen Emma. Open Monday to Friday, 9 A.M. to 4 P.M., Saturday 9 A.M. to noon. Closed Sunday, holidays. Adults 50 cents, children 25 cents, 2913 Pali Highway.

Sugar Mill Tours
10 A.M. and 2 P.M., Oahu Sugar Mill, call 273-349; Ewa Sugar Mill, 10:30 A.M. and 2:30 P.M., call 283-591. Seasonal.

Village of Ulu Mau
Hawaiian people showing their arts and crafts and telling of their ways of life. Open 9:30 A.M. to 4 P.M., Ala Moana Park. Closed Sunday and Monday.

Woodworking Factory Tours
9 A.M. to 4 P.M., 1207 Hopaka Street, call 586-727. Monday to Friday. Free.

Zoo
In Kapiolani Park, Waikiki. Largest tropical bird collection in the world plus standard animals. Open 9 A.M. to 5 P.M. daily. Free.

SIGHTSEEING AND TOURS

The following daily events can be booked through any travel desk or tour operator. Rates on request.

Barkentine *California*
Sail to Diamond Head aboard square-rigger for dinner, refreshments, and entertainment, 5:30 P.M.

Catamaran Sunset Supper Sail
Departs 5:30 P.M. from Hilton Hawaiian Village Hotel. Dinner, refreshments, and entertainment.

Circle Island Tour of Oahu
110-mile, seven-and-a-half-hour, round-the-island tour via Nuuanu Pali. Departs 9 A.M.

Glassbottom Boat Trips
11 A.M. and 2 P.M., Heeia-kea Boat Pier, Heeia, windward Oahu. Daily except Tuesday. Call 240-375.

Mount Tantalus Drive
Three-hour drive including Iolani Palace, Punchbowl Memorial, University of Hawaii. Departs 9:30 A.M.

Nite Club Tours
Nightly except Sunday, 8:30 P.M. to 12:30 A.M., visit to three exciting night spots. Leave from major Waikiki hotels.

Pearl Harbor Cruise
Conducted tour to historic site of U.S.S. *Arizona* aboard the *Adventure, Ale Ale Kai V, Kaimanu,* or *Leilani.* Depart Kewalo Basin 9:30 A.M. and 1:30 P.M.

Oahu: An Overview

Oahu means "The Gathering Place." Its two mountain ranges, the eastern Koolau and the western Waianae, are what remains of the volcanic domes from which the island grew. In the central valley of Oahu is the Wahiawa plateau. It was formed between the Koolau and Waianae mountain ranges by overflow lava from the old Koolau crater. Schofield Barracks, founded in 1908 and named after the general who took command at Richmond after Lee's surrender, is on this plateau. King Kalakaua also had a hunting lodge there. There is a saying in Hawaii that when the Waianae's Mount Kaala the highest point on Oahu (4046 feet) is free of clouds it is going to rain. Honolulu was once called Brown's Harbor in honor of a ship captain who broke through the coral reef to anchor his ship there. He is supposed to have called it Fair Haven, which, according to some, is the meaning of the city's name. The name itself, however, can be broken down into *hono,* which means "joining together" (the flat place that connects two higher places), and *lulu,* which means "a shelter from the wind." In this interpretation Honolulu's name refers to a wind-sheltered place in the flats between the two mountain ranges (which is *why* it is a Fair Haven!).

The Outer Islands HVB offices will probably hate me for this, but after all is said and done, Oahu, especially Honolulu, is what I love most of the Hawaiian Islands. It combines in a unique way the slower pace of the Outer Islands with the intensity of civilized life that inhabitants of Eastern-seaboard cities like New York and Philadelphia are in the habit of enjoying. And this civilized diversity is accessible not only to the affluent who can afford the splendor of the Waikiki hostelries or the "suburban" isolation of the Outer Islands. On a purely qualitative level it seems to me that the less you have to pay the better the attractions are. While this may be rationalization, I suggest that you test my hypothesis: you obviously have very little to lose!

The first way to save money is to take public buses instead of U-drives or tour limousines. If you don't have much time in Hawaii or even Oahu, take the Gray Line tour around the islands the first day and Honolulu Rapid Transit buses the following days.

GRAY LINE TOUR

If you prefer once-over-lightly sights to seeing a few things intensively, you should forgo the intellectual pleasures of scouting Honolulu's cultural attractions (described later in "The Egghead's Honolulu") for a more prosaic trip around the islands. The Gray Line air-conditioned-bus tour covers a hundred miles in seven and a half hours and costs $6.50. It leaves at 9:30 A.M. with pickups at the Waikikian, Hawaiian Village, Reef Tower, Royal Hawaiian, and Moana hotels in that order. You will see the best-known sights this way, and the tour drivers are fluent if sometimes idiosyncratic in their Hawaiiana. You will make a stop at the famed Pali Lookout, where you can buy bead leis, be photographed with scantily clad Tahitian dancers. You will lunch at Sheraton's Heeia, visit Bob Miller's House of Coral, and slake your thirst at Dole's Helemano stand right in the middle of the pineapple country.

HONOLULU RAPID TRANSIT TOURS

The city bus line also has a round-the-island tour, which leaves downtown from the Alexander Young Hotel at 8:45

A.M. with pickups at the Waikikian (8:57), Hawaiian Village (9:00), Fort De Russy (9:03), Halekulani (9:05), Royal Hawaiian (9:10), Moana-Surfrider (9:15), Kuhio Park (9:16), and the corner of Kalakaua Avenue and Ohua Street (9:17), daily except Saturday and Sunday. You can buy tickets on the spot for $5.50, tax included, if seats are available. The tour terminates in Waikiki about 4:45 P.M., just in time for a cool afternoon swim at Prince Kuhio or the Queen's Surf beaches. The Honolulu Rapid Transit publishes a very handy free map outlining its tour and, more importantly, showing what you can visit *inside* Honolulu by using public transportation. You should get this map as soon as you get ashore. Ask a bus driver for one, or go to the Rapid Transit offices at Beretania and South streets. Even if you plan to scout around town in a jeep, I think you'll find this map the best for a beginner to use in locating the most visited places. The free road maps you find at service stations are all made by the same mapmaker, but they can be confusing to a newcomer. Still it would be a good idea to drop a card to one of the major oil companies asking for its island map to study on the boat or plane. On one side you'll find Honolulu and vicinity. On the other side, clear topographical maps of all the islands you can visit. Write Chevron, Union 76, or Shell.

There are four basic Rapid Transit tours inside Honolulu and vicinity in addition to the round-the-island trip. Here are the highlights of the big four:

Kahala-Kaimuki-Maunalani Heights

Diamond Head	Lunalilo Home for Aged
Koko Head	Hawaiians
Pearl Harbor	Maunalua Bay
Kapiolani Park and	Waialae-Kahala residential
Aquarium	section
Natatorium	Kaimuki business and resi-
Kuapa Fish Ponds	dential areas
Kaiser's Hawaii Kai	

Three hours and three fares (25 cents each) plus 2 zone fares (5 cents).

Lower Tantalus-Maikiki Heights-Manoa Valley

Papakolea Hawaiian Homesteads
Punchbowl National Memorial Cemetery of the Pacific
Punahou School
Waioli Tea Room
Honolulu Academy of Arts
Alfred Preis's First Methodist Church
Mormon Tabernacle
Central Union Church

Two to three hours and three fares.

Nuuanu Valley-Alewa-Pacific Heights

Royal Mausoleum
Queen Emma Museum.
Soto Temple
Foster Botanical Gardens
Alewa and Pacific Heights residential areas

Three to four hours and five fares.

Bishop Museum-Fort Shafter-Tripler Hospital-Moanalua Housing

Bishop Museum
Fort Shafter
Tripler U.S. Army Hospital, largest in the world
Marine Camp Catlin, World War II staging area
Aliamanu-Moanalua residential areas, former
　Damon estate
Red Hill, underground oil storage

Three to four hours and four fares plus two zone fares.

Another advantage to taking public buses is that you can see and talk with Hawaiians instead of other tourists. And since these tours are strung together from regular bus routes (remember that you'll need the map and instructions for complicated transfers), you will see all of Honolulu, not just the glossy, flossy pictures of the travel brochures. If you plan to make more than one bus tour, you can save a little by buying five tickets for a dollar.

But you can also argue that, if Honolulu is the most interesting part of Hawaii, then the way to start exploring the fiftieth state is to scout everything within walking distance of the Aloha Tower dock—the way an Orient-bound one-day-stopover passenger would do—and then move out in wider and wider circles the longer you stay over. Therefore, I'm going to describe what to me were the most interesting parts of the city and county of Honolulu in the following order: downtown Honolulu, Ala Moana Shopping Center and Park, the University of Hawaii and East-West Center, International Market Place, Waikiki, Kapiolani Park, Hawaii Kai and Hanauma Bay, Windward Oahu, Laie Samoan Village and Mormon Temple, Kaena Point and Ewa District, Pearl Harbor, and Honolulu International Airport. It's frustrating, of course, to see how much more there is to highbrow and lowbrow Honolulu when you only have a week or so to spend looking. One way to soothe the frustration is to buy books and recordings at places like the Bishop Museum or the Honolulu Book Shops. Or find out in the basement of the Library of Hawaii how many excellent films about Hawaii have been made by George Tahara and other local film makers. There are more ways than by being there to get the aloha spirit.

Getting a Good Look

There are two fine vantage points for the new visitor to gain a good over-all impression of the layout of Honolulu, which sprawls twenty-five miles along Oahu's leeward shore. The first of these is the Aloha Tower, which dominates the slips where ocean-going boats dock. From here or from the top of the First National Bank Building, downtown Honolulu's first skyscraper, you can obtain a splendid view of all you will want to see in detail both in downtown Honolulu and in the outlying parts of the city. I think it is a good idea to begin one's visit to Hawaii with such a panorama by going either to the top of Aloha Tower or to the roof of the First National Bank Building. It orients the malihini much more quickly than a flat map can.

Seaward and slightly Ewa is Sand Island (you won't of course say seaward but *makai*); more directly Ewa (i.e., in the direction of the Ewa district when downtown) is the Iwilei district, where the Dole Company has a fascinating pineapple-packing-plant tour. As you look up Nuuanu stream, the notch in the distant mountain backdrop is the Nuuanu Pali, on the way to which you can visit the Royal Mausoleum and Queen Emma's summer home. *Mauka* (i.e., toward the mountains) and slightly Diamond Head is the Civic Center, with Iolani Palace, and across South King Street the Judiciary Building. Up South King Street you will see Kawaiahao Church. Across the street from it is the Library of Hawaii, where the leisurely visitor should begin his odyssey in Hawaii. Toward Punchbowl, which contains the National Memorial Cemetery of the Pacific, you will find the Academy of Arts on South Beretania Street.

As your eye follows Ala Moana Boulevard toward Diamond Head, you will see a high-rise office building with a revolving restaurant on it. That is in the Ala Moana Center across from Ala Moana Beach Park. Farther on the way to Diamond Head is Waikiki, which you can identify by the many high-rise hotels you will see. *Mauka* of Waikiki on the edge of the Manoa Valley are the University of Hawaii and the East-West Center.

Downtown

THE CIVIC CENTER

What promises to be the handsomest part of Honolulu's Civic Center remains to be built: the new State Capitol, which combines the latest architectural technology with modernized Oriental motifs. Until that striking center is completed, you can see a model of it inside Iolani Palace, which is billed as the only royal palace in the United States. Note the band shell on the Iolani Palace grounds, where King Kalakaua crowned himself after having taken a cram course around the world studying the latest fashions in royalty.

Across from the Iolani Palace is the Judiciary Building. In front of it is King Kamehameha's statue. It is the focal point of the King Kamehameha Day Parade each June.

IOLANI PALACE

The Hawaiian Senate now meets in what was the royal dining hall in Iolani Palace. Upstairs you will see what were the royal apartments, in a corner room of which the deposed Queen Liliuokalani spent a bitter year as a prisoner of the Hawaiian Republic. There is another room where Kalakaua, the Merry Monarch, is supposed to have participated with his cronies in pagan rites and old Hawaiian pastimes like the forfeit game *kilu*, which has been described as "like post office only more serious." This was perhaps the supreme example of Hawaiian hospitality.

KAMEHAMEHA'S STATUE

When the legislature of 1878 decided to commemorate the centennial of the discovery of the islands by Captain Cook, they resolved to raise a statue to Kamehameha. Kohala, on the Big Island, argued that it should be there where he was born. When the legislature rebuffed them, they replied: "You will see; the statue will still come to Kohala." When the statue had been molded by Thomas R. Gould in Florence, it was shipped aboard the German vessel *G. F. Haendel* in September 1880. The ship caught fire and sank off the Falklands near the bottom of South America. A junk dealer salvaged the statue, and a captain taking a shipload of Portuguese laborers to Honolulu bought it in Port Stanley on speculation for resale. So when the original arrived in Honolulu, a replica for Aliiolani Hale had already been purchased with insurance money. The original ended up after all in Kohala, where you can see it at Hawi on the Big Island.

The statue of Kamehameha the Great that stands outside Aliiolani Hale, across King Street from Iolani Palace, commemorates the momentous time in 1795 when the king summoned a great fleet of a thousand canoes off Upolu Point with a blast on Kihapu. This magic conch shell was embellished with the teeth of conquered chieftains whose groans were supposed to be heard in the blowing of the horn, which was so powerful that it could be heard from Waipio, on the northeast seacoast of the Big Island, to the mountain village of Waimea. At the base of King Kamehameha's statue in front of Aliiolani Hale, which is now the Judiciary Building, there are four tableaux from the great ruler's life: (1) the legendary feat of his catching several spears thrown at him at once; (2) his reviewing of a fleet of canoes off his birthplace near Kohala; (3) his first encounter with Captain Cook; and (4) his invoking the Law of the Splintered Paddle. The original of the statue stands on the courthouse lawn in the village of Kapaau.

KAWAIAHAO CHURCH

Inside Kawaiahao Church you can see tablets honoring missionary pioneers and the most ardent converts of Hawaiian royalty to Christianity. There is a bronze tablet, for example, to Binamu, which is as close as the Hawaiian could bring his language to Bingham. And there is a tablet on which are cast the dying words of Elizabeth Kaahumanu in her Manoa Valley home: *"Eia No Au, E Iesu E* [Lo, here I am, O Jesus], *E Nana Oluolu Mai* [Grant Me Thy Gracious Smile]."

LUNALILO'S TOMB

This is one of the most interesting structures near Hawaii's Westminster Abbey. Only two of the dynasty that ruled Hawaii are buried outside the Royal Mausoleum in Nuuanu Valley: Kamehameha the Great, whose burial place is a secret cave known to none, and Lunalilo, the King of the People, who desired to be buried by them in Kawaiahao Churchyard, where his mother also lay. You can see it there today, a little marvel of Victoriana. His tomb was not ready, so he had to be reburied on November 23, 1875. Kalakaua was so jealous of his predecessor that he forbade the gun batteries on Punchbowl to fire a royal salute during the reburial ceremony. The funeral procession, however, as it slowly marched the long route from the Royal Mausoleum to the center of the city, was treated to a display of thunder that appealed strongly to the Hawaiian sense of nature worship that flourished underneath a thin veneer of Christianity. An earsplitting crash had begun the display just as the party of troops, sixty wailing Hawaiian women, and plumed hearse followed by the aged Kanaina in his carriage left the royal burial grounds. Just as the coffin was being put into its crypt, a final blast of thunder shook Oahu. Several superstitious Hawaiians had counted the number of thunderclaps during the procession: twenty-one, the precise salute he was refused by his ill-natured successor.

LIBRARY OF HAWAII

To get the most out of your visit to Hawaii if you have more than one day, and to help keep the aloha spell long after you've returned to the mainland, start by spending a half hour at the Library of Hawaii's Central Library. It's kitty-corner from Kawaiahao Church, on King Street, just Waikiki of downtown. Even if you don't want to read anything this trip, you'll want to see how libraries were meant to be—the open courts for casual reading there are among the most relaxing places I've ever been. You can also get a mimeographed list of Hawaiiana there free. The Hawaiiana Room at the central branch will be most helpful, regardless of your intellectual interests: skin-diving, mythology, flora and fauna, or ethnic sociology.

One of the most attractive features of the library's services is its circulating artists' exhibits. In a typical year, from January to September, fourteen artists, ranging from University of Hawaii painting or photography instructors to the delightful "Grandma Moses of Hawaii," septuagenerian Popo Wong, exhibit their works for three weeks on a circuit that goes from the main branch through ten others. A schedule of who is showing where may be obtained from the publicity director of the library at the main branch, telephone 506-081, Ext. 17. The exhibits are open during library hours: Monday to Friday, 9 to 9; Saturday, 9 to 5; Sunday, 1 to 5.

Just a word about Popo Wong (Lee Kam Yee Wong). Popo means "Elderly One" in Cantonese. She started painting her delightfully colored primitives in 1960 after her artist son-in-law, Hon-Chew Hee, gave her several lessons. Not surprisingly, the mainland Moses' snow is replaced in paradise by Popo's sunny, strangely intense colors. Mrs. Wong paints strictly for recreation, first sketching a composition in pencil, then filling it in with oils in three or four weeks. Though she sometimes works from memory, more often she just looks around her for her subjects. Her garden is a rich source of paintings: pear and lichee trees, tangerines and mangoes, chrysanthemums and roses. Chickens are another favorite subject, perhaps, one critic writes, because "they remind her of the old days when the money from selling them meant five children could attend Punahou and the University of Hawaii." One of nine children of immigrants from Canton, Popo Wong is the silent kind of success story that makes Hawaii so satisfying a place to be. But don't try to buy her paintings; her five children and eight grandchildren are great fans of her work, and each has been promised one.

My favorite branch library is in Waikiki, on Kapahulu Avenue, just *mauka* and Ewa of the zoo. Architecturally, this is one of the most striking structures on the islands. It uses with great force the volcanic rock façade that has become a visual cliché in architectural hands less talented than those of Lemmon and Freeth. We often took the children to the Thursday-evening free films at the "Aloha Branch." A free brochure will tell you when they're showing the Hawaiiana films on surfing, local birds and flowers, the interesting George Tahara legends, so you don't spend precious island time seeing films they show at your local library back home. And come well ahead of the 7:30-P.M. screening time, because these are always well attended. We used to claim seats by posting a family sentry and then catching up on library business. By the way, you can borrow books as soon as you land if you pay a five-dollar deposit. Another service of the library that could interest you is the collection of films at the main branch.

Up the street at King and Kawaiahao you will find the three old mission houses where much of the early missionary influence was centered. There, for example, in 1822 was the first printing ever done in Hawaii. Behind these historic buildings with their well-informed guides is the combined Library Building of the Hawaiian Mission Children's Society and the Hawaiian Historical Society. These, together with the Archives on the Iolani Palace grounds and the Hawaiiana Room in the Gregg Sinclair Library at the University of Hawaii, are the three best sources for the serious student of Hawaiian history and culture.

Just beyond the mission houses where Kapiolani Boulevard joins King Street is a building of most interesting interior décor which is usually neglected by the tourist—the Advertiser Building, which now also houses the Honolulu *Star-Bulletin*. Note in the lobby how the traditional classical décor has been given a Polynesian twist. The Contemporary Arts Center in the court is a must for the artistically curious. It is the only art gallery in the United States set up and sponsored by a daily newspaper as a public service for local artists.

PUNCHBOWL

Punchbowl has been called the birthplace of Honolulu, for out of it once came the lava that filled in the place where the city proper stands today. In early days it had a name that meant "hill of sacrifice" so it is assumed that the gods were appeased by sacrifices made on the old *heiau* there. Today the parklike crater serves as a national cemetery for American war dead from World War II and the Korean conflict. On Memorial Day in Hawaii school children place leis as well as flags on the graves.

There used to be a very precipitous trail leading up to Punchbowl. The steep climb up this path became increasingly burdensome for people attending the Easter sunrise service. The boys and girls of the Honolulu playgrounds and public schools were equal to the task of making the ascent to Punchbowl a more gradual one. When it was recalled that the old *menehunes* were supposed to have built great fishponds or *heiaus* by passing stones from hand to hand in a human chain, the children of the city were pressed into similar service, making the gradient up the old crater less steep than it was. Over two thousand stones were passed up in this fashion. Even more spectacular in reviving the symbolism of the old days was the feat of the fifteen hundred students and faculty of McKinley High School: they relayed five hundred picked stones the one mile from their campus flagpole to the top of Punchbowl.

ORIENTAL DISTRICT

The Oriental District is on the Ewa side of downtown in an area bounded by Nuuanu Avenue and Liliha Street. There you can find in close proximity a wide range of Oriental shops, Japanese theaters (where Kurosawa's films are often shown years before they reach the mainland), dormitories for Filipino workers, and the temple shrines and other buildings of Chinese societies. The Chinese Chamber of Commerce sponsors a walking tour of shops and temples on Tuesdays at 9:30 A.M. It is possible to pick up a free walking tour guide at most of the downtown stores which directs you to the points of greatest interest in the Oriental section.

Kewalo Basin

Driving on toward Waikiki, stop for a moment at the Kewalo Basin, between Ward Street and Ala Moana Park. This is where chartered fishing boats and the sampan fishing fleet headquarter. If you want to see a sampan unloading for the tuna cannery, you must get there quite early in the morning, about 5:30. However, there are a few boats unpacking throughout the day.

Ala Moana Park

Farther up Ala Moana Boulevard is the extraordinary seventy-six-acre park built during the depression as a WPA project. Ala Moana Park has public tennis courts, picnic tables, lawn bowling, and swimming in a reef-protected lagoon, but I found swimming there much less attractive than at Queen's Surf, in Waikiki, or at Hanauma Bay, about a half hour's ride beyond Waikiki.

Ulu Mau Village

Surely the most interesting part of Ala Moana Park is Ulu Mau Village. Here you can see put into practice the fascinating skills and secrets of ancient Hawaii. These arts include *lauhala* weaving, lei making, poi pounding and quilt making. The words Ulu Mau mean "Ever-growing." Each year the dedicated Solomons (who have been sparking this drive to keep the old Hawaii alive) add something new to their ever-growing village. Many visitors are so impressed by the unwillingness of Ulu Mau to cheapen its search for a usable past by talking down to them that they decide to become Friends of Ulu Mau Village to help support its unusually objective educational entertainment. It is open Tuesday to Saturday from 9:30 A.M. to 4:00 P.M.

Ala Moana Shopping Center

Across the street from Ala Moana Park is a phenomenon most symbolic of the new Hawaii, the Ala Moana Shopping Center. In my judgment it is the most exciting place in all Hawaii. There you see what Hawaii will make of its future. First of all, it was a useless swamp before the Dillinghams made it a place to dump the fill they had dredged to make Honolulu Harbor. Today this man-made community contains perhaps the most valuable land in the islands.

For one thing you can shop for products of the entire Pacific world through its merchants. My favorite shop there was Shirokiya's, wedged in between Woolworth's on one hand and Sears Roebuck on the other. If your pocketbook cannot afford the prices at Shirokiya's, at the end of the same concourse there is a middle-class Japanese store, Iida's, and for those with minimum budgets a third Japanese store,

Hotei-ya. Also on the basement level are a fascinating Philippine handicraft shop, Gima's art gallery, where many local artists and some imported Asian ones are exhibited for sale, Hardwoods Hawaii, for monkeypod and koa-wood objects, and the Honolulu Book Shops, one of the best sources of books and records of authentic Hawaiian culture. If you would like to take a mynah bird home, you will find those and many other tropical pets in Birdland.

The Sears store at Ala Moana is like no Sears you have ever seen before. For in addition to all the standard hard goods and other amenities you have come to expect from Sears on the mainland, you will also find a wide selection of locally made goods. Next to Robert Hall, its aloha shirts and muumuus are the best I've been able to find at reasonable prices. Having shopped Sears up through the Mall level, walk down the concourse to Watumull's, one of the finest specialty shops.

One thing to note about this shopping center is the tremendously successful way art has been integrated into the total environment. I found it fascinating that the fish mobile outside the Sears store is the artistic creation of the construction engineer who put up Ala Moana Center.

Ala Moana was also attractive to me because of the continuing series of audience-attracting promotions the store stages. Aloha Week is a good example, but an even more interesting one is the annual exhibition of the Windward Oahu Artists' Guild, which exhibits on the lower level during the spring around Easter time.

I haven't mentioned what many people find most attractive at Ala Moana; that is its great variety of restaurants. The most spectacular is the so-called "Pie-in-the-Sky," La Ronde, at the top of the adjacent Ala Moana Center Office Building. A popular time at that place is Sunday brunch. You can get a complete dinner at La Ronde, say, *mahimahi sauté amandine*, for about six dollars. The Coral Reef Restaurant specializes in Chinese cuisine but serves all kinds of food. Another fine restaurant at Ala Moana is the Prince Kuhio. Again, however, Ala Moana is democratic in its offerings: The Crack Seed Center has fountain service as well as take-out orders, which allows people on limited budgets to sample Oriental foods.

ART AT ALA MOANA

For those with time to look closely at all of the art works Ala Moana enhances its center with, here is a list of the most significant. Bumpei Akaji's Fountain of the Gods is a prominent feature of the Mall, with colorful mosaic and bronze columns surrounding a chimney. Each side of the column represents one of the four principal Hawaiian deities.

In Edward Brownlee's Pool of Petroglyphs three waterfalls come from an exterior wall engraved with ancient Hawaiian figures. The humorous ostrich and giraffe, which have been constructed of welded reinforcing bars of scrap metal, are other examples of the art of the construction manager, C. W. Watson, who executed the fish mobile outside Sears. The relief map of Oahu which decorates the front of McInerny's store was done by Allen Girard, of the John Graham Company. Claude Horan, of the University of Hawaii, did the two ceramic fountains that are called the Fountains of the Twin Keikis. These symbolize the carefree spirit of play. Keiki is the Hawaiian word for child. Another Horan work is the Bamboo Fountain. In this one, ceramic figures in decorative tile symbolize the various cultures of the Pacific basin. The Japanese believe that the youthful bamboo symbolizes the ability to bend to changes in nature, at the same time growing strong through persistence.

There is also a Japanese Garden and pool next to the Coral Reef, designed by Takano Nakamoro. Just outside Shirokiya's Department Store is a kasuga stone lantern. This classical lantern and the stones and rocks and precast walkway were imported from Japan and are the work of Junzo Sakakura. One can also see the imaginative touch of the artist in some of the store fronts. For example, the façade of India Imports of Hawaii blends modern décor with Indian motifs. It is the work of designer John Bowen. Similarly, the Chinese Golden Palace is a reproduction of the façade of the Imperial Palace in Peking. It is hand-carved in teak and brilliantly enameled in Hong Kong by artist Sung Hoo. There is another fine sculpture right next to McInerny's store entrance, a monumental Tiki, an example of Polynesian religious art.

Finally, one must think of the extraordinary landscaping in Ala Moana as a significant art. Shoppers there are delighted by coconut palms, monkeypods, *lauhala*, rainbow shower trees, bougainvilleas, and other tropical flowers. To water all the plants and trees, a sprinkler system showering 12,500 gallons of water per minute for twenty minutes a day was designed especially for Ala Moana.

Ala Moana is a superlative example of how the urban environment can be economically productive as well as aesthetically civilized. Ala Moana has been so successful as a business venture that downtown Honolulu has been forced to come up with plans of its own to attract back to its stores the people of Honolulu who have overwhelmingly preferred the amenities of their new shopping center.

Manoa Valley

THE UNIVERSITY OF HAWAII

The University of Hawaii is another excellent example of democracy at work. Its academic specialties include tropical agriculture, marine biology, Pacific and Asiatic cultures, and sociology. The campus itself has a walk-in arboretum for which a free guide map is available in Bachman Hall, the Administration Building, to guide visitors to its numbered collections throughout the campus.

Another important aspect of the University of Hawaii is the stress that its faculty places on creative involvement in the arts. The clearest way to see this is by attending a play at the new John F. Kennedy Theater, the first theater in the history of the world to accommodate Oriental and Occidental theatrical traditions on a par, or the University Art Gallery in George Hall (open Monday to Friday, 8 to 4:30), which features student and faculty work, or musical performances in the new Orvis Auditorium of the Music Department.

THE EAST-WEST CENTER

This artistic richness has been greatly increased by the founding in 1959 of the East-West Center for Technical and Cultural Interchange at the university. To this center come Asians and Americans trying to understand each other's culture more adequately. Since the arts are one of the most effective means for breaking through communication barriers, the East-West Center has wisely put some emphasis on this cultural interchange while not forgetting that the major task is to modernize Asian countries by training Asians in the technical skills of industrialization.

Another interesting sight in the Manoa Valley is Robert Louis Stevenson's Grass House, at 3016 Oahu Avenue, which is open free Tuesday to Saturday, 8 to 5. It is now located on the grounds of the Waioli Tea Room.

At 3355 East Manoa Road is the Manoa Chinese Cemetery Pavilion, which has a composition of ten fresco panels on ancient Chinese legends by Tseng Yu-ho. The pavilion is a kind of combination entrance and meditation room for those paying respects to their departed ancestors.

Waikiki District

This district is an area bounded by the Ala Wai Canal, Diamond Head, and the ocean, and is about a half mile wide and two and a half miles long. At one time it was nothing but duckponds and taro patches. Its main street is named after the Merry Monarch, Kalakaua, a historic fact that the fun-loving king would have appreciated.

THE ALA WAI CANAL

The Ala Wai Canal is a man-made canal that helped drain the swampland. It is now a scenic waterway lined by apartments, palm trees, and a golf course which is among the best on the island. You can watch outrigger-canoe paddlers and

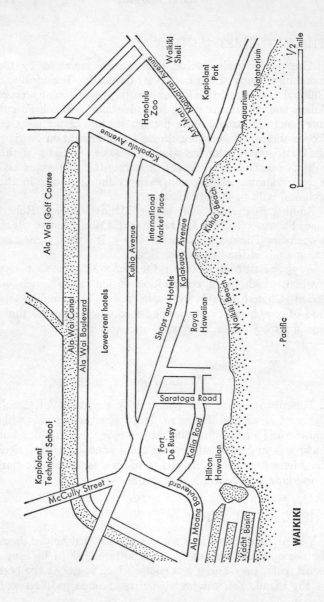

WAIKIKI

shell racers improve their skills there. And mullet fishermen sit endlessly on high, makeshift perches along its banks.

It is possible also to rent U-drive boats at the McCully Street Boat House, weekdays 3 P.M. to midnight, and weekends and holidays from 10 A.M. Another showplace in the area is the Kaiser Dome at 2005 Kalia Road. This first geodesic dome made out of aluminum is used as a movie theater auditorium and convention hall. There are many rather expensive shops adjoining it at the Hilton Hawaiian Village, but it doesn't cost anything to snoop.

CHARLOT'S MURALS

Look at the mural by Jean Charlot which depicts Hawaiian history on the walls of the First National Bank Waikiki Branch on Lewers Street just off Kalakaua. Charlot, whose internationally acclaimed works can also be found in the smallest churches of Kauai, was a young French cavalry officer when he went to Mexico in the 1920's to participate in the renaissance of public murals in that country. He came to Hawaii in 1949 and has since been one of the most important artistic figures in the islands. He teaches art at the University of Hawaii.

HAWAII VISITORS BUREAU

In front of the Royal Hawaiian Hotel on Kalakaua Avenue, you can find expert counsel on every problem besetting the tourist in Hawaii at the HVB office. Plan to drop in for a few minutes early in your visit so you don't unwittingly miss a special event or lead that might particularly appeal to you. A good example of the kind of serendipity you can expect there is one of the things I am most grateful to the HVB for. In 1957 as part of the centennial observance of the founding of the American Institute of Architects, the local chapter of the A.I.A. compiled a guide to architecture in Hawaii. While the supply lasts, single copies are free. A more recent pamphlet, by Harry W. Seckel, on "Hawaiian Residential Architecture" is available at the Bishop Museum. Together they give visitors a distinctive and authoritative introduction (with clear directions) to the fascinating regional architecture.

INTERNATIONAL MARKET PLACE

People with moderate budgets will find the International Market Place at 2330 Kalakaua somewhat expensive but certainly interesting to browse through. There are ethnic shows in the evenings at 7:30 Monday to Friday, where Polynesian, Samoan, Japanese, or Filipino dancing is featured; these fascinating performances are free. Possibly the best collection of strange Hawaiian ice creams is at Al and Dale's Ice Cream. Don't leave the islands before you have tasted guava sherbet or passion-fruit sherbet. Immediately to the rear of the International Market Place there is now a validated-ticket parking garage. At rear center is a visitor's information plaza and a place where you can arrange your Outer Islands trips.

THE DUKE'S

When visiting the International Market Place look for Duke Kahanamoku's night club. The 1912 Olympics gave the Hawaiians one of the greatest boosts, short of statehood, their morale has ever had. For it was there, at the games in Sweden, that the young Duke P. Kahanamoku, as the top representative of the United States, broke not one but two world records in swimming competition. The news of his victory unleashed a delirium of excitement in Hawaii when it got there. Since then, of course, the waters of Hawaii have been prolific in supporting American claims at such international contests. But there was never one like the Duke's victory. And, as the owner of a prominent night club, he is still one of Hawaii's most famous and respected citizens.

PRINCESS KAIULANI HOTEL

Queen Liliuokalani had a niece named Kaiulani. It was this girl after whom the handsome Princess Kaiulani Hotel in Waikiki was named. There's a good reason too for the room with a breath-taking view at the top of the hotel being called the Robert Louis Stevenson Room. When Kaiulani was a little girl, she played in the palace gardens under a big banyan tree. In those days, before it was a great tourist center, Robert Louis Stevenson then lived in a grass hut on Waikiki Beach. The author of *A Child's Garden of Verses* wrote poems for the princess and told her about his old home in Scotland. This interested her because her father, A. S. Cleghorn, was a Scot and she was sent to school there. When she left Hawaii, Stevenson wrote her a poem that runs in part:

> Forth from her land to mine she goes
> The Island maid, the Island rose
> Light of heart and bright of face
> The daughter of a noble race
> Her islands here and southern sun
> Shall mourn their Kaiulani gone
> And I in her dear banyan shade
> Look vainly for my little maid.

When Princess Kaiulani did arrive back in Hawaii, Stevenson had gone for good. He had left for Samoa, where he died. Kaiulani was the daughter of Princess Miriam Likelike, sister of the reigning King Kalakaua, and was considered heir apparent to the throne.

KAPIOLANI PARK

The Kapiolani Park Zoo has most of the standard big animals, but the world's best collection of tropical birds is what makes it a must for the visitor. Notice the striking new entrance building, designed by Alfred Preis, the same man who designed the extraordinary Pearl Harbor Memorial for the U.S.S. *Arizona*.

THE ART MART

There is also a free Art Mart on Saturdays, 10 to 4, at the Honolulu Zoo fence *mauka* of Prince Kuhio Beach. On Sunday across the street there is a free concert at 2 P.M. by the

Royal Hawaiian Band. This is the band that meets the cruise ships, a melodic thrill that jet airplane travel deprives you of.

Where to Swim

A beach is not a beach since they are really all very different; and the true Hawaii buff has an encyclopedic knowledge of their minute differences. The newcomer needs only two things: an introduction to the major beaches and a healthy respect for signs warning about the dangers for even the experienced. And, of course, a sense of moderation about exposure to the tropical sun, which the trade winds tend to make newcomers unconscious of. The best guides to the fewer organized beaches of the Outer Islands are the free maps that HVB will give you at each of the airports on the less populated islands. Start the tour at Ala Moana and circle Oahu counterclockwise.

Ala Moana Park. Extensive bathhouses. Exceedingly crowded and murky on weekends. The new Magic Island, a manmade beach, may clear things up, but as far as I'm concerned its main advantage is its proximity. Fledgling spear fishermen like the shallows just Diamond Head of it for poking around at octopi and eels when the tide is out.

Hilton Hawaiian Village Lagoon. I could find no particular virtues in the beach in front of this hotel, although I noticed a great many parents with small children on the enclosed lagoon between it and the Waikikian.

Fort De Russy Military Reservation. Much beach is under the control of the military. Too much, some think, as the bikini explosion continues. Meanwhile, you'll have to get a private to take you to this one just Ewa of Waikiki.

Halekulani Cove. Strictly speaking, the beaches Ewa of Prince Kuhio are for those staying at the hotels behind them. But it's hard to keep foot-loose Americans from following a sandy beeline, even if it means high-wiring it along the narrow cement breakwater at the Moana Hotel. If the tiny cove in front of the Halekulani isn't floating away with patrons who have paid, I like to sun and snoozle in the surf there. Which is to say I stay away on weekends, but exert a genteel right of pre-eminent domain during working hours. Next to Hanauma Bay (of which more later) it's my favorite float.

Prince Kuhio Beach. The public beach at Waikiki is where to learn how to surf, cheaply and safely. Outside of that it's strictly Crowdedsville or Ogler's Alley. Fun watching homemade surfboard riders from the dock.

The Queen's Surf. For the person who tans best with a well-replenished alcohol content, this is the beach for him. Because the Queen's Surf Bar stands at hand to offer medical counsel. This is also the near beach for families with small children. Just Ewa of the beach is the grassy sward across from Kapiolani Park, ideal for diapered crawling campaigns.

Sans Souci Beach. In front of the hotel of the same name, it is also a private strand. But spear fishing is excellent beyond the reef, and that's international water as far as the scuba troupe is concerned.

Diamond Head Beach Park. Strictly for the marine biologist as far as I'm concerned. But for him it's very good.

Waialaie Beach Park. In spite of some high praise from the locals, this always struck me as mud flats with picnic tables. Marginal.

Maunalua Bay. The spear fishermen rave about this watery turf. They can have it.

Hanauma Bay. A half-hour drive from Honolulu, this in my judgment is the nicest play in Hawaii. The strand gets quite crowded on a Sunday, but that would never dissuade even a professional crowd-hater like myself. The coral comes in very close, making a safe shallow for the children. The coral itself is open enough in spots to make learning how to skin-dive a cinch for the nonathletic. If you never did anything in Hawaii but have your first afternoon of communion with the tropical fish, your trip would have been a success. (Fortify yourself with basic research on the way out at the biggest 25 cents in Kapiolani Park, the admission to the University of Hawaii Aquarium.)

Makapuu Point. Before I had sense enough to read signs, I went romping into this surf at the easternmost tip of Oahu. I almost didn't get out. Body-surfers thrill to the astonishingly powerful thrust of the waves in this cove. But if you don't know when to roll with the breakers, at best you come up with a nose full of sand—at worst with a broken neck. If the surf is high and you're an amateur, be content with exploring the fascinating tidal pools. Or watching the daredevil body-surfers.

Waimanalo Beach Park. Good for all-day weekend swims. Generally considerable surf casting.

Kailua Beach Park. A well-developed family park. Eating facilities. Highly regarded for finding shells and floats, early in the day. There are small parks for swimming from here on all along the Windward Coast to Kaena Point. About the only reasons for going farther from Honolulu to these beaches are privacy and professionalism. Privacy is obvious, but the close-in beaches tend to clutter up with learners—surf-casters, surfers, body-surfers. And the expert flees the amateur, savoring the special qualities he as an *aficionado* finds at the more arcane places. Be particularly careful about the safety signs on deserted beaches.

Camp Erdman. This is about as far as you can get away from man and all his works and pomps on Oahu. I urge you to get out and hoof it on your Kaena Point trip. It's so clean you can't even imagine the idea of smog. And the shearing back of veils of spray from the cresting breakers is something I could watch for hours.

Makaha Beach. This is the world's capital of surfing. However much you've watched TV coverage of this sport, it doesn't get a sniff of the thundering terror of it. Look, don't touch.

Pokai Beach Park. Oahu's center for small, crafty skippers.

Surfing: The Safe Way

Don't try this sport without a lesson first. They are easy and inexpensive to obtain at the Public Center at Prince

Kuhio Beach at Waikiki. To get in the mood, walk down Kalakaua toward Diamond Head to the jetty that is between Prince Kuhio Beach and the Queen's Surf. There you can see the Little League of Surfing in action. Kids just breaking into the sport and not well heeled enough to afford a real surfboard (about a hundred dollars) go sliding down the waves on short, fat, gaily painted homemade surfboards. If you're in the islands in the winter months, you should find out whether the International Surfing Championships at Makaha, Ewa of Pearl Harbor, will be held while you are there. Even to watch champions from Hawaii, California, and Australia practice on the big waves up to thirty feet high is a wonder I shall never forget. Keep the kids away from the action, though. Children have a tendency to drift transfixed down toward the edge of the shore, where the sudden lift of incoming waves is incredible. The undertow there could suck them out like toothpicks. Notice how the surf makes projectiles out of riderless surfboards, another reason for the faint of mind to stay clear unless they're experienced surfers.

Perhaps the easiest way to surf vicariously is to attend the surfing movies often shown in the islands. I have found, too, that the admirable Thursday-evening film programs at the Kapahulu Library, just *mauka* of Waikiki, often feature surfing films as well as other fascinating Hawaiiana. So if you are the unathletic type, try your surfing via celluloid.

Diamond Head

Diamond Head, which dominates Waikiki, is Hawaii's trademark. It got its name from the excited sailors who found little calcite crystals in the old crater. They soon found out that their imaginations had run away with them, but the name stuck. Inside the crater today there is a military installation. It is possible to go hiking up the sides of this mountain.

Hawaii Kai and Hanauma Bay

A twenty-minute drive past Waikiki on Route 72 brings you to Hawaii Kai. If Ala Moana Shopping Center is the vision of what a civilized commercial development can become in the United States, then Henry J. Kaiser's Hawaii Kai is a glimpse into the residential development of the future. As Kaiser himself explained: "From the moment I first saw the magnificent Koko Head area I knew that here at last was the place in which to bring to life my dream of a complete, perfectly planned place for living." His dream is unfolding before you now. It is Hawaii Kai—one of the island's unique ways of life enhanced by every beauty, every facility and convenience that the most progressive community planning can provide. Its motto "By design . . . the most beautiful community in the world" is now already partly a reality. By deciding ahead of time how to use every part of the natural terrain for housing and other developments at various levels of income, Kaiser's planners have been able to avoid the stereotypes of many mainland settlements that have become one-class communities. There, more than two thousand families will be able to enjoy Kuapa Pond, an island lagoon with waterways that wander mile after mile into the valleys of the Koolau range.

Just beyond Koko Head, perhaps five minutes by car, is surely the most beautiful swimming beach on Oahu. Hanauma Bay was formed when one side of a volcano blew out, letting in the sea. A coral reef makes it perfectly safe for youngsters to swim and for adults to learn how to skin-dive. Both seaward ledges are favorite spots for the expert fisher. (These experienced Hawaiians also know enough to stay away from the ledges when the surf is high; not a few lives have been lost by the treacherous big waves' backlash.) I would say that anyone who had only a day in Hawaii (off ship or between planes) and who wanted to be certain to have a touch of the tropics could find no better place to have lunch and a swim than at Hanauma Bay. Make it the center of a round-the-island trip.

Hawaii's Sea Life Park

The newest educational entertainment is a Sea Life Park, about an hour's drive from downtown Honolulu along Route 72 past Koko Head to Makapuu Point—which is the beginning of Windward Oahu. At this park, natural habitats for various kinds of sea life have been arranged to give visitors a realistic view of how these creatures live. Nearby Makapuu Point is a favorite haunt of body-surfers, a kind of sophisticated tangling with waves which is not recommended for the inexperienced but which is great spectator sport when the waves are high. The tidal pools at the State Park here are also fun to walk through with *tabis* on.

Round-the-Island Tour

The great circle route around Oahu is approximately ninety miles. It takes a good day to cover the main route, more time if you get sidetracked. And there are many things and places to tempt you off the main road. Starting from the center of the city, it is seven miles up Nuuanu Avenue to the Nuuanu Pali; drive around Dowsett Highlands, the fine residential area en route, before you begin to ascend in the interesting rain forests that also help conserve Honolulu's water supplies. You miss the best of this on Route 61 superhighway—through the mountains beneath the Pali. You must take the old winding road to see the really tropical flora. One thing to watch for in the upper valley is the Upside Down Falls. When the wind is strong right after a heavy rain, falling water will be blown back up the cliff.

The Pali Lookout has Oahu's most spectacular view. The gap itself is some twelve hundred feet high, but there are cliffs between two and three thousand feet enclosing the green valley. The constantly shifting kaleidoscope of greens and blues as you look windward to the towns of Kailua and Kaneohe is one of the great scenic delights in the world.

On Windward Oahu itself you will find many miles of sandy beach from Mokapu Point through Lanikai. Although these beaches along Routes 61 and 63 are lined with homes, there are many right-of-ways for swimmers to gain access to the beach. Kailua itself has a first-class public beach and park.

The Marine Corps Air Station at Kaneohe has an exciting water carnival every June with boat races and other festivities. Also in Kaneohe Bay are coral gardens that can be seen from glass-bottom boats available at the Heeia-kea Boat Pier. Driving north on Route 83, look for the Royal Fishponds along the shore where fish used to be trapped to await His Majesty's prerefrigeration dining pleasure.

You can visit the Hulalei Perfume Factory and House of Coral at Kahaluu. There also is a poi factory, farther north on Route 83 at Waiahole, where mornings you can see taro roots being made into the staple food of the Hawaiians.

Kaneohe Bay ends at Kualoa Point, where you will notice Chinaman's Hat Island just offshore. This is near an abandoned sugar mill where a hundred years ago the Windward coast had thriving sugar plantations that the mechanization of agriculture later put out of business.

PUNALUU

The Punaluu district was famous as a home of a god named Kamapuaa. "Sometimes he would look like a big hog," said Herman Bach; "sometimes he would look like a big handsome man. When he was a big hog he would run around and have fun eating up the crops of the rich people he no like, but when he was a handsome man he would fool around with the ladies that belonged to the rich people." It's this kind of lore that you can expect if you take a tour with a native tour driver.

Beyond Hauula Beach Park you will notice a marker for Sacred Falls, which is at the head of the Kaliuwaa Valley. By walking a mile through a cane field road, you discover a fresh-water swimming pool at the base of the Sacred Falls. This is a most fascinating retreat and a side trip well worth the hour to hour and a half it takes. It is a most enchanting place to have lunch.

Farther up the coast is the Mormon village of Laie, where the Church of the Latter-Day Saints had established a rehabilitation project back in 1865. A lot of the sugar cane land that the original colonists planted is now leased to a commercial firm. Between 10 and 4 daily you can visit the Mormon Temple, where the colony's history and Mormon religious beliefs are both explained.

The Church College's Polynesian Entertainment Center opened in the fall of 1963. It is authentic because the college attracts students from its missionary outposts on Samoa and Fiji. These students then sing and folk-dance their ways through college.

Past Kahuku Point, Route 83 along the coastline turns in toward the south. On your left above Paumalu is a stone called the George Washington Stone. A Hawaiian legend explains that it is actually not the father of our country but a prince turned to stone when he was chasing a lover to whom he had been unfaithful. Also in the bay area are the ruins of the largest *heiau* in Oahu. Puu O Mahuka Heiau had a 520-foot wall—which must have taken some dragging in a culture without the wheel. There is another sacred place on the edge of the cane field south of Waimea Bay.

KAENA POINT

While the sand dunes look attractive along Waimea Bay, *malihinis* should be advised that the currents here are notoriously dangerous for swimmers.

The long hard way back to Honolulu of course is to take Route 99 out to Kaena Point, then down on Route 90 to Makaha Beach. As suggested before, don't try this during the rainy season, and make sure that your car and disposition can take a goodly bit of rattling. It is well worth the inconvenience in any case. If you don't like to be shook up, you might try driving up Route 99 as far as Camp Erdman. Park your car there and walk along the beach.

BARBERS POINT

Barbers Point, off Route 90 between Makaha and Pearl Harbor, is named after a sea captain who unsuccessfully tried to water the rum Kamehameha purchased from him. Captain Barber set before the king some unusually good Jamaican rum. Tasting it and liking it, Kamehameha ordered several cases. When they arrived, the king held them up to the sun and found them several shades too light. Not long after, Barber's ship was wrecked off the point that bears his name, on the southwestern tip of Oahu. When Barber came to ask favors about his cargo, he found Kamehameha giving his canoe builders a round of rum. The ordinarily generous king did not offer Barber any. When the captain asked why, he got the chilly reply "You don't like rum, Barber, you like water." Kamehameha was not the soft touch for white traders so many of his chiefs were.

WAHIAWA

If you don't have the courage to try Kaena Point, you should return to Honolulu through the central Wahiawa Plain. There are two roads, the Kamehameha Highway (Route 99) and the older Kaukonahua Road (Route 75). Both provide excellent vantage points to see Oahu's highest peak, the 4025-foot Mount Kaala, and the only break in the Waianae Mountains—Kolekole Pass. Wahiawa is a shopping center for the small agricultural villages and for the military personnel at Schofield Barracks and Wheeler Field. There is a good picnicking place at 1396 California Avenue, the Wahiawa Botanical Gardens.

Modern Pineapple Culture

While driving through the Wahiawa Plain, don't fail to note the technological virtuosity of modern pineapple production. Like the highly automated sugar industry, pineapple cultivation is one of the glories of Hawaii's brilliantly scientific agriculture. The complex process begins with soil preparation about six to eight months before actual planting; huge tractor plows dig a foot down into the soil, repeating the operation several times. In the last plowing, DDT is injected six to eight inches down to fumigate the soil.

Pineapples are generally planted in fall and spring; hence production is a continuous cycle. Pineapple seeds are rarely available, since they would be scattered throughout the fruit and spoil it for canning. Hence new fruit is grown from slips found near the base of the fruit, or from suckers growing lower on the stem, or from crowns. Slip-grown pine (the standard nickname for the fruit) matures in about twenty months; crowns, in twenty-two to twenty-four; suckers, between sixteen and eighteen.

Mulch paper strips laid across the field in rows not only keep weeds to a minimum but they also conserve moisture and fertilizer and increase soil temperature, all of which make the fruit grow better. Planting is still done by hand by plunging a narrow steel trowel through a marked spot on the tar-paper mulch, 17,500 slips per acre. When the mulch paper has disintegrated, frequent weeding by mechanical cultivators, chemical sprays, or hand hoeing is necessary. An organic insecticide has been developed to do in the pineapple's greatest enemy, the mealy bug. Twenty months after the hand planting, a five-pound fruit can be plucked from rows three to four feet apart. In early summer, trained pickers snap the pineapples off the stalks, cut off their crowns, and place the fruit on the long narrow boom of a mechanical harvester with a conveyor belt. Bins full of fruit are detached from the mechanical harvesting machine and taken to hydraulic dumping units. There they are tilted into spiral grading units. Thence to the remarkable Ginaca machines, which core one hundred pineapples a minute. The cylinders slide to trimming tables and, after hand trimming, proceed to slicing machines. The sliced fruit goes into cans where it is trucked to syruping machines. Next the cans are hermetically sealed, pasteurized, sterilized, and packed on trays for the labeling department. Juice is also extracted, shells ground up for livestock feed, and citric acid obtained from shells and trimmings. About 15,000 Hawaiians work during the peak of the canning season; half that number year round. In 1962 these 22,500 accounted for about 30,000,000 cases of fruit and juice.

Pearl Harbor

From Schofield to Honolulu, the Kamehameha Highway is a fast-paced multilane highway passing through forested hills arching the deep Kipapa Gulch. Soon you begin to see Pearl Harbor; the highway itself goes past part of it. Pearl Harbor is what is known as a drowned valley, a dual estuary of the Pearl River, so called because pearl oysters were once abundant there. The old Hawaiians thought that it was the home of a shark queen who protected her people by keeping all man-eating sharks out of the harbor. To appease the Hawaiian superstitions, when the Navy workers starting to dredge the harbor had to destroy a fishpond and fish god shrine, they made a ceremony of taking the stones out to sea and burying them. When a dock foundation collapsed in 1913, the Hawaiians were certain that this had happened because an old Polynesian religious shrine had been violated.

The best reason for visiting Pearl Harbor today, however, is to see a truly superlative modern shrine to the sailors entombed inside the U.S.S. *Arizona* on Pearl Harbor Day.

A TRIP TO THE ARIZONA MEMORIAL

Don't miss the free Navy boat ride to the Arizona Memorial. About seven hundred lucky people can make the trip each day. I was fortunate enough to take the ride in the company of the monument's architect, Alfred Preis, who explained its symbolism to me. Preis, a naturalized citizen from Vienna, cares very deeply about democracy and is one of the most articulate architects I have ever talked to. He believes that the 1100 sailors trapped in the hull of the U.S.S. *Arizona* are in effect the real memorial. His first concept for a shrine was to create a subterranean chamber with glass walls so that a visitor could descend beneath waters still entombing the sailors and thus in a small way be confronted physically with the enormity of the sacrifice these people made to protect our freedom.

Preis was very worried that tourists coming to the memorial would only respond on a sentimental or cliché level, that the depths of their beings would not be touched. As a good architect who regards his art as something nearly religious in its most successful expressions, he wanted the experience of paying respect to these national heroes to be a profoundly felt personal one. Not just a mumbo-jumbo ritual, but a unique, maturing act for each individual who went there. That is why he first started with the water-chamber idea, where the rusting, encrusted old hulk could shock people to a fresh response.

The idea that was finally approved by the naval authorities is more ethereal but every bit as interesting. First of all the concrete shell is built right over the bridge of the sunken battle wagon. If you look over the *mauka* side of the concrete canopy, you will see the stub of the old flagstaff of the ship. There is a slight declivity in the central floor. This is meant to symbolize the disadvantage a democracy like ours suffers because it will not start wars and thus can be victimized as it was on the Day of Infamy, when the Japanese made their surprise attack. There we were beginning a war with our entire Pacific Fleet paralyzed. How did we manage to win? Notice the thin vertical concrete piers that rise from the floor and gradually flare out to meet the ceiling and then join with the piers on the opposite side and return to the floor, one continuous flow of concrete. The thin separate piers, which have surprising strength, stand for the unity and diversity that is the democratic miracle that wins our wars. Thus even though we start at a disadvantage because of our peaceful traditions in the democracy, the strength of one for many gives us unique powers of resilience and combativeness once aroused. Hence the soaring concrete, which forms an abstract frame for the flag flying overhead.

Just before you go into the chapel at the Ewa end of the memorial, notice the well surrounded by railing, looking into which you can see the submerged ship. This is a vestige of Preis's underwater-chamber concept. When you read the names of the heroes, notice something else: they are not in order of rank but are arranged alphabetically. That is also a reflection of Preis's democratic ideas.

Most memorials in America have been rather slavish and uninspired imitations of classical motifs. For the first time in our history, I think, Preis has created a memorial that uses new materials and construction techniques in achieving a brilliant new form that is, paradoxically, ethereal yet enduring, just like the democratic ideas all these men died for.

The boat makes six trips a day, every day but Monday. The first leaves at 9 A.M., the last at 3:30 P.M. The trip takes twenty minutes, with ten minutes spent in contemplation at the memorial itself. Children under eight are not allowed. You may take pictures of the memorial, but you should not shoot pictures of the naval installation. Aliens must be logged in before they leave. You do not need reservations for this ride. Enter Pearl Harbor at the Halawa Gate off Route 90, with parking on the Pearl City side of the gate.

This ride should not be confused with the Navy's long-established boat ride around Ford Island, which takes a half hour. You need a reservation for that, which can be secured from the Public Information Office of the Fourteenth Naval District.

Honolulu International Airport

If the air traveler to Hawaii missed the thrill of the Royal Hawaiian Band meeting his ship at the Aloha Tower, then the ship traveler too often overlooks the pleasure of visiting the gardens in the new Honolulu International Airport, between Pearl Harbor and Honolulu off Route 90. There are three of them—Japanese, Chinese, and Hawaiian—and it is well worth the extra time to arrive several hours before flight departure either overseas or to the Outer Islands. It gives one a chance, not only to visit these striking tropical gardens, but to eat in the relaxing restaurants at the airport.

Where to Eat

In addition to the inexpensive places I suggest in this section for getting a taste of Hawaii's culinary riches, there are of course a good many top-flight restaurants, one of which—Canlis' Charcoal Broiler Restaurant in Waikiki—has the coveted Holiday Magazine Fine Dining Award. The best way to sort out the culinary possibilities of the fiftieth state is to take them genre by genre—the luau, first in time and first in the hearts of Hawaii's mainland countrymen; Japanese food; Chinese cuisine; and general international dishes including American.

A WEEK OF LUAUS (if you can stand it!)

Sunday

2:30 P.M., the pig goes into the *imu* (open-air oven using hot stones) at the Queen's Surf, at the Diamond Head end of Waikiki. Served on the ground if your back can stand it. $8.50 includes *kalua* (or roast pig), highballs or Polynesian rum punch. Call 937-387. Authentic entertainment.

6:30 P.M., Royal Hawaiian Luau. Okolehao Punch. $10 includes continuous entertainment at Waikiki's most prestigious hotel. Casual Hawaiian dress. Call 937-311. Somewhat more formal than Queen's Surf.

6:30 P.M., Duke Kahanamoku's, International Market Place. $10 includes the Duke's special rum punch. Continuous dance music. More night clubby in tone. Casual dress acceptable. Call 973-377.

Wednesday

6:00 P.M., Hilton Hawaiian Village Hotel. Three hours of Polynesian ritual, stressing things like blowing the ceremonial conch, and MC'd by Danny Kaleikini. A three-hour party for $8.50. Call 994-321. Also on Sunday.

Saturday

Noon, Church College, Laie. $4.50 plus whatever it costs you to drive or be driven to this charming place ninety minutes away from Honolulu on Windward Oahu. You eat in a simple church hall, but the luau proper was the best I ever had in Oahu. Besides, the Polynesian Entertainment Center, just opened by the college, draws on students the Mormon missionaries have sent to the college from all over Polynesia. Their performance of native crafts, and the *hukilau* (community fish gathering) make this a must-visit spot on your Oahu itinerary.

OTHER POLYNESIAN EATERIES

Trader Vic's, Ward Avenue at King Street. Hawaii's first Polynesian restaurant. It is near the Academy of Arts between downtown and Ala Moana. It also specializes in rum drinks, Cantonese dishes, and planked *mahimahi*. Lunch 11:30 to 2:30 P.M. (except Saturday and Sunday). Dinners 5 to 10:30 P.M. daily. Call 576-428.

Tahitian Lanai, poolside at the Waikikian Hotel, Ala Moana Boulevard next to the Yacht Basin. Papeete Bar is a favorite rendezvous. Dinners from about $4. Call 999-954.

Fisherman's Wharf, Kewalo Basin. Specialty: poached *opakapaka*, and *mahimahi*. Lunch 11:30 to 2 except Sunday. Dinners 5:15 to 10 daily. Several entrees under $3.00. Fascinating nautical décor.

Tiki Room, Waikiki Biltmore, Uluniu Avenue at Kalakaua Avenue. Exotic drinks in Polynesian atmosphere. Coffee shop open until midnight. Call 935-711.

JAPANESE RESTAURANTS

Ishii Garden, 1720 Huna Lane. Teahouse. Reservations (minimum of four) necessary. Call 65-430.

Mochizuki Garden, 647 Kunawai Lane. Interesting tropical atmosphere. Call 586-498.

Kyo-ya, 2057 Kalakaua Avenue just beyond Fort De Russy. Not as authentic as above but closer to Waikiki. Call 968-485.

CHINESE RESTAURANTS

Lau Yee Chai, Waikiki. Its gaudy architecture is a strange and delectable treat for the eyes, a foretaste of what goes on inside. Definitely a must-go in Honolulu. Reservations helpful. Call 992-487.

Wo Fat, 115 N. Hotel Street, downtown Honolulu. A good perch for seeing the festivals in Chinatown if you get close to the windows. Excellent and not nearly as expensive as Lau Yee Chai's. Reservations less necessary. Call 57-260.

Golden Dragon, Hilton Hawaiian Village. Nine-course dinners at tables for ten. Dinners 5 to 10:30 P.M. Entertainment starts at 7. Call 994-321.

INTERNATIONAL CUISINE

Canlis' Charcoal Broiler Restaurant, 2100 Kalakaua Avenue, Waikiki. Probably the most highly regarded restaurant in Hawaii. A George Wimberley architectural gem integrating native materials and flora in a unique way. Cocktails from 4 P.M. Dinner nightly 5:30 to 11:30 P.M. Piano bar entertainment from 7:30 P.M. Domesticated waterfall a spectacle! Call 932-324.

Pikake Terrace, Princess Kaiulani Hotel, Waikiki. A delightfully airy place in the central court of this modern hotel. Breakfast-lunch 12 to 2. Dinners 6 to 9.

The Willows, 901 Hausten St., five minutes by car from Waikiki. Luncheon 11:30 to 2:30 P.M. Dinner 5:30 to 9:30 P.M. This is a completely captivating spot that serves a wide range of foods at reasonable prices. It has a unique setting around a tropical pool teeming with huge goldfish. A classic, cheap Willows lunch is a hamburger and iced tea with pineapple spear. At least have lunch here once. Try dinner if you have time. Completely different and equally satisfying. Call 94-808.

The Vikings Restaurant, 1140 Twelfth Avenue, Kaimuki. A ten-minute ride from Waikiki to the district behind Diamond Head. Excellent Scandinavian food. Try it just to remember there is more to Oahu than Waikiki. A fine evening is to combine a foreign movie at the nearby Queens Theatre with an after-movie dinner there. Call 772-055.

The Hofbrau, 2448 Kalakaua Avenue, Waikiki. Daily from 11 A.M. Piano Bar Sing-a-Long with Mitch Mueller. Wide variety of German beers. Call 938-033.

Waioli Tea Room, 3016 Oahu Avenue, Manoa Valley. Fifteen minutes from Waikiki, up past the University of Hawaii, is a quaint tearoom run by the Salvation Army. Robert Louis Stevenson's grass hut is there. Reservations must be made on the morning of your visit. Lunch 11:30 to 2. Tea 2:30 to 4. Bakery and gift shop are also on grounds. Call 982-131.

La Ronde, atop the Ala Moana Center Office Building. Prices, like the location, are fairly steep, but you miss a unique thrill if you don't go at dusk with a map of the city in one hand and a tall cool one in the other. "Pie-in-the-Sky" makes one complete revolution per hour. A dramatic way to end your stay, guaranteed to have you returning for more as soon as possible. Call 97-138.

A Pauper's Guide to Eating in Honolulu

It's not hard to spend a lot of money eating well in Honolulu, and your Carte Blanche, American Express, and Diners' Club directories will steer you to the best places immediately. Pick up a copy of the Honolulu *Snooper* to get a fast view of the best restaurants. But for a minute, think of eating differently and cheaply in Honolulu.

Ala Moana Park's Shoyu Chicken. While I don't think much of swimming at this beach across the street from America's most beautiful shopping center, do plan to eat there once —maybe when you visit Ulu Mau Village. Their dinner plate of *shoyu* chicken, rice, and trimmings for 75 cents is one of the tastiest best buys on Oahu.

Chunky's teriyakiburgers. Across the street from the Honolulu Stadium on Isenberg and South King streets is a hot-dog and fish-and-chips drive-in where you can sample the most astonishing Americanization of Oriental cuisine you will ever experience—the teriyakiburger. New Zealand beef, imported because local meat is expensive, has a gamy taste but is very tender. But, fortunately, marinating it in *teriyaki* sauce produced a delicacy the most humble can afford. I used to make a complete lunch out of two of these and an orange splash, a weird kind of near sherbet.

McCully's Chop Suey. At the corner of McCully and South King streets is the poor man's answer to Wo Fat's and Lau Yee Chai's, good but inexpensive Chinese food. The Golden Duck across the street is not bad either. The secret is to have each person order a different dish, because there's always too much for one to eat, and then you can go platter-swapping, the only sensible way to eat Chinese food.

Sampan Inn. In the low-rent district (or Diamond Head side) of Kewalo Basin, that is to say, the opposite side from Fisherman's Wharf (an interesting but expensive restaurant) is the lowly Sampan Inn. There you can get an evening meal for a dollar in the Japanese style. Since this is the tuna and *mahimahi* landing area for the fishing fleet, you can count on having superb fish at very low cost. Not fancy, even a bit forbidding for the squeamish, but a cheap place to eat well.

Kapiolani Technical School. This is a culinary sleeper. Young Honolulans learn here how to serve you at the luxury hotels and regular restaurants of the city. If you don't mind helping them learn to be waiters and waitresses, chefs and dietitians, you are in for a treat. Their school is on the *mauka* side of the Ala Wai Canal just where McCully crosses it. The highlight of the season here is the International Food Fiesta the students put on by way of graduation in June. It is absolutely essential to have reservations for that particular feast and indeed advisable to phone for noontime reservations the morning of your weekday visit. Not open during summer, weekends, or holidays.

University of Hawaii Hemenway Cafeteria. In addition to the marvelously permissive ethnic atmosphere where faculty and students eat side by side, this cafeteria has chiffon pies using native fruits, such as guava and papaya, that are out of this hemisphere. No children, please.

Atherton House University Y.M.C.A. Lunch at A-House is 99 cents for all the Orientalia you can cram on a plate. The students (from all over Asia) are even more interesting.

Don't fail to try local food products: island juices, such as papaya, guava, or passion fruit; macadamia nuts, poha jam, Kona coffee, ti-root liquor. And for recipes to last you a lifetime, get Napua Stevens annual Hawaiian Food Contest in a special issue of the *Star-Bulletin*.

A Pauper's Guide to Shopping

The first thing one wants to do in Hawaii is to get a taste of the native foods. The second fascination is with interesting clothing. Let me tell you a secret. On your way in from the airport on your left you will see the Pepsi-Cola Company plant. Turn right onto the Sand Island Access Road for a Robert Hall store with a difference. Spend a half hour looking at their aloha shirts and ladies' muumuus. Don't expect all of the shifts or dresses to be attractive. There is an old vulgar tradition of borax design (dating from soldier and sailor tastes in World War II), which one fashion designer contemptuously refers to as "garbage." But if you know what you're looking for, you can find shirts and dresses at literally half the price you would pay for the same things in downtown Honolulu, or at Ala Moana shopping center, or at Waikiki. The only other place where I have found such bargains in clothing was at the Kauai Rehabilitation Center just Hanalei of the Wailua River where the Coco Palms Hotel is.

If you are curious about what clothes you should bring to Hawaii, the trusty old HVB has a folder on that subject, too. Basically, the rules are to travel light, with spring and summer mainland clothing of a resort rather than city flavor. Women wear hats and gloves only on formal occasions. Either high heels or sandals will do with dressy clothes. Straw or raffia sandals or *zoris* will do for casual daytime hours. Light fur stoles or dressy sweaters will be welcome on cool winter evenings. Trips to the mountain or volcano areas of the Outer Islands make warm sweaters a must for men and women.

Men can leave their dinner jackets at home, even though there are some places when a light jacket is worn in spring, summer, and winter and a dark one in winter. More to the point is what to try in the way of new clothes. For the man, I recommend three Japanese things I've grown to love to wear. The *hapi* coat is a kind of finger-tip-length bathrobe with no buttons and with full sleeves, a smoking jacket with a Tokyo fit. *Tabi* shoes have separate toes like mittens; they are ideal for exploring coral or stepping on an eel by mistake. *Zori* sandals are rubber soles held loosely on the foot by bright-colored rubber thongs. The most interesting *hapi* coats (and kimonos for the ladies) I found were at Shirokiya's in Ala Moana Shopping Center. *Tabis* and *zoris* are fairly cheap everywhere, but Long's, at Ala Moana, or Ben Franklin's, in Kaimuki, had the best buys.

Neckties are not *verboten* in the land of aloha shirts; indeed you would be well advised to see how freshly Polynesian motifs have been adapted to the fabrics of the more expensive ties sold there. One thing you've got to get used to is the lack of vest-pocket space for wallets when you're wearing aloha shirts. The First National Bank of Hawaii has thoughtfully provided its customers with a miniature wallet suitable for the breast pocket of an aloha shirt. Cash your American Express checks there and they may give you one!

HAWAIIAN DÉCOR

Hawaiian interior décor borrows from many cultures, East and West. Hawaii supplies *punees* and *hikiees* (low couches). The Chinese have furniture made of teak or bamboo, the Philippines supply mahogany or island monkeypod; there are Chinese rugs and scrolls, Japanese screens and native *lauhala* floor mats, Chinese and Japanese porcelain side by side with Polynesian wooden bowls and vases, lacquer ware, prints, and other exotics from every part of Asia. Look for these in the downtown Oriental district, Ala Moana Shopping Center, and Waikiki's International Market Place.

HAWAIIAN QUILTS

One of the finest minor arts of the Hawaiian Islands is the splendid quilts created there. The best collection I ever saw was in the gym of the Kawaiahao Church after the King Kamehameha Day luau. Prices begin at thirty dollars for a bedspread. *Woman's Day* offers a set of instructions for designing and cutting, appliquéing, assembling, and quilting an authentic Hawaiian quilt and actual size patterns for making the Maui Beauty and Breadfruit patterns for 75 cents per set (P.O. Box 1000, Greenwich, Connecticut).

The Hawaiians started in the late nineteenth century to create these quilts, which characteristically have an intricate center medallion cut from a square of folded bright cotton and an appliquéd border of the same material against a sharply contrasting ground. The figures are generally stylized flowers, royal emblems, and other local motifs. Colors run to strong reds, oranges, yellows, usually in violent contrast, such as the clashing royal yellows and reds (as in feather cloaks) found in the Breadfruit pattern. Try Sears, Ala Moana, for the best selection.

HAWAIIAN JEWELRY

Quite by accident Hawaii Silversmiths came upon a new "semiprecious" stone to add to their repertory of indigenous materials for jewelry. Paul de Marrionne, co-owner and designer for the firm, recalls that early in 1962 he introduced a line of olivine jewelry. One of his suppliers of this material found those little gems among the vast waste of lava cinders on the Big Island. When he brought a shipment of olivine he showed De Marrionne a handful of small, prismlike pieces of obsidian. This glassy volcanic rock of smoky shades of gray is known in Mexico as "tears of the Aztec," in American Indian country as "Apache tears," but in Hawaii, in honor of the goddess of the volcano, "Pele's tears." De Marrionne quickly saw that by simply polishing these tiny (up to a half inch) stones to highlight their smoky brown and gray tones to almost crystal clarity he had a unique new fashion element of native Hawaiiana.

For the geologically curious, the stone is a result of a process that recalls hot cereal boiling: tiny flecks of molten silica spewed out by the volcano hit the air and solidify quickly into these crystalline structures. You can buy these and other Hawaiian Silversmith creations at Sears, Ala Moana, and Liberty House jewelry departments, Pierre of Waikiki, and other specialty shops. And if you're hard up, look intently as you walk down Devastation Trail in Volcano National Park: you might just turn up a few of Pele's tears, which is something to cry home about.

The Egghead's Honolulu
A Day on Oahu for the Intellectually Curious

Ocean liner and jet leave increasing numbers of visitors free on Oahu for the better part of a single day. The standard gambit is for a shop and a swim. Let me suggest an alternative—to get a fast and penetrating look at why Hawaii is a unique mixture of East and West. Morning at the Honolulu Academy of Arts; lunch in the cool green oasis of Foster Gardens; and an afternoon at the Bishop Museum.

THE HONOLULU ACADEMY OF ARTS

The Academy of Arts is just a short cab or bus ride from the ship piers downtown. Roughly six to ten major exhibits are staged there each year. Two of the most interesting, usually in the fall, are the Hawaiian Art and Prints exhibit, and the Annual of Advertising Art in the islands. There are also major exhibitions in the house specialty, Oriental art, as well as traveling shows from the great national museums of Asia. The academy is one of the lucky small museums to have a Kress collection. Robert Griffing, the academy's long-time director until 1963, explains that the institution was formed to bridge the East and West: its collections make it possible for Hawaii's Orientals to have a strong sense of their traditions and at the same time to be exposed to the Western ideas, and vice versa for the haole. In this way, as Hawaii creates a new composite culture, it can draw on the insights of both streams of historical development. "We don't want any of these people to lose sight of the good things in their past," is the way he put it to me in an interview, "and their pride of having been a part of that past, or coming out of the past which created these great monuments." Operating on an annual budget of a quarter of a million dollars exclusive of acquisitions, the Honolulu Academy depends on the benefactions of its users and endowments; no public funds support it. It has a lively publication program and a store selling books and reproductions that is worth a long, leisurely visit. About 40,000 of the 100,000 to 150,000 visitors a year by the way are tourists, so don't be bashful. There's a rule of thumb, too: you can recognize the tourists as the ones wearing Hawaiian clothes! The Bishop Museum-Pali tour stops at the Academy.

Quite apart from the collections themselves, the buildings and grounds are most pleasing to be in. The architect was Bertram Goodhue, and he has used stylized Polynesian motifs in roof lines and ornamentation. The garden courts, like those at the Library of Hawaii central building, are among the most pleasant places in the islands. Quiet, cool, relaxing. In the 1920's the Honolulu Academy of Arts was founded through the benefactions of Mrs. Charles M. Cooke and her family, another instance of the contributions of missionary-derived individuals to the islands. It has a Kress collection of Italian Renaissance painting, and one of the best collections of Korean ceramics outside the Orient. But as much as one admires the works of art there, the tourist will truly value the serenity of its courts and galleries. For heaven's sake, don't go to this place on a tour. Plan to stay at least an afternoon.

FOSTER GARDENS

For ship stopovers who would like to look intensively in the downtown area rather than use their day ashore frantically trying to see all of Oahu, Foster Gardens is a must. For botanists, for nature lovers, for photographers—for those in search of an astonishing green coolness—this horticultural show place on the Vineyard Expressway is a remarkable testimonial to Nature's Greenest of Thumbs. And it's a marvelous place to eat lunch.

Dr. Hildebrand, a German physician, started the place as a private garden over a hundred years ago. He was physician to the queen and a botanist who wrote the first book on the flora of the Hawaiian Islands. The original plantings by this famed student are still standing on the main terrace. In 1930 the Foster family gave it to the City of Honolulu. Included in the gardens' annual budget of a quarter million dollars is provision for three five-man tree-trimming crews who also take care of seven hundred miles of tree-lined streets on the island of Oahu. This is a new concept you might well tell your home town about if you like it: having a botanical garden dress up the entire surrounding area. Foster Gardens, then, has a kind of "extension service" in its work on Honolulu's roads. There is a city-beautification master plan guiding a program for the entire island.

The Outdoor Circle ladies, who incidentally man the reception desk at Foster Gardens, are one of the most powerful factors behind Hawaii's success at keeping commercialism from killing the Golden Goose of tropical beauty. Having waged a classic struggle against billboards over fifty years ago, they are among the most stalwart anti-uglies in the country. The gardens are closed only two days a year, Christmas and New Year's; the rest of the year, seven days a week, fifty-two weeks, the Outdoor Circle ladies are at their Foster Gardens posts. Before these doughty ladies took their posts in 1954, vandalism and theft were common at the gardens. Kindly old men and women would be discovered, gunny sacks and shovels in hand, absconding with rare plants—on the grounds that they paid their taxes and therefore were entitled to reap a tithe for their own home gardens!

Four men take care of the nine acres of plantings at the gardens. About a thousand new species of tropical flora are brought into the collections each year by director Paul Weissich, a personable and articulate landscape architect trained at the University of California. Partly these are to expand the holdings, and partly the new species are evaluated for their potential for Honolulu's street tree program. A new master plan for the gardens has been devised by Honolulu architect Harry Seckel so that a visitor can wend his way through the place with maximum dispatch and horticultural insight. They also are planning a 240-seat lecture hall without walls, a "plantetarium," the enclosure for which will be massed flower banks.

Foster Gardens is organizing its collections into several educational displays, one of the most promising of which is to illustrate the history of oil. A display of prehistoric plants that go back 250,000,000 years will form the heart of this exhibit. They were the basis for what are now deposits of coal, oil, and natural gas. Although the volcanic origins of the Hawaiian Islands did not include such plants, they can grow in the tropical climate of the islands.

The orchid exhibit on the School Street side is another specialty. About a third of an acre in the mauka-ewa corner is set aside for a landscaped orchid garden. This simulates as much as possible the conditions under which orchids are grown in the wild. The species will be organized geographically; e.g., those from the Philippines, Southeast Asia, and Malaysia will be grouped together. They will be grown on trees, rocks, and shrubs, as in the wild. The purpose of this is not only to show basic species and primary hybrids and how they are genetically related, but also to reveal their ecological differences. Microclimates are created by jets of air and water.

One of the most interesting projects of Foster Gardens is its "coolhouse" idea. In the rest of America, to get the kinds of rare things that grow naturally in Hawaii and other tropical areas, horticulturists create hothouses. But in Hawaii, to show some of the most interesting endemic plants (which happen to grow at high altitudes), Weissich needs a "coolhouse."

The range of flora in Foster Gardens is truly remarkable. Look for the bo tree. Under such a tree the Buddha meditated for six years and met his disciples. Buddhists plant the tree in symbolic remembrance next to their temples throughout the world. The bo tree in Foster Gardens, however, is something special because it was grown from a cutting of the very tree under which Buddha sat. There is also an asoka tree, the kind under which Buddha was born.

Other conversation-starting trees include the henna tree, from which the dye is made. The chicle tree, from Mexico, is the source of chewing-gum sap. But more people in the world are addicted to chewing betel nuts, so don't forget to look at that tree, either. For the culinary at heart, there are cinnamon-bark trees, vanilla vines, pepper, chocolate, coffee, clove, and nutmeg trees. The raffia palm furnishes its leaves for hula skirts. The carnauba palm is the source of shoe polish and candle wax. The fish-poison tree has pods that the ancient Hawaiians smashed to make a substance that would stun the fish and make them easier to catch. The sandalwood tree is there too. There is a giant bamboo that grows a hundred feet high and to eight inches in diameter; it can grow as much as eighteen inches in a single day. The tree that grows the world's biggest coconuts is there too, but it takes fifty years for it to bear mature coconuts. The oldest tree in the gardens is the giant kapok tree, the kind used in market squares in Latin America. It may even be the oldest tree in Honolulu, because it was planted about 1855, when the gardens were still a private estate.

BISHOP MUSEUM

There is a new look at the Bernice P. Bishop Museum. Dr. Alexander Spoehr, the former director, was chancellor of the East-West Center for two years. Before he left he brought the young and energetic Dr. Roland Force from Chicago's Field Museum. He has a fascinating TV show on Channel 13, has already mounted a dazzling Art of the South Seas room, and plans to refurbish Hawaii Hall.

Dr. Force reported that more than 147,000 people visited the museum during 1962 and more than 40,000 visited the planetarium. He noted that a common disability of museums is that people feel no need to return once they have been there, and it is therefore essential that a museum change if it is to survive. There are no plateaus—you either go up or go down. New ideas and new programs must be projected in order to meet competition. He said that fortunately Bishop Museum had changed through the years and will continue to change. Recent changes include a retirement plan for the staff, an admission charge, being open seven days a week, a new planetarium-observatory, and a science education emphasis, two guards, a new, endowed research chair, a new quarterly publication—*The Conch Shell*—new paint and plaster, a museum TV program, a new research building to be started soon, and new research programs.

In addition, the museum contemplates the following future changes: more temporary exhibits, new permanent exhibits, a health education program, an educational extension service, a greater emphasis on history and technology, a musicological training center, authentic reproductions for sale, consultation and codevelopment of the Hawaii exhibit at the 1964 New York World's Fair, aid to other museums in the state and the Pacific in general, and reprints of out-of-print museum publications.

Research Expeditions

For years the Bishop Museum's Dr. Kenneth P. Emory was the only American student of Polynesian archaeology. In 1950 he inaugurated the Bishop Museum program for using modern excavation techniques in Polynesia. His eleven years of excavation have provided unique data for studying the history of Hawaii. The earliest evidence of settlement in Hawaii is on South Point, on the Big Island, the closest point to Tahiti. The stone adzes Emory found at the second, lower level of his excavation there were so much like Tahitian tools as to establish the point that these settlers or their immediate ancestors came from there. Radiocarbon dating estimates this settlement at about eight hundred years before anyone had thought that man had appeared in Hawaii. Another interesting result of these excavations was that skeletons of the fabled *menehunes* were *never* found. These "black dwarfs" have been explained in a fascinating way: they were commoners who were darker in skin because they worked out in the sun doing the hard labor; they were smaller because they ate inferior foods! Human imagination and exaggeration did the rest. Radiocarbon dating places the first Oahu settlement at A.D. 1000 and Kauai A.D. 1200. Language and temple designs suggest that Kauai was a kind of cultural backwater keeping alive older cultural patterns. Even those stern forbidding near-islands northwest of Kauai, Nihoa and Necker, show evidence of early settlement uncovered by the indefatigable Emory and his colleagues. The Nihoa and Necker settlements were inexplicably abandoned about the twelfth or thirteenth century. The remains haven't even been covered over with much vegetation, the setting is so marginal to vegetative life. However the temples are of a type common in Tahiti at the same period, indicating that there was still intercourse over the forbidding two-thousand-mile waterway.

Survival Wisdom

Thousands of soldiers who participated in the Pacific war against the Japanese should feel a debt of gratitude to the Bishop Museum. For Dr. Emory wrote a small booklet, *South Sea Lore*, which was the basis for "survival training" instruction for more than 150,000 men. In this booklet the old techniques of adjusting to the Pacific environment devised over millenniums by Polynesians were remembered to give soldiers stranded and on their own resources in nature a better chance to come through alive.

Highlights at the Bishop Museum

Look for Kamehameha's war god at the Bishop Museum. Kukailimoku is the name of this fierce image with pearl-shell eyes and a leering smile made from dog teeth. The bust is covered with red feathers of the iiwi and the yellow of the o-o. And if a warrior weren't completely demoralized by a look at that horrifying image, he might even stand a chance against the brave Kamehameha.

Royal Feather Cloaks

About 125 Hawaiian royal feather cloaks are known to exist today. Quite a few of them are in the hands of English families; several in fact are in Windsor Castle. More than twenty of them are at the Bishop Museum, mostly under lock and key, but some are always on public view, for these are the most glamorous treasures of this Museum. It is estimated that Kamehameha I's cloak had so many feathers it must have taken a hundred years to gather them. One of the splendid feather cloaks at the Bishop Museum has an estimated eighty thousand feathers. Sometimes the birds were caught with a sticky gum from the breadfruit tree or from blue grass beans, but fiber nooses were used oftener. The Bishop Museum is full of other items of interesting Polynesiana to look for:

Kahili staves were sometimes made of the bones of defeated chiefs.

The precious royal leis made of fine strands of human hair with pendants of whale's teeth on display in the Bishop Museum are called *lei niko paloa.*

The Hawaiians had neither metals nor the technique of weaving with a loom.

The new surfboards made of plastic weigh from twenty-five to forty pounds. The ancient wooden ones you can see in the Bishop Museum were much heavier, by three or four times.

The new planetarium, Kilolani, specializes in Polynesian sky lore. Be sure to visit it.

Chapter IV

THE BIG ISLAND: HAWAII

One of the first things the *malihini* learns to do in Hawaii is to distinguish between the state and the largest island, which gives the state its name. The Big Island is also known as the Orchid Island and the Volcano Island, from two of its most distinctive products. A diversity that runs the gamut from orchids to volcanoes is the hallmark of the biggest member of the Hawaiian chain. The Big Island has its garden spots to rival Kauai, history enough to compete with Lahaina, ranches like those on Molokai, but it's also big enough to have something of all of them. And above and beyond these it has what no other island here has, live volcanoes able and willing at the drop of a geological fault to improvise pyrotechnics so awesome they make the biggest Fourth-of-July fireworks seem like a single sparkler.

Hawaii's land area of 4030 square miles makes it bigger than all the other islands combined, almost twice as big in fact. It was formed by five volcanoes, two of which continue to add land to the island. At its longest north-south point it is 93 miles long; its greatest east-west width is 76 miles. It is 216 air miles from Honolulu, a 65- to 90-minute flight, depending on whether you land at its northernmost extremity, at Upolu Point, Kohala; or near the Parker Ranch at Kamuela; on its western coast at Kailua-Kona; or at its biggest (and the state's second biggest) city, Hilo, on the eastern shore of the island.

The best plan for exploring the Big Island is to (1) land at Hilo and explore its attractions, (2) drive on to the Volcanoes National Park and stay overnight, (3) continue on to the Kona coast, stopping at its many interesting sights on the way to Kailua-Kona, (4) the next morning explore the Parker

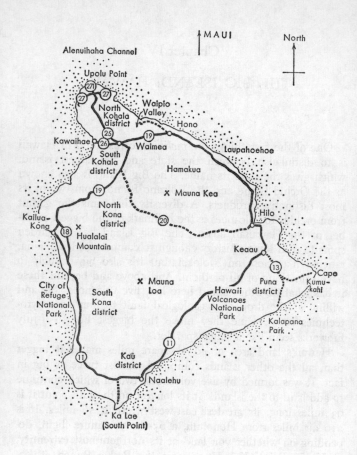

MAUI

North

Alenuihaha Channel

Upolu Point

27 27

North
Kohala
district

Waipio
Valley

Hono

Kawaihae

25

26

Waimea

19

Laupahoehoe

South
Kohala
district

Hamakua

19

✕ Mauna Kea

North
Kona
district

20

Hilo

Kailua-
Kona

18

✕
Hualalai
Mountain

Keaau

13

Puna
district

Cape
Kumu-
kahi

City of
Refuge
National
Park

South
Kona
district

✕ Mauna
Loa

Hawaii
Volcanoes
National
Park

Kalapana
Park

11

Kaū
district

11

Naalehu

Ka Lae
(South Point)

0   10   20
miles

HAWAII

Ranch area and on up into the North Kohala district, (5) double back to Waimea to cut across the island to the eastern, or Hamakua, coast, (6) drive down the coast to Hilo for a return flight to Honolulu.

Another day could be spent driving back a different route: over the rough saddleback road between Mauna Loa and Mauna Kea after driving up the Hamakua Coast in the morning (having driven it in the opposite direction the previous afternoon.) These are the basic outlines of the touring suggestions that follow. As everywhere in Hawaii, the best fun is had letting your U-drive car take you where a whim dictates. But the itineraries suggested will give you a broad understanding of the diversity of the Big Island.

Hilo and Vicinity

As your plane comes down to land at Hilo, look out the right side at Mauna Kea. If it is winter, you may see snow on its peak; some hardy types even ski there. Glacial evidence indicates that this 13,796-foot peak was covered with a glacier 250 feet thick during the Wisconsin glacial age. The large mountain on the other side of Hilo is Mauna Loa, 13,680 feet. Hilo is located about thirty miles east of the saddle between the two great mountains of the Big Island. It has a population of 25,000, less than a tenth that of Honolulu. There are many interesting things to see in Hilo itself.

In front of the Hawaii County Library on Hilo's Wainuenue Avenue are the Naha Stone and Pinao Stone. The huge rectangular Naha Stone was a kind of Hawaiian Excalibur. It was put in front of the Temple of Pinao for chiefs to prove they belonged to the Naha blood. If you did belong to that family, you were supposed to be able to budge it. Anyone who could turn it over not only became a king like those who moved it, but he also would unify all the islands. Kamehameha the Great, who did not belong to the Naha family, did turn it over and later fulfilled the prophecy. The Pinao Stone was the entrance pillar of the temple and was near the present library site.

Liliuokalani Park, named after the last royal ruler of Hawaii, the queen deposed by the sugar interests in search of the American market, is opposite Hilo Bay between the Wailoa River and the Naniloa Hotel. It is an authentic Yeddo-style Japanese garden with the traditional ponds and statuary, bridges and tropical plants. There are picnic grounds there, too.

At the mouth of the Wailoa River are the sampan moorings where fish auctions are held between 7 and 7:30 every morning. You enter the auction shed from Lihiwai Street.

Another attractive picnic place is Coconut Island, in Hilo Bay which is approached by a footbridge. Along the point that juts out in Hilo Bay opposite Coconut Island Park is the Banyan Drive. Each tree on the shaded parkway has a plaque saying what famous visitor planted it. In Wailoa River Park there is a Hawaiian village that completely reconstructs an early settlement.

Another village is at Keaukaha, south on Kalanianaole Avenue; it presents a free Hawaiian show at 8:30 P.M., Tuesday, Wednesday, and Thursday.

About a mile from downtown Hilo on the Wailuku River is Rainbow Falls. Morning is the best time to see the falls, when its spray and mist often form rainbows. Drive beyond the Hilo Memorial Hospital to get there. In the cane fields about two miles inland from the city center on the Wailuku River are the so-called Boiling Pots. There the river has cut pot-shaped holes in a lava stream bed. Agitated water bubbles up from connected holes from beneath the surface to give the illusion of boiling.

Another interesting lava formation is Kaumana Cave, on Kaumana Drive (or Saddle Road), about five miles from downtown Hilo. This cave is a lava tube, ten to sixty feet wide, that ranges in height from two and a half to fifteen feet. You can walk in it for about half a mile. This tube was formed in the 1880–1881 flow, which lasted for nine months and came closer to Hilo than any other eruption.

In Hilo itself, don't miss the Lyman House Memorial Museum. It used to be the home of the missionaries David Belden Lyman and his wife, who came to the islands in 1832. Their house was constructed in 1839, using hand-hewn local timbers and stones mortared with lime burned out of coral. It is located at 404 Haili Street and is open free Monday, Thursday, and Friday 10 to 12; Tuesday and Wednesday, 10 to 4; and Saturday and Sunday, 1 to 4.

One of Hilo's prime attractions is its complex of commercial orchid gardens. Here are some of those you can visit to see how anthuriums and orchids are grown and shipped to the mainland. They are open during business hours weekdays; a few even on Sunday:

Aketa Gardens, 1744 Kinoole Street
Hawaiian House, 1528 Kalanianaole Avenue (specializes in dry arrangements)
Hawaiian Tropical Flowers, 1538 Kalanianaole Avenue
Hirose Nurseries, 46 Josephine Lane
Hirorchids, 45 Wainuenue Avenue
Jewel Box Flower Shop, 277 Haihai Street
Kong's Floraleigh Gardens, 1477 Kalanianaole Avenue
Mauna Loa Orchids, 514 Kamehameha Avenue
Ogawa Orchids, 1454 Kilauea Avenue
Orchids of Hawaii, 580 Laukapu Street
Tanaka Anthurium Nursery, 99 West Kahaopea Street
Senator W. H. Hill's Garden (private but open to public), Keokea Loop Road off Kalanianaole Avenue

Almost a quarter of a million packages of exotic flowers are air-mailed out of Hilo a year. If you're looking for planters with a Polynesian touch for some of these flowers, go to Hawaiian Fern-Wood, Ltd., at 300 Manono Street, open daily. Orchid Isle Gift Shop, 2196 Kilauea Avenue, has a good collection of crafts for sale. At Hale Manu Crafts, four and a half miles from the center of Hilo on the road to Hawaii National Park, you can watch natives making hats, purses, and baskets by hand from *lauhala* or the leaves of the pandanus tree.

Also off the road to the national park is Keaau Orchard, a macadamia-nut farm open weekdays from 7 to 3:30. It's about seven miles to the gate from the Hilo Post Office and three more miles on a side road. Macadamia nuts are one of the many specialties, such as Kona coffee, orchids, and bagasse, that the Big Island is cultivating to diversify its agricultural base against the expected decline of sugar and pine (as the succulent cash crop is affectionately abbreviated).

There are two phenomena of nature in its wilder moods in Hawaii of considerable interest to people from less "primeval" parts of the country: the tidal wave and the volcano. Both of them are most visible in the Hilo and Puna districts of the Big Island. Before the present *tsunami* (Japanese for the big waves) warning system was installed in 1946, the unexpected violence of these unannounced visitations from the sea was truly terrifying. Paradoxically, the gently erupting volcanoes in Hawaii, far from provoking terror, start a field day for tourists and journalists, since they are safe to watch. (Since volcanoes give more forewarning than tidal waves, the local airlines have plenty of time to arrange for special "overflights" to provide the best possible view of the fiery spectacle.)

Most of the *tsunami* that damage Hawaii originate at mountain-building belts that surround the Pacific Ocean, especially from the Aleutians, Kamchatka, and South America. Hilo, facing the faraway western coast of Latin America without intervening protection, has been hardest hit by tidal waves. Today as you drive along the waterfront highway at Hilo you will be astonished at the gigantic forces you can infer from the hollowed-out buildings resulting from the buffeting of the last disaster, in May 1960. Ironically, much damage comes not from the force of such waves striking but from the tremendous undertows that go out to sea as the waves crest.

It helps to understand the origins of tidal waves if one knows how an earthquake happens. In this, rock layers in the earth's crust are deformed under pressure until they reach a breaking point. When this fracture occurs, elastic energy stored in the rock during the bending is suddenly released. The vibration or trembling of the earth that follows is called an earthquake. The break causes a fault. Such faults gradually spread by repeated small movements, and each such movement may cause an earthquake because of the large amount of friction involved in rocks slipping along a fault. (Except for the Big Island itself, Hawaii is not a highly seismic—i.e., subject to earthquakes—area. Even the Big Island quakes are usually small and do little damage.)

The tidal wave is not really "tidal" at all. Its proper name is *tsunami*, or seismic sea wave. Several conditions can lead to such waves, which travel across the deep ocean at speeds approaching five hundred miles per hour, but most, and especially those which do damage over a long distance, come from sudden fault movements on the ocean floor. If a block of rock is suddenly pushed up out of the sea floor, it pushes the water violently to form a seismic wave; if a block drops, water rushes in and rebounds, causing a shock wave. Thus both earthquakes and tidal waves are the results of fault movements, but since only a small number of submarine "earthquakes" are accompanied by tidal waves such quakes are useless as warnings against tidal waves.

The Puna District

At Keaau on Route 11 to the Hawaii Volcanoes National Park area, turn off onto Route 13 for an interesting side trip to the Puna district. Puna is perhaps best known for the 1955 and 1960 eruptions along the eastern flank of Kilauea. The 1955 affair was the first eruption in this area in 115 years and the first in a populated area of the United States. For three months, lava spread over eleven hundred acres of pasture, truck gardens, coffee farms, sugar cane, and papaya orchards as well as over six miles of public roads. In spite of all the physical damage, no one lost his life in the disaster. It is really eerie, and something that children enjoy wide-eyed, to drive through the Puna district today with still smoking remains visible at the side of the road. For a unique experience by all means spend the half day you'll need to make the side trip. It is just over twenty miles down to the Kalapana Black Sand Beach from Keaau, and just over seven miles from Kalapana to MacKenzie State Park, up seaside Route 137. At Pohoiki, on Route 137, you can turn inland or follow Route 137 up to Route 132 through Lava Tree State Park, which is eight miles from Pahoa back on Route 13. This

Pahoa-Kalapana-Pohoiki triangle is full of scenic surprises that those in haste to get to the Hawaii National Park miss.

Now to spell out in detail some of the things to look for in the Hilo-Kalapana side trip. The Mamalahoa Highway from Hilo to Olaa (Keaau on newer maps) goes through the lower reaches of Panaewa Forest Reserve, so you'll find thick forests growing right down to the edge of the highway. (Be careful when driving in this area. The roads, even paved ones, tend to be exceedingly narrow with whimsically skinny shoulders. I had a couple of close calls before I realized what the matter was.) Olaa is the little plantation town where you leave the highway for the road to Pahoa. The Hawaii Volcano Observatory set up shop in the school at Pahoa during the Puna eruption of 1955. They had a seismograph there that recorded up to several hundred earthquakes a day just before the blowup.

At the Pahoa school intersection you can go either to Kapoho Cinder Cones or south to Kalapana. (The village of Kapoho was buried by the 1960 eruption.) We have already recommended that you take the southern loop. At first the Kalapana road goes through tropical forest. It is interesting to go along the old lava-barricaded road as far as you can. By walking a few hundred feet beyond the barrier across the old road you find deep cracks caused by explosions. Grayish-silver lichen, the first thing to grow in the posteruption desolation, is already flourishing there. A twenty-foot spatter cone blocks the road farther on, and it is safe to climb up its sides for a peer into its still-steaming insides. Just off the road is Pele's Kitchen, so called because gases hot enough to cook over come out of the tree molds in this area. Especially interesting here is Kamaili Crater or the hole in Nii's cucumber patch, a 135-foot-deep pit crater. Watch out when walking in this area because it's difficult to spot hot mud, cracks, and holes from the recent holocaust.

After passing less spectacular, much older flows you will reach the sea; by turning right you discover one of the most photographed sites in all Hawaii: the Kaimu black sand beach next to Kalapana Black Sand Beach Park. This kind of sand is formed by the action of waves on small bits of lava, and all the Kodachromes you have seen of it will not diminish scrunching around in bare feet on its surface. My sons and I had a most idyllic game of catch with the coconuts that had dropped from the palms edging this unique crescent. We didn't swim because we were told that it wasn't very safe. There is good wading for children in the tidal pools that adjoin the lagoon of Kalapana Black Sand Beach Park.

Just beyond the park is one of the famous painted churches of Hawaii. These are the Roman Catholic places of worship that Alfred Frankenstein has written of with much affection and insight in *Angels over the Altar* (University of Hawaii Press, 1961).

Inside this church, Our Lady, Star of the Sea, and especially inside St. Benedict's over at Honaunau on the Kona Coast, plain house paint has been used to spell out the Christian story to the simple parishioners who worshiped there. I'm especially fond of the strikingly modern, plain panels of stained glass in the Kalapana church. Although the church's interior was painted in 1927, it is already flaking away, but the colored windows are still very fresh. Don't fail to walk past the open-walled gym behind the church to the splendid view of the sea.

Also in this Kalapana neighborhood are the Queen's Bath, a pool the size of a bathtub made by a volcanic crack; palm-fringed Punaluu pond, a fair-sized natural swimming pool; and also a lava tube the old Hawaiians used to hide in called the Cave of Refuge. Eventually there will be a road connecting this spot with Volcanoes National Park. Two miles down the Halape hiking trail leading west from Kalapana is the Wahaula Heiau. This is supposed to have been first built in the eleventh century by a *kahuna* from the Society Islands and later repaired about a decade before Captain Cook's visit by the King of Hawaii. This is also supposed to be one of the last places where human sacrifice was offered before Kamehameha II abolished the *kapu* system in 1819.

As you drive along the coast from Kalapana toward Cape Kumukahi, easternmost point of Hawaii (island *and* state), you will cross three paths the 1955 lava flows took to the sea. On your left is a hala forest. Just before Opihikao you can see a small graveyard with concrete tombs on top of the lava. MacKenzie Beach Park has a very cool stand of ironwoods beyond Opihikao. Isaac Hale Park at Pohoiki is another good spot on the Puna Coast for fishing, picnicking or camping.

Near the intersection of Route 132 which goes back to Pahoa you will see Kapoho Cinder Cone. It antedates the 1955 eruption. In the center of this cone there is a ten-acre lake that looks green because of the algae there. Since it is almost hidden by jungle growth, you'll have to walk down from the rim of the cone to see the lake. When we talk about Hawaii as the growing island, we must also realize that it also loses established places during its periodic eruptions. In the 1960 flow, for example, the entire town of Kapoho (about seventy homes in the vicinity) was buried under what is now solid rock. The new highway goes *over* the village nowadays. Nearby a favorite tourist attraction also lost was Warm Springs Park. Now it is gone. On Cape Kumukahi, the lighthouse almost got buried. The lightkeeper's house *did*, and the paint on the tower was blistered; it was that close. Beyond Kumukahi toward Hilo is a place called Honolulu Landing. Local lore says that it was named after a chief who then went to Oahu and the town was eventually named after him.

As you drive back on Route 132 toward Pahoa, look at Lava Tree State Park. It is the site of stone forms that look like statues built up when lava flowed around green tree stumps. By the time the interior tree had burned up the outer lava had hardened. Pele is supposed to have come this way looking for something to eat. When the villagers committed the cardinal Hawaiian sin of being ungenerous by refusing her, Pele turned the uncharitable ones into stone.

One other side trip *between* Hilo and Keaau is that up Stainback Highway (about four miles out of Hilo) to Kulani Prison. You have to call ahead to have the gate unlocked. This honor camp has a hobby shop selling tree-fern and woodcraft products made by the prisoners. The prison is exactly a mile high in elevation. Farther up, at eleven thousand feet, are a geophysical laboratory and a weather station; permission to visit this place is secured at the Hilo airport weather bureau. You need a four-wheel-drive jeep or a constitution of iron to hike to the top.

En Route to Hawaii Volcanoes National Park

Now that Puna has prepared us for Pele's prowess, let us drive on to Hawaii Volcanoes National Park. The park was established in 1916 to protect this fascinating outdoor geology course from abuse or exploitation. At first the park had two sections, Haleakala on Maui, and the Mauna Loa-Kilauea area on Hawaii; but in 1961 Haleakala got separate status. In all, these two parks constitute about three hundred square miles of the globe at its primeval, earth-forming stage. Besides the volcanic specimens, there you can see giant tree ferns (as you enter the park from the direction of Hilo on Mamalahoa Highway, the ferns reach heights of twenty feet with ten-foot single fronds), rain forests of hardwood trees, and rare birds and plants. The park headquarters, near Kilauea Crater, is about thirty miles from Hilo, ninety from Kona. To get to the Mauna Loa section, choose one of two approaches: the Kulani Prison road or Stainback Highway, already mentioned, and a park trail from Kilauea.

I stayed at the Volcano House on both my visits to the park, but I advise large families to find other lodgings because of its prices. When dining at the Volcano House, try to get a window table—it becomes any other restaurant several rows in! If you have breakfast there, you can see their unique vista on the precarious rim of the volcanic area. Early supper will give you another interesting view, and the free movies of eruptions shown after dinner are worth staying around for. To families of moderate income, I'd suggest camping at one of the three public areas with water, fireplaces, and rest rooms: one along Hilina Pali road (which skirts the southeast Pacific coast below Kalapana at the start of Halape Trail), another near Kilauea Rim Drive by the Kilauea-Iki crater, and one as you come in from Hilo off Mamalahoa Highway west of Bird Park. If you are in the military you have no problem, for the armed services operate a rest and recreation camp just a mile from Volcano House.

Be sure to start your exploration of the volcanoes with a visit to park headquarters. They have an excellent short film,

Nature on the Rampage, bracketed by an explanatory talk by a park ranger, that will explain the connections between tidal waves, volcanoes, and earthquakes and will greatly increase your capacity to understand the spectacular phenomena of this area. A huge relief map of the volcano area is invaluable for visualizing the process of eruptions. You will also find it worth your while to invest in some of the literature on sale there. Among the most useful I found were Gordon Macdonald's and Douglass H. Hubbard's *Volcanoes of the National Parks in Hawaii*, with its useful volcanic glossary and many informative pictures, *Trailside Plants of Hawaii National Park* by Douglass H. Hubbard and Vernon R. Bender, Jr. (Each costs fifty cents.)

It is natural to regard volcanoes as destructive, but a little reflection convinces one of their positive aspects; Hawaii's very islands are the peaks of submarine volcanoes. For even though an island appears to be made of reef limestone and sand, it is resting on a volcanic pedestal that gradually rose to the surface of the ocean, allowing the corals and related aquatic life that form limestone to exist.

Of Hawaii's Big Five volcanoes, Kohala is the longest extinct. There, the unending northeastern trades have dumped rain into streams that have cut deep canyons like Waipio Valley, while waves powered by the same winds have cut back the lava to form steep cliffs. Mauna Kea, next to the south, has not been active since the arrival of the Hawaiian people. Over near the Kona Coast, Hualalai last erupted in 1801. The two southernmost volcanoes, Mauna Loa and Kilauea, can go anytime. Thus we see that the volcanic activity has been gradually moving southeastward along a rift in the Pacific floor.

There are two basic kinds of lava flows in Hawaii: *pahoehoe* (pah-hoe-eh-hoe-eh), which has smooth, ropy, or billowy surfaces, and *aa* (ah-ah), which is very rough and rubbly. Lava generally comes from the vent as *pahoehoe*, changing into *aa* as it is stirred up advancing down a slope. We can see this clearly when a *pahoehoe* flow going down a smooth slope stays *pahoehoe*, but if some drops off a cliff, it changes to *aa*.

Because Hawaiian lavas are so freely flowing, speeds of thirty-five miles an hour have been observed in main feeding channels, although the whole flow advances much more slowly, commonly a few tens of feet to a thousand feet per hour. In other parts of the world, where lava is more viscous, advances are more like a few feet or tens of feet per day. Another feature of these smooth flows is that they spread out over great distances from their vents. These thin, far-reaching flows build broadly rounded, dome-shaped volcanoes known as *shield volcanoes* because of their shapes. Mauna Loa and Kilauea are good examples of this type.

The sunken crater of a volcano is a *caldera*, oval in shape, ringed by steep cliffs, and possessing a nearly flat floor because of the lava flows within the depression. Even though not much is known about the insides of Hawaii's volcanoes (the deepest exposures on the oldest islands allow observation of only the upper few thousand feet of shield), still it appears probable that two or three miles down beneath the active shields are collections of *magma* (or molten material) shaped like broad lenses. New magma rising up from beneath can inflate this reservoir, causing the volcano to swell. This tumescence forces the shield walls to rise up and tilt outward, a sign that the volcano may erupt to relieve this pressure.

Eruptions can also occur along cracks or fissures that extend across the summit of the volcano and far down its flanks. For example, the main vent of the 1942 eruption of Mauna Loa was eleven miles from the summit, and Kilauea's 1955 eruption was more than twenty miles from its top. The cracks through which the magma emerges are part of a zone of fissures known as a *rift zone*. The surfaces of these zones are marked by many open cracks and by long, low ridges of spatter cones.

When an eruption ends, the magma just about to be spewed aloft freezes in these fissures and forms a more or less vertical septum of rock up to ten feet thick. These are called *dikes*. Rift zones in Hawaiian volcanoes are generally half a mile to a mile wide and contain hundreds of these dikes.

Along rift zones you can also find smaller craters that have collapsed, called *pit craters*. The theory goes that magma works its way almost to the surface and then is drained away, possibly by a fissure lower on the flank. This causes the undercut rock to fall in. Near Mokuaweoweo, the caldera of Mauna Loa, there are several pit craters, and you can easily see a whole row of them by Chain of Craters road, in Volcanoes National Park along the east rift zone of Kilauea.

Lava tubes are formed when a *pahoehoe* flow crusts over to form a roof and the lava stream flows within this tunnel of its own making. At the end of an eruption most of the lava may drain out of the interior, leaving a tunnel from ten to as much as fifty feet in diameter. The Thurston Tube at Volcanoes National Park is a good example. Don't miss it.

You may also want to know what explains the black sand beaches like those at Kalapana. Where aa lava enters the sea, water may get access to the hot central part of the flow. The outrushing steam may carry a cloud of liquid lava drops with it. These are chilled into bits of black glass when they hit the air or water. Sand-sized and larger particles can wash up in sufficient quantity to form a black sand beach. Ironically, although the prize beach at Kalapana makes handsome travel magazine photos, it is treacherous for swimming.

After you have spent some time over the park headquarters relief map to get thoroughly oriented, you are ready to explore the drive along Kilauea's rim, which circles the crater with side trips like these that follow clearly marked. The children will especially like the Sulphur Bank, a third of a mile west of Volcano House, where gases and vapors emitted from volcanic fumaroles leave colorful deposits when they cool. About a mile and a half beyond the Sulphur Bank and just off the highway are more Tree Molds.

Kipuka Puaulu is about a mile from the Sulphur Bank. This Bird Park was an oasis created when a lava flow from Mauna Loa split in two, surrounding about a hundred acres of rich earth covered with deep foliage. Some of Hawaii's most unusual and even unique specimens are growing here, including forty varieties of trees, many found nowhere else in the world. This is made for do-it-yourself naturalists, since an exhibit at the start of the mile-long self-study trail dispenses free booklets to tell you what's what. You can picnic in this tropical display case, too.

Back on the rim road, you will soon come to Uwekahuna Bluff, a four-hundred-foot-high section of Kilauea Crater's west wall. It is the site of the only permanent volcano observatory in the United States. Look in the window at the seismograph, a silent sentinel keeping track of all agitations large and small that foretell eruptions.

Many visitors wonder how a seismograph works. Its basic element is a freely suspended weight that tends to stand still because of inertia when the earth moves under it. If the earth were still and the weight vibrated, you'd get basically the same effect. The apparent movement of the weight can be recorded in any of several ways: by a beam of light focused on photographic paper, by direct mechanical means, or through electricity. Weights are arranged in such a way that they vibrate along north-south, east-west and vertical directions. The small movements are magnified and recorded on paper attached to a revolving drum.

Another interesting device at the observatory is the tiltmeter. Early in the history of this observatory it was noted that the ground surfaces on the volcano slopes were always tilting in one direction or another. Later it was discerned that such tilting could be correlated with volcanic activity. Before an eruption, for example, the entire volcano starts to expand as if it were a balloon being inflated. Hence there is an outward tilting of slopes that can be measured in the same way land is surveyed. They found that between 1912 and 1921 a bench mark rose three and a half feet. After the outward tilt collapsed following steam explosions in 1924, they releveled their bench marks in 1927 and found that the same point had *sunk* three and a half feet and that another point of reference near Halemaumau's rim had descended thirteen feet. Many smaller changes in angle of slope can be discerned, not with surveyor's equipment, but with a tiltmeter. At the observatory, for example, tilts of less than one-tenth of a second can be determined. (To get a sense of how tiny a movement this is, imagine a board ten miles long one-quarter of an inch higher at one end: this forms an angle of one-tenth of a second!) Tiltmeters can measure angles of several seconds of arc. If there is strong outward tilting of the ground surface, this indicates magma rising to create a volcanic explosion.

A few miles beyond this observatory there is a place to

park so that you can get a good look into Halemaumau, the "House of Everlasting Fire," Pele's homestead. If you are the conservationist type, you'll want to join (for an honorary dollar) the Hui O Pele, or Pele's Club, sponsored by Honolulu's Outdoor Circle. Your life membership will not only help keep up the park, but will put you on Pele's side in case the going gets rough during an eruption while you're there.

Bob Krauss tells an amusing anecdote about the old Greek innkeeper of Volcano House called Uncle George. His Volcano House, of course, was only as valuable as the number of eruptions, which brought tourists in droves to watch the Drive-In Volcano. When Pele seemed to have gone into premature retirement, Uncle George Lycurgus, by then a firm believer in Pele—he professed to have seen her on two occasions—took a bottle of his best Gilbey's gin and threw it into the crater. By this supreme sacrifice he hoped to *start* some eruptions. (The old Hawaiians used to placate her with offerings asking her to lay off for a while!) Uncle George's prejudices were confirmed when the gin did its work, and Pele soon went on another toot, one that hasn't stopped yet.

You'll find the murals about Pele in Uncle George's Volcano House interesting, too. Among the other Pele lore is the belief that it will rain if you pick a red lehua blossom from the ohia tree. Try it and see. This flower is sacred to Pele and her sister Hiiaka. So is the red ohelo berry (which you shouldn't pick in the park even though they make fine pies, baked). The first blossom you do pick, by the way, should be offered to Pele.

As you continue to drive around the Crater rim road you will see 1894 lava deposits on your left, 1924 explosion debris on your right up to Keanakakoi Crater. Beyond it is 1877 lava. Bear right *off* the rim road just beyond the campground sign to see other parts of the park located on Chain of Craters road. It has two spurs at its end, one terminating if you bear right at the Hilina Pali, the other taking you to Makaopuhi Crater, where the easy-to-negotiate twelve-mile Kalapana Trail begins. Makaopuhi means the "Eye of the Eel." At the bottom of the eel-shaped pit there is supposed to be a mineral of the blue color of that fearsome sea serpent's eye. (I haven't yet gotten over the lump in my snorkel when I ran into such an eel loose at Hanauma Bay.) All told, there are nine pit craters and several cinder cones along this seven-mile stretch from Byron Ledge to Makaopuhi.

An easy trail walk to the left of the southeast spur is Puu Huluhulu, which means "Shaggy Hill." It is the largest cinder cone in the park and gives you an outstanding perspective, including a look inside several of the smaller craters. You can picnic at the end of the southwest spur on the Hilina Pali at Kipuka Nene. "Kipuka" is the Hawaiian term for an oasis spared a lava flow; literally it means "Opening." Don't try the trail down to the sea, since it is extremely arduous. Be content with the splendid vista of the southern coast or adjacent Kau district it provides. The Kau Desert is the leeward or dry slope of Kilauea. One "advantage" of such a desert is that foliage does not obscure unusual formations.

Now drive back to the fork where the spur roads branched off the Chain of Craters road. The first crater on your left is called Kokoolau. The next, on your right, is Puhimau. Puhimau means "Always Blowing," and it is assumed that this crater's vents were full of hot air but not much lava! The Hawaiians use the same term to refer to what we would call a "blowhard." And finally on your left is Lua Manu, or "Bird Pit," Crater. Turn right as you rejoin the circle road. You will then begin to drive around "Little" Kilauea, or Kilauea-Iki. Stop for a walk through the vegetation around the Thurston Lava Tube. Compare the dense tropical foliage of the adjoining fern forest with the bleakness of the leeward Kau Desert you saw just a few miles away when you drove out to Hilina Pali. The roads along the northeast rim of Kilauea Crater and the Chain of Craters road are in the upper edge of a tropical rain forest where the northeast trades dump an average of a hundred inches of rain a year. The many different kinds of ferns are shaded by a heavy stand of ohia trees. This forest has been undisturbed by lava flows for centuries; on the other hand there is a very young rain forest beginning along Chain of Craters road.

The Thurston Lava Tube itself is a wonder. There is a display at the start of the quarter-mile trail which explains what a lava tube is. An electric light makes it more civilized and a lot less eerie than I suspect it should be. This is a must if the kids are restless from aeons of geology all morning. And don't fail to let them walk the Desolation Trail. This is the most surrealistic landscape I've ever followed. The Park Service has put a boardwalk down over an area covered by the 1959 eruption of Kilauea-Iki. As you approach the end of it, you can see how the lava flow petered out. The trees there are not bleak, bleached gray abstractions as they are in the midst of desolation, but are just seared or scorched. Now you can follow the road back to park headquarters. If you're a really budding volcanologist, you could try a hike on the three-mile Halemaumau Trail, which begins near the Volcano House and proceeds into Kilauea Crater to the very rim of the Halemaumau fire pit. There are numbered points of interest to follow on a free map available from the park headquarters.

For the truly Himalayan types who have to climb it because it's there, save three days for a round trip to 13,680-foot Mauna Loa. You reach it by driving to 6000 feet at the end of the road up from Kipuka Puaulu. There are a shelter and an overlook at that elevation. You can reserve completely furnished cabins at the 10,000-foot level and at the summit through park officials. You will be trudging most of the time over barren lava. Some ice remains in shady spots during the summer at the top. If you're lucky enough to reach the top on a clear day, you have an unparalleled view of the southern and eastern parts of the Big Island waiting for you. It's breath-taking (like the hike itself at 13,000-plus feet).

The ninety miles between the volcano area and Kona are not the most exciting in the islands, but don't make the mistake of driving them at night and missing things at each end of the drive. For the curious there are places to be seen in the Kau district. If you have the single-mindedness of the tour driver, you can cover the distance in three hours. Bring a lunch if you don't stop for it at the plain lunchrooms in the plantation village of Naalehu, three miles beyond Honuapo on Route 11.

The first historic spot to look for as you drive toward Kona from Volcano House is about seven miles from the park headquarters. On your left off Route 11 you will see a sign pointing to "Footprints Trail." This is where Kamehameha got his first big psychological break from Pele. In 1790 Keoua was retiring to his Kau headquarters after an enervating but undecisive struggle with Kamehameha the Great over control of the Big Island. As the army passed Kilauea, the crater uncorked one of the two steam explosions it has had in historic times (the other was in 1924). Keoua's troops panicked at the continuing series of explosions caused by water that had seeped into lava vents and turned to superheated steam. When Kilauea "blew its top," it tossed ton-size stones a thousand feet into the sky and pushed a cloud of dust ten thousand feet high. The steam caused thundershowers that turned the dust cloud into mud balls like viscous hailstones. For years the footprints of Keoua's soldiers were recorded in the hardening mud. In the pavilion at the end of the trail, less than a mile long, a set of the prints has been preserved away from the effacing pressures of the wind and rain. The soldiers presumably died of asphyxiation from the hot gas and dust that Pele's favoritism set loose on Kamehameha the Great's behalf. With such divine allies, how could he lose?

About fifteen miles farther along on Route 11 is the side road right down to the sea at Punaluu Black Sand Beach. It used to be an open roadstead sugar-shipping port. There you can see outrigger canoes under palm-roofed sheds and buy shell and seed jewelry at the stands. It's a fine place to swim. One of the interesting aspects of Stone Age interior decoration there are the water-smoothed stones used to make "paved" front lawns on top of the jagged lava.

Down the road from Punaluu is Honuapo Landing, where sugar used to be loaded for shipment from a now abandoned wharf. Beyond the plantation town of Naalehu is the town of Waiohinu, which has a precarious title to literary fame as the place where Mark Twain planted a tree on his visit to the Big Island in 1866 when he was a correspondent on the sugar industry for the Sacramento *Union*. The lectures he then gave on "Our Fellow Savages in the Sandwich Islands" put him into literary orbit as a humorous lecturer. You'll still get a kick out of his Hawaiiana in *Roughing It*. Sorry to report to the Huck Finn societies everywhere that at last report Twain's tree had been subject to an intense dose of applied lightning. But a new tree is reported growing from the roots of the original, blown down by the wind in 1957. Stop at the green and white church, Kauahaao, in that town. It was the first one I went inside, and the surprise of seeing the Bible in Hawaiian on the lectern there got me interested in the whole missionary story.

About four miles from Waiohinu you should look for the South Point turnoff from Route 11. Ten miles down this side road you reach the sea and the spot that radioactive-carbon dating techniques have established as the oldest known human habitation in all Hawaii—an incredible A.D. 214, a date that pushed back the start of human habitation several hundred years when Bishop Museum archaeologist Kenneth Emory established it a few years back. And for those who like the ironies of history, this southernmost tip of the islands, like the westernmost one at Kokee on Kauai, is the site of a space-tracking station. From Polynesian navigators to Mercury-tracked astronauts, a kind of microcosm of the human story.

About three miles northeast of Ka Lae (South Point) are the so-called "green beaches" of Papakolea formed from olivine sands, larger gobs of which make the striking jewelry sold in some of Hawaii's better shops. Other sights of interest at South Point and vicinity are canoe-mooring holes chipped into the edges of the rocks near the unoccupied Coast Guard base and the large Kalakea Heiau, once used by Kamehameha the Great.

As you keep west on Route 11 beyond the South Point turnoff, you will drive over many dated flows from Mauna Loa on your right. Almost twelve miles past the turnoff and just before your route swings north in the South Kona district there is the excellent Manuka State Park, its entrance beautiful with white ginger during summer. It is on top of a slope near Mauna Loa's 1907 flow and has an arboretum for flowering trees and another for native trees and plants.

On Route 11, heading north into the South Kona district about ten miles above the Manuka State Park turnoff, is a complex of small villages—Papa on the highway, Milolii and Hoopuloa off the highway toward the left to the sea. Hoopuloa was wiped out by the flow of 1926, which you will cross; luckily no lives were lost in that eruption. Milolii is a fishing village whose natives exist by bottom fishing or trolling from outriggers powered by outboard engines. Up Route 11 twelve more miles is the turnoff to Hookena, another small seashore village on Kauhako Bay. What used to be a thriving village has now dwindled to a few old houses, a broken-down wharf, and (worth the effort if you can get a local person to jeep you in), an old earthquake-wrecked Catholic church nearly reclaimed by the jungle. I was lucky enough to have as my guide Norman Carlsen, who took the extraordinary color pictures of the painted churches for the book *Angels over the Altar*. We got to the Kealia site just about twilight, and the absolute desolation of the structure and its surroundings, with tropical foliage gradually covering over the effects of the earthquake, was a spectacle I shall not soon forget. I don't think I'd try to find it, though, without someone who really knew the way.

Your next stop should be the most famous painted church in Hawaii: St. Benedict's, at Honaunau. Turn off Route 11 at Keokea Junction and bear right to the church at the first side road. Some of the points worth noting in this church, decorated with regular house paint by Belgian priests, are the symbolically painted palm fronds—with green edges toward the altar and brown ones away from it, representing to the native Hawaiians the power of the Church's grace; the Hawaiian translations of Christian messages circling the poles down the aisles, and especially the illusionistic backdrop painted behind the altar. Art critic Frankenstein engaged in a fascinating detective exercise tracing the sources of the sophisticated European paintings and buildings Father John copied to give his parishioners the illusion of being in a great cathedral instead of a tiny missionary settlement ten thousand miles from his native Belgium. It is a touching story of faith. Also spend a few moments in the cemetery, with its splendid prospect of the sea. Note the shifting ethnic composition of the congregation from the headstones. The Maryknoll missionaries who now run the parish are most congenial men and are always ready to chat on the front porch about their famous church.

Now double back to the road you got on at Keokea Junction and turn right toward the sea to visit the City of Refuge at Honaunau. This is one of your newest national parks. When I visited there, I found archaeologists scanning the area for old Polynesian artifacts (some of their recent finds were in the information center inside the park proper). And, most amusing irony to me, three Hawaiians were busy using power tools (planers and sanders) to make an "authentic" outrigger canoe! There were also great cranes lifting about the huge boulders (up to several tons in bulk) that once were carted on crisscrossed scores of *wiliwili* poles. This fortress city is much larger than the one on Kauai. It could hold thousands of families. The price of leaving the refuge under safe-conduct of the gods was to offer certain sacrifices at the *heiau* inside the City of Refuge.

For sheer Polynesian paralysis I have yet to find a place as conducive to total regression from civilization as the green-carpeted grove of palms to the right of the central wading lagoons at the park. Don't hurry through this place. Curl up in that grove of palms with the pamphlet the National Park Service has written. There you'll find that the real name is Pu'uhonua-o-Honaunau in Hawaiian. Literally "Pu'uhonua" means "Fortified Place" or "Hell." It is located on a twenty-acre shelf of lava jutting into the Pacific Ocean. The City of Refuge is roughly square in shape, with the ocean fronting two sides and a huge wall extending along the two others. This was only one of at least six cities of refuge on the Big Island, but it was the most important one in the entire chain, each of whose islands had such places in every major inhab-ited district. The Honaunau refuge is supposed to have existed before 1492. The great wall itself dates from about A.D. 1550. A Kona chief named Keawe-ku-i-ke-ka'ai is ac-counted by tradition the builder of both the wall and the *heiau* 'A-lea-lea, whose stone platform still stands within the refuge. The wall, about ten feet high and seventeen feet wide, extends for about a thousand feet. The largest single stone is six and a half feet high, five feet wide, and two feet thick. The gods of those places of refuge were supposed to be the spirits of dead chiefs who could lead the souls of men to safety or destruction. Some chiefs became deified after death. For example, after 1650 the chief Keawe became the major deity of the refuge. A third temple, built for this chief turned god, was called Ka Iki 'A-lea-lea (or "The Small 'A-lea-lea"), but it was better known as Hale-o-Keawe ("The House of Keawe") after King Keawe-i-Kekahi-alii-o-ka-moku, who reigned in Kona about 1650. His bones were put in the temple to make it sacred.

Later chiefs were deified in the same way. The last *alii* so honored was a son of Kamehameha the Great in 1818. By that time twenty-three chiefs and kings had been so honored by having their bones put into separate containers inside the thatched temple. Lesser nobles had their bones thrown in a heap like firewood in a corner. Because women were considered inferior, none of their bones were ever interred in Hale-o-Keawe.

When the temples were destroyed along with the *kapu* system in 1819 after Kamehameha the Great's death, this one was left, because of its use as a royal mausoleum, until the bones were removed to a secret hiding place in 1829. Because for a decade it was the only extant temple in Hawaii, many Europeans sketched it. Much of the park area's 180 acres is now covered by a thorny kind of vegetation introduced in the last century. The Park Service is removing these nonnative plants to approximate more closely the barren lava of the original Honaunau, relieved by pockets of pili grass for thatching and coconut, pandanus, and kou trees along the coast.

You can take the self-guiding tour with twelve numbered markers:

1. *Palace Gounds:* Here a king of Kona might have as many as ten separate huts to his name, each for a different purpose. If a commoner so much as let his shadow touch the sacred palace grounds, he died. To get into the Place of Refuge, one had to take the trail from the south or swim across the bay from the north. The coconuts date from historic times, planted by the Paris family of Kona.

2. *Kauwalomalie:* The two stone bowls carved out of solid lava were used to mash and strain awa root, a ceremonial drink. Near here in 1782 Kamehameha met Kiwala'o to purify him because the latter had touched his dead father Kalaniopuu, late king of the island. A few days later Kame-

hameha's troops killed Kiwala'o during the battle of Moku-o-Hae at the Keei Battleground north of the City of Refuge, which you will see on your drive from Honaunau to Napoo-poo. Kiwala'o's death made Kamehameha king of the Big Island, the first big step to his eventual hegemony over the entire chain in 1795.

3. *Keone'ele*: This cove was the Royal Canoe Landing. Here Kamehameha I arrived to purify Kiwala'o.

4. *Heleipalala*: In the Royal Fishpond certain ocean fish were reserved for the king. They were put here until the King had the urge to eat them!

5. *The Great Wall*: Built entirely by hand without mortar of volcanic rock, it has survived almost five hundred years of tidal waves, earthquakes, and human use. It formed two walls of the twenty-acre Pu'uhonua.

6. *Hale-o-Keawe*: Standing until 1829, when it was destroyed by Queen Kaahumanu, it was sketched and described completely by the Rev. William Ellis, ensuring the authenticity of the forthcoming reconstruction of the grass temple, which was the most sacred spot in all Hawaii.

7. *Refuge Area*: Not even a king could bring the spear of revenge into this compound of compassion.

8. *'A-lea-lea Heiau*: Probably abandoned about 1650 except for a games *heiau* for the use of chiefs and kahunas.

9. *Keoua Stone*: Reputed to be one of the stones of King Umi's tomb *ca*. A.D. 1450. Partly squared with stone tools, the stone has six holes that, according to legend, supported poles for the canopy of Kona high chief Keoua's bed. Keoua was the father of Kamehameha I.

10. *Queen Kaahumanu Stone*: The queen is supposed to have hidden here from her husband, Kamehameha I, after a bitter quarrel.

11. *Papamu*: This was used for the Hawaiian checkers game called *konane*, played with black and white pebbles placed in the small depressions.

12. *Old Heiau*: Site of the first *heiau*. Lack of large stones explained by their probable use in constructing the second *heiau*, or 'A-lea-lea. Park Service archaeologists are planning to determine its exact size and form by a dig in the near future. Hikers can follow this anthropological sleuthing with

a three-mile round-trip hike down the coast to Kiilae, an abandoned ruin of a Hawaiian village. Tidal pools along the route will give amateur biologists a field day. The Park Service advises you to take two things: good hiking shoes and a canteen of water. Remember you're on the dry Kona Coast.

The Kona District

The word *kona* means "south" (or by extension "leeward"), as most of the islands have dry sides of their mountains away from the prevailing northeast trades. It refers on the Big Island to the thirty or more miles of coastal region between South Kohala on the north and the Kau district in the south. About nine thousand people live in the region; eight hundred of them in the "capital," Kailua. But before going on to Kona-Kailua, visit another small village with history coming out at its ancient seams. I mean Napoopoo, three miles north on the seacoast road (which parallels Route 11) from Honaunau. Notice the HVB marker of Keei Battleground, where Kamehameha started his rise to power.

At Napoopoo itself you can buy a cool bottle of pop while you haggle at the various stands for seed and shell necklaces much cheaper than similar jewelry on, say, Waikiki. And it's free and fun to talk about things in general with the people running the stalls. Right behind their stalls is the platform of the Hikiau Heiau, where Captain Cook unwittingly let himself be invested as the returning god Lono. Climb up on the platform and look across Kealakekua Bay until you see a tiny white obelisk. It was erected in 1874 to honor Captain Cook, and each year a British warship pays its respects to the great navigator. The easy way to get to see the monument up close is by a cruise boat that leaves from Kailua-Kona up the coast. You transfer to a glass-bottom boat to see the submarine Coral Gardens of Kealakekua Bay. You can't walk around from Napoopoo because the cliffs are sheer drop-offs into the sea. Look high up their sides and you'll see why chiefs jealous of the integrity of their bones had themselves buried there. Some of the burial caves have not been opened to this day. At Napoopoo also look for two historical plaques: one honors Henry Opukahaia, the young Hawaiian who urged the first Boston missionaries to come and convert his people, and the other shows where the first Christian burial was held (that of an unlucky associate of Cook).

But if you want a thrilling way to see the Captain Cook Monument (and actually go ashore there, which the tour boats *don't* do), hire one of the local boys to take you there in an outboard motor outrigger. When I dropped in on a former student of mine who teaches high school at nearby Konawaena School, he expressed an aloha by arranging to have one of his students take us out by motor canoe.

On your way back to Keei Junction on Route 11, note the Captain Cook Coffee Mill on your left. You can visit it during working hours to see why the Kona district is grossing about $3,000,000 a year on its 10,000,000 to 12,000,000 pounds of green coffee. The 5000 acres of Kona coffee are worked in small five- to ten-acre plots at elevations ranging from 1000 to 2000 feet "up *mauka*," as they say to distinguish the area from the seacoast. The last time I was there, friends gave me a three-pound can from K. Ogata's General Store in the village of Captain Cook. He got it from his own orchards and wrapped a plain can in very handsome tapa-cloth paper, so striking that my wife puts regular coffee (decidedly inferior to Kona, which is excellent stuff) in the Kona container now. Take a pound or so home.

Drive north on Route 11 toward Kailua, past Kainaliu, until you come to a cutoff down to the sea again on your left. Watch for the HVB marker showing where the royal slides were in Keauhou. Chiefs took a rocky ride into the bay on wooden sleds down this natural trough covered with pili grass. There is a most attractive cove, with a fisherman's dock at the southern end of this road. Tourists can get a ride on Captain Machado's *Jeanie Marie* to Kealakekua Bay from here. A monument marks this as the birthplace of Kamehameha III.

Now double back toward Kailua on the seacoast road. On your left on the shore of Kahaluu Bay is the tiny photogenic St. Peter's Catholic Church. It was built on the site of an ancient *heiau*. Some of the seaside Polynesian-style and A-frame houses along this stretch of coast are among the most attractive residences in all of Hawaii. Past St. Peter's, look for White Sands Beach, also called "Come and Go" or "Disappearing Sands" beach. At times the action of the waves completely exposes the lava base under the shifting sands. It is a favorite subject for the amateur artists who abound in the islands. A few miles out of Kailua is Kauakaiakaola *Heiau*, which was rebuilt in 1947 with a grass hut for the kahuna to live in and a wooden oracle tower he used to chant the worship service from. It was originally built in the sixteenth century and restored by Kamehameha. If you like the idea of Stone Age restorations, leave a small donation in the box for the private party who restored it on his own property.

John Lenk publishes a uniquely lively mimeographed ten-cent weekly newspaper, the Kona *Torch*: it sees the world as centered in Kailua-Kona. Don't forget to read a copy as you sip a Whaler's Punch in the Sea Lounge of Kona Inn.

Kailua's main street is called Alii Drive, the road of the chiefs. The Big Island's oldest church is on the right as you drive towards Kailua-Kona Airport, across from Hulihee Palace. Mokuaikaua Church was at first a thatched temple built by the missionaries who first came to Kailua in 1820. When they built this church in 1837, it was done without nails by using wooden pins, to join the beams, and mortar made from coral. The coral slabs came from the offshore reef; the ohia timbers, from the mountains "up *mauka*."

Hulihee Palace, across the street, was a summer place for the royal family. It was built in 1838 by Governor John Adams Kuakini. There you can inspect the solid rock medicine ball Kamehameha used to keep his waistline under control, stone lamps, and ancient implements of war. King Kamehameha the Great first came to Kailua in 1782, before he was sovereign ruler of the islands. His grass house was where the present pavilion is located. Although he later moved across the bay to the Kamakahonu area, the Hulihee grounds remained a consorting place for high royalty.

Kuakini, who built Hulihee Palace, was the brother of Queen Kaahumanu, Kamehameha I's favorite wife. He became governor of the Big Island when the capital of the kingdom was moved from Kailua to Honolulu in 1820. Kuakini was a great help to the missionaries in establishing schools, because he believed that *hoonaauao* (education) was their greatest gift to the native Hawaiians. At one time he even had a school under his personal care in his own yard. He helped translate the English Scriptures into Hawaiian. For a long time he was the only man on the island to wear a hat, and it is thought that his directive that women could not enter either Mokuaikaua Church or the Palace Grounds uncovered led to the widespread use of coconut hats. It was he who persuaded the Hawaiians to start building Mokuaikaua, when an unknown arsonist burned down the large (4800 seating capacity) ti-leaf and ohia-post church in 1835. After Kamehameha's death in 1819 this imposing (tall and weighing over five hundred pounds) figure was the most influential man on the Big Island.

When Kuakini died in 1844, his adopted son inherited both his property and his office. Next in office for fourteen years was the son's wife Princess Ruth, the great-granddaughter of Kamehameha I. Under the Great Mahele of Kamehameha III, she and Princess Pauahi (later Mrs. Charles Bishop) became large land-grant holders. With the lands she inherited from her half brother Kamehameha V, Princess Ruth became the largest landholder in the islands. Her and Mrs. Bishop's wills bequeathed their holdings to the founding and support of Kamehameha Schools in Honolulu. When Princess Ruth died in 1884, King Kalakaua secured Hulihee Palace for a vacation residence and it became world-famed as his summer palace. He stuccoed the outside, plastered the inside, and threw house parties for visitors from all over the world. Prince Jonah Kuhio Kalanianaole was the last beneficiary of Kalakaua's will. Since he lived most of the time in Washington as the Territorial Delegate for twenty years, Hulihee was neglected. Most of the furnishings were sold in 1916 at a benefit for Prince Kuhio.

In 1925 the Daughters of Hawaii got the Territory to acquire Hulihee as a museum. They raised $17,000 to restore it; members and friends gave objects of historical or scientific interest. Thus restored, it was opened to the public in the summer of 1928. The Daughters have tried their best to recapture the décor of King Kalakaua's days. There are imported German chandeliers, a huge Victorian-style sofa from Peru, a sandalwood wardrobe inlaid with ivory from China, and a wardrobe in the Kawananakoa Room made in England of koa and kou woods from Hawaii.

The *heiau* where Kamehameha the Great died in 1819 is on the point beyond the wharf. It is called Ahuena. The king used to keep his war god on the black lava point visible from the King Kamehameha Hotel today. The destruction of this *heiau* by Kamehameha II in 1819 signalized the end of the *kapu* system.

Of course to those for whom the thrills of today's sports are more invigorating than the memories of bygone historical eras, Kona means one thing: F I S H. Really big ones. An *a'u* (or marlin) over 900 pounds is the Kona Coast record since 1957, although the world record with rod and reel is a 1002-pound monster caught off Oahu. The *ahi* (or yellowfin tuna) is known for its initial run, which may take out as many as seven or eight hundred yards of line. The world's record is $266\frac{1}{2}$ pounds for sports fishing even though commercial fishermen have caught them up to 450 pounds. The *ono* (or wahoo) is a hard-biting game fish of from 30 to 50 pounds often caught in Hawaii. The *mahimahi* (or dolphin) is noted most for its great speed and aerial acrobatics when hooked. Many fishermen would prefer a fight with a smaller dolphin than with a larger one of other species. (As a nonfisher, I must put in a plug for the fish as a food, plain or in a sandwich; but also check for bones, I report to my own personal sorrow.) The *a'u lepe* (or sailfish) is not very prevalent in Hawaii's waters, but a few are caught each year. The *aku* (oceanic bonito) is a terrific fighter; a thirty-pounder caught on light tackle can take thirty minutes to land. If you do have dreams of establishing some kind of record or another, be sure to have your big ones weighed on a certified scales and have the record signed by the official representatives of the International Game Fishing Association. When I inquired at the convenient game-fishing desk in the lobby of Kona Inn, there were thirteen boats in the charter fleet. A boat can be rented for up to six people for $85 a day, including gear. The biggest time of year there, of course, is the International Billfish Tournament in late July and early August.

If you belong to the anti-Isaac Walton League like myself, you can save yourself a sunburn and aching muscles by sport fishing vicariously: join the crowd at the end of the day to watch the catch come in. Amaze your fellow-nonfishers by knowing what the signal flags mean: dark blue announces a marlin aboard; a white flag, *ahi*; canary yellow, *mahimahi*; and red, *ono*. Other kinds of hunting on the Outer Islands should probably be confined to the Big Island, since only there are guides easy to find. (Slim Holt, Box 1425, Hilo; Lloyd Hing Lai, Box 248, Hawi, up in North Kohala; Henry Ota, Box 51, Holualoa, "up *mauka*" from Kailua; and Kenneth Kohata, 284 Silva Street, Hilo, are recommended on the Big Island.) It costs about $90 per person for a two-day hunt. Before 1964 Hawaii required a guide if you hunted the 300,000 public acres. About 20,000 of the islands' 100,000 wild pigs are taken a year; and about 2000 of their goats and mouflon sheep. An all-inclusive hunting license costs $10.

For an interesting twilight trip take the road "up *mauka*" to Holualoa from Kailua. There, after you turn left onto Route 18, is an old Congregational church almost hidden by *kiawe* trees on a bluff to the right of the road, a Catholic church on the left which has made a shrine of the bell tower, miraculously saved when its old wooden church burned. But the most interesting view from here is at a Buddhist cemetery overlooking the Pacific far below. Try a sunset from here after watching the catch come in at Kailua.

At Honokohau, the Mamalahoa Highway becomes Route 19, and you are ready to see the country of the Hawaiian cowboy, or *paniolo*. After Kalaoa the route turns northeastward into the South Kohala district and Parker Ranch country, next to the King Ranch in Texas the largest such enterprise in the United States. On your right just before Puuanahula you can see Puu Waawaa. Up ahead is the town of Waimea (Kamuela Post Office—for the way the first name of Samuel Parker sounded to the Hawaiians new to English). There your itinerary splits three ways. Left on Route 26 is Kawaihae, the cattle port village near which Laurance Rockefeller is planning a destination resort area; ahead on Route 25 to Hawi and Upolu Point; and right on Route 19 to Honokaa, where the Hamakua Coast drive down to Hilo begins. But before trying any or all of these trips, tarry a while in the "capital" of the Parker Ranch, Waimea.

Parker Ranch and North Kohala

PARKER RANCH: KAMUELA

A sight that will surprise you on the Big Island is Richard Smart's plan to Victorianize the architecture of his Parker Ranch and its related towns. The idea behind the refurbishing is to make these places look as they did in the days of the Hawaiian monarchy. With this end in view, Smart has ordered gingerbread added to porches in the vicinity. Since men who work for the Parker Ranch have their choice of paint, pink, blue, green, yellow, red, and brown houses are beginning to dot the dazzled countryside.

This startling showmanship in the rather staid business of large-scale ranching can be traced perhaps to the Broadway career of the forty-nine-year-old Smart, who has sung in *Bloomer Girl* and appeared in other Broadway productions. The Parker Ranch's 262,000 acres make it one of the world's largest family-owned ranches. Its several spreads extend along the eastern, southern, and western slopes of Mauna Kea and west to the Pacific. Nearly 40,000 cattle graze on its acres. One of the most striking tableaux in all of Hawaii is to watch the cattle being loaded on board ships for Honolulu at Kawaihae.

When you drive through the Parker Ranch country, don't fail to stop in Kamuela, the "capital" of the Parker Ranch. There you should take a leisurely visit through the incredible diversity of the general store run by Ken Hayashi and his wife. With an encyclopedic memory for inventory, the Hayashis will astonish you with their facility at locating precisely what you want in the apparent chaos of their merchandise.

On the way out of town, stop at the "village green" on your left, with its remarkable complement of churches, each made necessary as the work force changed in Hawaii: first a Congregational church for Hawaiians, then a temple for Orientals, then a Catholic church for Portuguese and Filipinos, and finally a Mormon church for converts to that faith. This religious pluralism was one of the striking things to me about the many small towns here and down the Hamakua Coast.

The Waimea-Kohala district, which lies between the Kona Coast on the west and the Hamakua Coast on the east, is primarily a region of truck farming and ranching. Waimea was famous in olden days for its huge warriors, who, along with the white man's cannon, helped Kamehameha conquer. Mamalahoa Highway, or the Belt Road around the island which is Route 19 between Honokaa at the Hamakua turnoff and Waimea (fifteen miles in length) and between Waimea and Kailua (thirty-five miles), goes through only a part of this district. While the region is most appealing to hunters and horsemen, there is good swimming on the west coast and interesting exploring in almost inaccessible regions like the historic Waipio Valley.

First explore Kawaihae, which is a fifteen-minute drive down Route 26 to the sea from Waimea. It was a thriving port in the early nineteenth century. (The first horses in Hawaii, gifts of a California sea captain to Kamehameha, were brought ashore here in 1803.) Spanish longhorn cattle, protected by royal *kapu*, became so wild and numerous that Kamehameha ordered stone walls built in Waimea to protect crops and people. Nowadays cattle are led down the slopes over the "potato trail" (so called because that's what early Hawaiians grew on these hills). Before the hot and dry Kawaihae became a deep-water port, these critters were forced into the water to be raised off shore on a belly sling to the ship that took them to Honolulu. While fur traders and whalers gave the early-nineteenth-century port economic vitality by stopping for salt (dehydrated in pans now covered by wharves) and supplies, sugar and cattle are the main sources of activity today.

On your way down to the sea look on your left for Puukohola Heiau. It was dedicated with eleven human sacrifices in 1791 to Kamehameha's war god Kukailimoku (now on display at the Bishop Museum) because of a prophecy that he would become ruler of the entire island chain if he built a *heiau* there. This is also where he perfidiously slew his rival Keoua, who came on a peace mission.

Turn left along the beach to two attractive parks for picnics and swimming. The Samuel M. Spencer Park has showers in its beach pavilion and a coolness compounded of sea breezes and the shade of *kiawe* trees that is a godsend in the oven of Kawaihae. About three miles farther down is Hapuna Beach, ideal for those who can't stand the clutter of the prestige beaches on Oahu and, more and more, on the neighboring islands. Hurry, for soon it will succumb to the groupiness of the jet age. At Kaunaoa Beach nearby, the Laurance Rockefeller interests are planning a twelve-million dollar, two-hundred-room luxury resort done in an architectural style that has been described as late Shangri-La. And there is something indecent to a Calvinistic sort like myself in this resort's plans to furnish motorized gocarts for visitors to get from one end of the beach to the other. One of the side benefits of being poor is not having to participate in that kind of elegance! The hotel is scheduled for opening late 1964 or early 1965.

Down the swirl of dust that deludes itself into thinking it's a road is the village of Puako. From there on it's strictly beach trail down the coast to Kailua. Puako is best known as one of the three missions of the saintly Lorenzo Lyons, who from 1832 to 1886 carried the Christian gospel over the dusty plains of this region. His Kawaihae church is torn down, but you can see his Waimea Imiola Church ("Seeking Life") on the road to Honokaa. Lyons, whose name the Hawaiians hear as "Laiana," translated the standard hymns into the natives' language, and you can still see his hymnals at Imiola. The Puako church was built of homemade cement and of coral. Behind it is the old schoolhouse of the same materials. Lyons was known as the Poet of the Mountain Country because of his translating and composing hymns.

NORTH KOHALA

Now double back to the Route 26 junction with Route 25 and turn north for a tour of the North Kohala district. On your right as you climb into the mountains is the splendidly sited Hawaii Preparatory Academy. Your children will love the cactus and the cowboys they see along the road in this Texas *cum* aloha shirt country.

Soon you will come to Hawi, a sugar plantation town, twenty-two miles from Waimea. If the weather is clear, you can get a splendid view of Haleakala on Maui across the Alenuihaha Channel, and, looking south on the Big Island, of Hualalai, east of Kona, as well as the big peaks of Mauna Kea and Mauna Loa. A little six-mile side trip on Route 27, past Upolu Airport, and down the northwest tip of the island will bring you to Mahukona Landing, which used to be a shipping port for the Kohala Sugar Company before Kawaihae took its business away. While the lee side of the island is dusty and dry, it is also excellent for fishing, swimming, and skin diving because it doesn't get rough, as the windward side does. A little over five miles from Hawi is Kapaa Park, known for excellent skin diving. On your way back to Hawi cut off to your left toward Upolu Airport. On your left look for Mookini Heiau, where you can still see a grooved stone for beheading human sacrifices. This is supposed to be one of the only two *heiaus* built by a priest from Tahiti in the eleventh century. The other is Wahaula, in Puna. Kamehameha I was born just west of the *heiau* at Kokoiki.

Drive back to Hawi. If you take Route 27 north, you can get a great view of Maui and realize why this was a staging area for attacks between the islands. Drive through Hawi on Route 27 toward Makapala, Niulii, and the remote Pololu Valley. At Kapaau, three miles east of Hawi, you will see the original of the statue that stands across from Aliiolani Hall in downtown Honolulu, the one symbolically garlanded with leis on Kamehameha Day. At Waikani Gulch, six miles beyond Hawi, the villagers still tend their own taro patches, irrigated by a community stream. Then drive to the end of Route 27 for a glimpse of country like the Na Pali Coast of Kauai and produced by the same geologic and climactic forces of pounding surf and eroding streams. Kamehameha I was probably secreted in one of these valleys when the king tried to kill the infant prophesied to become ruler of all Hawaii. You can climb down to the floor of the Pololu Valley by trail in fifteen minutes. If you want to go deeper into the series of

The Fern Forest in Hawaii Volcanoes National Park on the Big Island is a fascinating place to explore tropical ecology. (HAWAII VISITORS BUREAU)

[9]

The City of Refuge on the Kona coast is the newest national park. Here Polynesians fleeing punishment found sanctuary. (UNITED AIR LINES)

The Painted Church of Honaunau translated European religious culture into Hawaiian imagery. (PATRICK D. HAZARD)

More recently, Roman Catholics have erected splendidly simple churches like this A-frame (using telephone poles) building at Hanalei, Kauai.
(PATRICK D. HAZARD)

[11]

Devastation Trail is the hellish landscape left in the wake of the 1959 eruption of Kilauca. Look for traces of life reappearing. (PATRICK D. HAZARD)

[12]

Maui's Haleakala ("House of the Sun") Crater is another landscape from the prehistory of the earth. Overnight camping for the hardy. (PAN AMERICAN AIRWAYS)

Maui's Iao Valley is famed for its towering needle, the myths that explain it, and the bloody battles fought there. (PAN AMERICAN AIRWAYS)

The Hanalei Overlook on northern Kauai is a reminder of how the old Hawaii with taro and later rice patches probably looked. (HAWAII VISITORS BUREAU)

Halawa Valley, on the remote eastern tip of Molokai, is a part of Hawaii most removed from the hectic bustle of modern America. (HAWAII VISITORS BUREAU)

gorges, you must make advance arrangements for guides from the Kohala Ditch (irrigation) Company in Hawi. The ditch itself is as impressive a bit of hydraulic engineering as the other irrigation feats on Oahu and Maui.

On the way back to Hawi look on your left for signs pointing out Kala-hikiola ("Day of Salvation") Congregational Church, less than a half mile off the main street. It was completed in 1855 after herculean labors by the parishioners of the Rev. Elias Bond, D.D., and his wife, Ellen Howell, who arrived from Boston in 1847. Bond designed the stone church himself and described its difficult construction well: "The stones were gathered from the neighboring ravines and brought on men's shoulders. Men in canoes with ropes and sticks for loosening up the bunches of coral, would go into three or four fathoms of water. Some would dive, loosen the coral and attach the rope thereto, while others in the canoe would draw up the rock. After being piled on the shore it was carried on the shoulders of the people to the church site. Then the wood for burning it was brought in the same way from eight to ten miles *mauka* up in the mountains. A fathom of coral required the same measure of wood for burning. Then came the sand, hundreds of barrels. It was brought by women and children from all along the coast, from Kawaihae around to Pololu, in bits of kapa, small calabashes, small lauhala bags. . . ." The Rev. Bond had grown tired of replacing grass churches leveled by Kohala's strong winds. Beyond the church is what is left of a female seminary for training Hawaiian girls from the Kohala area. Like the saga of the kindly Lorenzo Lyons on his Waimea-Kawaihae-Puako circuit, the dedication of the Bonds' parish is inspiring.

If you want to go to Waipio Valley the hard way, start with a guide and mules at the Pololu Valley entrance. Otherwise double back through Waimea and east on Route 19 to Honokaa through territory originally settled by immigrants from Portugal and the Madeira Islands. They have given a Mediterranean touch to the winding highway with their plantings of loquat, peach, sour lime, and rose-apple trees and swarms of little red roses. (Gastronomically they add to Hawaii's cornucopia of foods a round sweet bread, *malasadas,* and hot pork sausages; the latter I find puts Sunday-morning eggs on an entirely new plateau of tastiness.)

At Honokaa turn left onto Route 24 and go about eight miles north through Kapulena and Kukuihaele to the end of the road and the overlook into Waipio Valley. In this half-mile-deep valley, which extends six miles from the sea to the Kohala Mountains, there is a historic Hawaiian village. The name means "Curving Water," an apt description of the way its river wanders to the sea. The women fishing here use nets or woven baskets to scoop fish out of the still lagoon. You can make a horseback tour in four hours or sleep overnight. Another way of approaching it is via the trail just before Kaaihue on the Waimea-Honokaa road. On the cliff opposite the overlook there is a switchback trail that leads across thirteen smaller gulches into Waimanu Valley. This valley is supposed to be where Kamehameha was given the war god Kukailimoku for safekeeping. Umi, an ancient *alii*, is reputed to have sacrificed eighty men to the gods in this stronghold of the ancient kings. At one time a hundred years ago seven thousand people lived in this beautiful valley; less than half a century ago, there were seven hundred residents; today fewer than a dozen live there. Some taro is raised commercially and carted out on muleback. Not long ago you had to camp out or stay with friends overnight, but a three-bedroom Waipio Lodge, with kerosene lamps and cookstoves, running water and inside plumbing, takes the roughness off this tour. Waipio Valley Jeep Tours, billed as the valley's "only public transportation system," manages the cabin. See Raymond Arraujo at Kukuihaele if you're interested.

Coming back down the coast road, Route 24, you will see sugar cane plantation after sugar cane plantation because the rich red earth of this plateau land on the windward wet side of the island is ideal for raising cane. If you are hooked on macadamia nuts from following my suggestion to make your first Oahu breakfast macadamia nut pancakes, stop in the Honokaa Macadamia Nut Factory (Monday to Thursday 7:00 A.M. to 11:00 A.M. and 12 noon to 2:00 P.M.; Friday 8:00 A.M. to 11:00 A.M.). Honokaa is the second city after Hilo and the site of an annual rodeo.

Next stop down the coast after Ookala is Laupahoehoe,

where the tidal wave of 1946 swept twenty teachers and students and four other citizens out to sea as they arrived for classes in the morning. The site of the old school is now a public park. The new school is by my favorite Hawaiian architect, Viennese Alfred Preis, who did the U.S.S. Arizona Memorial, the entrance to the Kapiolani Park Zoo, and the First Methodist Church on Beretania Street, Honolulu. This is also the place where the sailors from the *Hornet* fire landed and gave fledgling newsman Mark Twain his first really big scoop. If you decide to swim here, remember what the name of the place ("Leaf of Lava") implies: there is no protecting reef here.

At Hakalau there is an interesting sugar mill to which some of the cane still comes on the photogenic water flumes. After you pass through Wailea, look for the Akaka Falls sign at the Honomu turnoff. As you climb the hill to the main street, take a turnoff to the left until you come to a streetful of churches of exquisite design; note especially the Japanese temple. Now get back on the Akaka Falls itinerary, which is about four miles from the highway. In this sixty-six-acre state park there is the most luxuriant growth of tropical vegetation I have seen with the exception perhaps of the Fern Forest in Volcanoes National Park. Akaka is much more variegated, though, and hence ultimately more attractive scenery. Its four-hundred-foot waterfall is a marvel. There is a pavilion (from which you see the Pacific in one direction and the falls in the other) which is ideal for picnicking. By the way, you'll have to keep your eyes peeled for the signs through the cane fields to Akaka Falls unless the HVB has improved the situation since we tunneled through there, feeling like lost leaf hoppers in the tall, tall cane. And don't miss Kahuna Falls on the trail.

There is one trip left for the hardy type that doesn't mind jouncing on near-roads, the fifty-five-mile Saddle Road between Hilo and Waimea, known as Route 20. It crosses a broad pass between the slopes of Mauna Kea on the north and Mauna Loa on the south. Each lava flow is marked by HVB signs, including a nine-mile stretch you cross of the 1855 flow, which lasted for thirteen months, the longest historic eruption. You'll also pass the 1935 flow that threatened the city of Hilo's water supply until aerial bombers diverted it. Near the Humuula Sheep Ranch junction you can see Puu Huluhulu, a cone surrounded with the ropelike form of lava from Mauna Loa in 1935. If you're a Douglas fir enthusiast, take the gravel road at Humuula to the northeast, over open grazing land where a jeep trail goes near a monument to David Douglas, the botanist and explorer killed under mysterious circumstances near here. The fir is named after him. At 9500 feet there is Halepohaku Camp, where about sixty persons can stay overnight with barracks-type accommodations. Make arrangements at the Hilo office of the Board of Agriculture and Forestry. Be sure to be warmly dressed, as the temperature is extremely cold day and night even in summer. At 10,000 feet there is an attractive picnic area at Kilohana Lookout. Six miles from here by extremely rugged trail (you will sink to your ankles in cinders, so wear high shoes) is the summit of Mauna Kea. The air is so rare it takes a tough day to make the twelve-mile round trip. Keanakakoi Cave, on this trail, is an abandoned mine where ancient Hawaiians chipped spear points and other tools out of hard lava. Back on Route 20 about seven miles beyond Humuula is Pohakuloa Camp, where Hawaiians are succeeding in fighting the extinction of the bird of the state, the *nene*, or Hawaiian goose. For a dozen miles beyond Pohakuloa you will be riding through the Parker Ranch until you reach Route 19, the Mamalahoa Highway, five miles Kailua of Waimea. The variety I have been describing in this chapter is the reason I consider the Big Island the most interesting part of the chain, second only to Oahu itself in fascination. Remember to get on the starboard side of the plane back to Honolulu to get the best view of the city. Do it after dark if the weather over Oahu is reported clear. It's a sight you'll never forget.

Chapter V

MAUI: THE VALLEY ISLE

Maui is a fascinating blend of history and scenery. The Valley Isle boast that it is the best seems a trifle strained to one familiar with the vitality of Honolulu and the greater variety of the Big Island. But there are some incomparable aspects of Maui that fully justify a visit.

Among my most pleasant recollections are the patchwork taro plots seen from the Wailua overlook on the road to Hana; and just past Hana on the south coast the Ka Iwi Pele hill, where Pele is supposed to have left her bones when she went to the Big Island in another form; the Seven Sacred Pools just before Kipahulu; the incredible views on the rough but negotiable Piilani Highway between Kipahulu and Ulupalakua; the marvelous vista of pineapple and sugar plantations in the Central Valley from Route 37 along the shallow slopes of the astonishing mass of the dormant volcano Haleakala—"the House of the Sun"; the unexpectedly un-cliché-ish quality of Iao Needle; the constantly changing panorama of the offshore islands of Kahoolawe, Lanai, and Molokai, visible from Route 31 on the way to Lahaina; the striking view of Lahaina from Lahainaluna, the "first academy west of the Rockies."

Before you leave for Kahului Airport, phone from Honolulu and reserve the kind of car you want. The U-drive dispatcher will say that you can't get a definite confirmation—until you threaten to go to his competitors, of which there are many. Otherwise you may end up paying for more car than you want to. If you're the bazaar type, you may enjoy waiting to haggle at the airport. It's part of the fun if you don't care for the prefabricated spiel of the many good tours.

We rented a Vauxhall for seven dollars a day, first fifty miles a day free, the rest ten cents a mile. We paid about

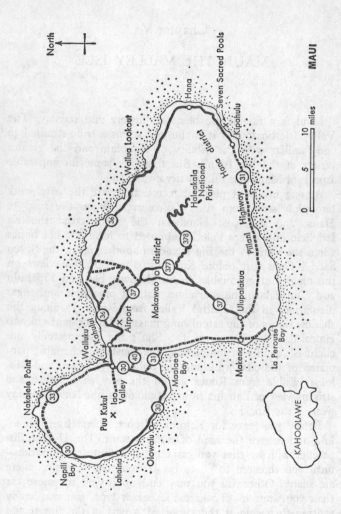

North

MAUI

0   5   10 miles

Hana

Seven Sacred Pools

Kipahulu

31

Hana district

Wailua Lookout

Haleakala National Park

378

Pillani Highway

36

Makawao district

377

Ulupalakua

37

37

Airport

Kahului

Wailuku

36

40

31

Makena

La Perouse Bay

Nakalele Point

30

33

Puu Kukui

Iao Valley

Maalaea Bay

Napili Bay

30

Lahaina

Olowalu

30

KAHOOLAWE

forty dollars for almost four hundred miles of Maui. If you like to root around, get a jeep. It's the best way to do the main stretches of rough road (Route 31 between Kipahulu and Ulupalakua on the eastern tip and Route 30 between Honokahua and Waihee on West Maui). Route 31 revealed what was for me the most satisfying scenery on the whole island. Be sure to take the complete collision insurance coverage (a dollar a day extra) if you plan to jeep it. And check to see that you have the comprehensive coverage. I lost a tail pipe just beyond Kaupo, but the sight of the old lava flows broaching the sea would have been worth a busted transmission—much more satisfying visually than similar flows on the Big Island, where you're on flatter ground and the denser foliage keeps you from seeing as much. The lava blackness touching a Pacific blue is the most splendid sight.

Try to avoid these bad roads after a big rain, which in drought-seared Maui isn't very often these days. The cinder cones on the flanks of Haleakala just before you reach Ulupalakua Ranch are also unparalleled geological displays. This sere stretch of sulphurous and ferrous earths set off here and there by flowers and shrubs is one of the finest pleasures of Maui—and in astonishing contrast to the lush valleys you just passed before and after Hana.

Allow yourself a full day to drive from Wailuku to Ulupalakua with lunch in Hana. If you want to pack a lunch, there is a very handsome spot to eat just before Route 31 gets rough at Hui Aloha Church (1859). This old coral Hawaiian Congregational church is intrinsically interesting, and it's set on a small peninsula with a beautiful view of both Haleakala and the ocean. The more you see of the immensity of Haleakala on this trip, the more you will want to see its innards.

The tour drivers claim that the best time to see the crater is in the early morning. Fog very often takes over by the early forenoon. If you want to avoid the deep pique of a vocal lady from New York who groaned the day we were there that she had come five thousand miles to see nothing but high-altitude smog, you should check the weather at Haleakala as soon as you arrive at Kahului Airport. Hardy types will want to hike into the crater for a few hours (or several days, as a Boy Scout troop was preparing to do when we visited the observatory).

There are free cabins "down there," courtesy of the management of this, our newest national park.

The observatory has an excellent geological display showing how at one time Lanai and Molokai formed a single island with Maui. A bank of windows facing the crater clearly explains the various formations. Plan to spend at least an hour at the observatory, taking a do-it-yourself cram course in geology. The Hawaiian mythology here, as usual, is as fascinating as the modern science.

Don't forget to pack a sweater for your trek to the House of the Sun. Paradoxically, Old Sol hasn't solved the problems of central heating in his own digs. And don't expect to find a place to eat at ten thousand feet. There isn't any such, though on the way down at six thousand eight hundred feet you'll find the Silversword Inn.

One of the rare sights at Maui's ten-thousand-foot Haleakala is the silversword, which like the *nene*, or Hawaiian goose, barely escaped extinction due to human carelessness. On the walls and within the crater grows this rare plant with long, narrow leaves that glisten like frosted silver. Each plant produces one flower stalk, which can reach a height of six feet, with hundreds of small purple flowers. When the seeds mature, the plant dies, like the agave of the Southwest desert. Sixty years ago you could see an entire crater floor covered with this exotic species; thirty years later they had all but disappeared, due to the kleptomania of visitors. Now you must shoot your pictures and movies of them from behind a wire fence enclosure; and don't make the mistake of trying to snitch one of the rare blooms. The rangers are most jealous of the flora they saved from extinction.

But in your silversword trance don't overlook the less publicized flora. Excellent pamphlets on them are available at the observatory, but you need only your eyes to glory in their variety and profusion. And keep an eye open for the curious evergreens in reforestation areas on the way up to Haleakala.

The second most interesting natural feature of Maui is the Iao Needle, a few minutes' drive from Wailuku, the twin city of the airport and seaport town Kahului. We had an inexpensive lunch of fine *mahimahi* at the Iao Inn, which has a splendid view of its namesake. Near it is a very satisfying Japanese formal garden. The Iao Valley is famous in Hawaiian history because here Kamehameha—the Napoleon of the Pacific—consolidated Maui by defeating Kalanikupule in 1790. From there he went on to mop up Oahu by forcing the native warriors to jump over the Nuuanu Pali.

On the way back from Iao Needle you should stop at Hale Hoikeike, the home of the Maui Historical Society. There are relics there from prehistory through annexation. An excellent little bookstore will put you in touch with authentic books on the history, language, and arts of Hawaii.

More highly touted as a historical site, but still very much in the planning stage, is Lahaina, the old capital and once center of the Pacific whaling industry. An unusually good historical guide to Lahaina has just been published, and you can get it for a dollar by writing to the Maui Historical Society. Read it before you go and it will increase your pleasure. You can drive to Lahaina from the airport in less than an hour. The greatest pleasure I had in Lahaina was visiting Waiola Cemetery (1823), where you can muse among the archaic headstones for hours. There you can reconstruct in your imagination over the grave of the Rev. William Richards his fierce fight with the boisterous tars who wanted him to lift the taboo off the dusky but newly Christianized wahines. Down the street is the Hale Paahao (Old Prison) (1852), where the whalers on shore leave sobered up after painting the town. If you want to see a more enduring way of raising cane, you can visit the Pioneer Sugar Mill by appointment.

As sugar gets into deeper economic trouble through mainland mechanized competition, Lahaina and many other towns in Maui are looking for alternative sources of income. Lahaina is packaging its own fascinating and fast receding history (Ozymandias types will have a field day here). *Heiaus* and petroglyphs can be studied in the fields at nearby Olowalu.

It is also near what the State Planning Department grandly calls a "destination resort area," which is to say a hotel *not* on Waikiki Beach. Architect George Wimberley has created a jewel, the Sheraton-Maui, at Kaanapali, up the beach a few miles from Lahaina. It has a golf course Bing Crosby has already beatified with his divoting. Wimberley has an interesting concept—he is building an elite hostelry up against the side of a hill. You enter this conversation piece from the top (physically and financially). A six-story façade of saucer-shaped lanais (porches to *malihinis*) faces a far distant Haleakala and the adjacent sea. Honolulu sculptor Edward Brownlee has distinguished its fountain with a version of the harvest god Lono's sunken outrigger emerging, as promised, from the sea.

If you like good, old as well as handsome, new architecture, there are many surprises in store for you on Maui. The old wooden churches are an unappreciated glory of all the islands, and Maui has its share. Note especially the octagonal church near Kula; striking Buddhist temples at Hana, Paia, and Makawao; excellent Catholic churches at Waiakoa and Waihee. Wailuku's Congregational Church is also striking.

You will also like the plethora of the kind of American architecture Mark Twain claimed had "Queen Anne fronts and Mary Ann behinds." The Iao movie house in Wailuku is also a glorious variant on what one wag has called "Early Balaban and Late Katz." The plantation society's use of classic revival to remind the immigrants whose sugar they were growing is also very evident in the Kahului Railroad terminal, the Lahaina Court House, and the old courthouse in Wailuku. There is a smattering of fine modern: the Lahaina Library next to the Pioneer Inn, a new federal building in Wailuku, a promising Veterans Memorial on the road between Wailuku and Kahului. There is less stylized Polynesian than one would expect from having seen a lot of Honolulu. One fine example is Hale Kini, an easy-to-overlook motel midway between Lahaina and Wailuku just off Route 31 on Maalaea Bay. Rising early at Hale Kini one morning, I got a rare vision of Haleakala and realized why that volcano dominated the mythic imagination of Maui.

And in a class by itself is a curious and unique Japanese folk shrine in Haiku. Don't miss it.

These, then, are the main attractions of the Valley Island: (1) Wailuku-Kahului; (2) Haleakala; (3) the road to Hana; (4) Hana to Lahaina; and (5) beyond Lahaina. Now for a closer look.

Wailuku-Kahului Area

The Maui office of the Hawaii Visitors Bureau has an excellent forty-page pamphlet you can get free at the Kahului Airport. They also provide the best map with HVB historic site markers on it. Both will help you get more out of your visit to the Valley Isle. On your way in to Kahului from the airport on the right is the Kanaha Bird Sanctuary, which is one of the two protected areas in the state for native wild life and migratory waterfowl. You can arrange to go on a guided bird-watching tour here by calling state wild-life expert Joseph Medeiros at 726-585.

Kahului itself is Maui's port town and the second largest city on the Valley Isle. It is Maui's only deep-water port. When we were there, in addition to ships and barges, there was the Japanese Naval Academy's square-rigged sailing ship making its annual summer visit. It's open for tours during scheduled hours and is well worth a visit. During plantation operations, the bulk sugar plant, first one on the islands (1942), is a half-hour tour. Call the main office of the Kahului Railroad (72-112) to make arrangements. Other sights worth exploring: the Maui Pineapple Cannery, the Kahului Shopping Center, where entertainment for tourists is offered now and again on a mall shaded by giant monkey-pod trees, and the Hawaiian Fruit Growers' Exchange on Each Road, where passion fruit, guava, and papaya concentrates are packed (call 33-714 mornings between June and January for tours).

About a mile from Kahului, in Puunene, is the Hawaiian Commercial and Sugar Company mill, founded in 1882 and the largest cane sugar plantation in America, where you can tour every weekday afternoon during the season at 2 P.M. If sugar is too tame for you, there's a Joseph Seagram and Sons rum distillery next door included in the tour. If there are more than twenty people in your party, call the Hawaiian Commercial and Sugar main office at 76-511. On the way to Puunene you will pass the Maui County Fair grounds, site of the oldest such event in the Pacific area.

Haleakala

It is thirty-six miles from the airport at Kahului to the observatory at Haleakala and takes about two and a half hours one-way driving. A guided tour costs over nine dollars per person to Haleakala alone, and you can't set your own pace. On the other hand you can cover more and get oriented better on such a tour. Haleakala is a 26.7-square-mile area within an elevation range of 3847 feet at Kaupo Gap to over 10,000 at the summit of the mountain.

A helpful National Park Service leaflet explains the geology of the area. East and West Maui used to be separate volcanic islands; they are now separated by an isthmus about seven miles wide. There is geologic evidence to show that Haleakala was more than 11,000 feet high at one time before erosion wore it down. While the last eruption was some time in the mid 1700's, there are still earthquakes in the Haleakala region, indicating that it should be still regarded as a dormant rather than an extinct volcano.

For a dollar you can buy a most useful *Guide for the Haleakala Section*, prepared for the Hawaii Natural History Association by George C. Ruhle. It is on sale at Hale Hoikeike in Wailuku and at the park itself. There you can get the basic information on the greatest scenic attraction of Maui. It is a volcano thirty-three miles long and 10,025 feet high. Stream erosion cut two deep valleys, the Keanae and the Kaupo, into the volcano during a long period of inactivity. Later activity covered the valley floor with a blanket of cinders and flows of *aa*-type lava.

At the 6800-foot level Silversword Inn offers a place to stay or eat. Hiking and riding are popular in the vicinity of the inn, which is a half-hour from the crater itself. There are three paved roads leading to the park entrance at 6740 feet, eleven miles from the observatory. The shortest is called the Pukalani Road; the others—Paia and Haiku—veer inland before making the final ascent but go through more interesting country. The three routes converge at Pukalani ("Hole in the Heaven") Junction, a poetic way of observing that the sun often breaks through at this point even though there is a general overcast.

As you wend your way up to the top, don't fail to note the ever-changing view of the 6000-foot West Maui range at the other end of the island, and even more spectacularly the shifting panorama of the islands to the west—Molokai, Lanai, Kahoolawe, and Molokini. You can see Haleakala from three outlooks on the way up: Leleiwi, at 9000 feet; Kalahaku, two miles below the top, and the Park Observatory, almost at the top. There are three cabins maintained by the National Park Service in the crater itself; the closest is Holua Cabin, then Kapalaoa, finally Paliku on the park's southeastern edge.

One other place you should know about if you're packing a lunch is Hosmer Grove Campground and Picnic Area, a half mile from Silversword Inn. It has a rainy-weather cover over two tables and two charcoal burners. Four other tables with burners are uncovered. Eight parking places, running water, and tent sites are also available. There is charcoal for sale at Silversword Inn. You can walk through Hosmer Grove with the aid of a self-guiding nature trail. The grove commemorates the experimental efforts of the Territory's first forester, Dr. Ralph S. Hosmer, who made notable efforts to plant temperate-zone trees at high altitudes on Mauna Kea, on the Big Island, and on Haleakala. Native birds are plentiful in the park, but wild pigs and goats, mongooses, rats, and mice are the only mammals living there. If you plan to take pictures of these animals, the silversword, or the constantly changing colors of the cinder cones, underexpose color film by one stop to compensate for the intense sunlight at this altitude and reflections from clouds above. Best shots from the crater rim are during midafternoon except when overcast. Incidentally, the Park Service tells visitors not to be discouraged by their inability to see Haleakala from the airport because of clouds. Thick clouds often form up to 6500 feet. The top of the mountain, however, is usually clear.

The popular route into the crater is called the Sliding Sands Trail. It begins at the observatory parking area and goes along the south side of the crater for six miles to Kapalaoa Cabin. Another trail, four miles long, connects Kapalaoa with Paliku Cabin. Another trail is Halemauu, which goes down the west wall, or Leleiwi Pali to Holua Cabin, four miles from the eight-thousand-foot elevation of the main highway or six miles from the lodge. Halemauu Trail then continues easterly beyond Holua along the north side of the crater to Paliku, six miles distant. There are other branch trails making a total of some thirty miles of well-marked trails for hikers and horseback riders. For example, Kaupo Trail goes through Kaupo Gap from Paliku Cabin and descends the southern sun-drenched slope of the crater.

The three cabins for visitors have running water, woodburning stoves for cooking, firewood, kerosene lamps, cooking and eating utensils, and twelve bunks with mattresses and blankets. While you can telephone the park for possible last-minute reservations, its increasing popularity, especially during summer months, makes it safer to write ahead to P.O. Box 456, Kahului, Maui, Hawaii, giving the trip you propose to make, the number in your party, exact calendar dates, and which night you want to use which cabin. During June, July, and August, under a policy begun in 1962, cabins may not be reserved for more than three consecutive nights by one group, with not more than two nights to be spent in any one cabin. Not more than one cabin will be assigned to a group, either. These rules apply from June 1 through Labor Day. Everyone except those going in with Silversword Inn guides needs a permit to descend into the crater. The hiker is advised to use good walking shoes, warm clothing, and a light raincoat. It's also a good idea to bring sunburn lotion along.

The short walks recommended for the casual visitor are along the Halemauu Trail from the highway to the Crater Rim, a distance of three-quarters of a mile. Here there are views down Keanae Valley, of the trail itself, and across Koolau Gap to Hanakauhi. Another one is to go down the Sliding Sands Trail, remembering that it is very exhausting to climb back at this altitude. Finally, there is a walk to the top of White Hill, past old Hawaiian stone-walled encampment sites. Longer all-day, overnight, and two- to three-day hikes are outlined in George Ruhle's *Guide*.

At the Leleiwi overlook near the 9000-foot contour you may be able to experience the Brocken Specter phenomenon. In the afternoons clouds roll into the gap and a person's shadowy image appears within a circular rainbow that is projected against the cloud bank.

The Kalahaku overlook at 9325 feet was the site of an overnight resthouse in the days of horseback and foot travelers before the road you took was built. The name Kalahaku, given to the rugged cliff that forms the crater wall at this point, means "Meeting Place of the Chiefs."

Beyond the observatory erected in 1937 at 9865 feet is White Hill or Pakaoao. It gets its name from the formation of andesite that caps its peak. This volcanic rock is lighter in color than the common basaltic lava of Hawaii. Notice the sleeping shelters or oval stone-walled enclosures along the trail. They afforded protection against the unkindly elements (wind, fog, cold) that prevail here. It is speculated that they were used a long time ago by travelers, or perhaps by sentries, or even by the professional robbers, or aihue, who ambushed travelers in out-of-the-way places.

Red Hill, at 10,025 feet, is the summit of Haleakala. Its original English name was Pendulum Peak. It is a recent cinder cone. There is a pointer table by the road to identify the many islands and peaks visible from this point.

Halemauu ("Grass House") Trail gets its name, it is supposed, from a grass house that used to be located at the head of the trail. The trail descends at a gentle gradient down the 1500-foot Leleiwi Pali to the bottom of the crater. If there is fair weather, you can get superlative views of Windward Maui (northeast) and the Keanae Valley. Evening cloud formations in Koolau Gap will often produce the Specter-of-the-Brocken effect. Also look along this trail for the small silver geraniums peculiar to Haleakala called hinahina.

Holua Cabin is near Holua Cave, which was used for shelter at night before the cabin was built by the National Park Service. The grasses you see in the meadow were introduced. The strangely pale "moss" you see growing on the rough lava is a lichen called Hawaiian snow.

There is a quarter-mile detour off Halemauu Trail called the Silversword Loop because of the many clumps of that rare plant which find the old, weathered red lava congenial to growth. Toward the eastern end of the loop is Keahuokaholo, a sacred place for the Hawaiians which has many piles of markers, platforms, stones, and *ahus* put up by the ancient people. Don't touch these antiquities; they are too rare to be scavenged into valueless pieces on a thousand coffee tables across the country. Read about them if you want to take home something that lasts.

The Bottomless Pit isn't, but it should be approached with caution nonetheless. It is a pit ten feet in diameter ringed with small lava spatter mounds. Though you can't see it, it is choked with debris sixty or seventy feet below. Custom has it that umbilical cords were thrown here to make a child strong or, as on Kauai, to keep him from becoming a thief.

Take the Ka Moa o Pele Trail at the foot of Sliding Sands to join Halemauu on the other side of the crater. There you can see flowering silverswords from June to September on the red cinder cone Ka Moa o Pele. Pele's Pig Pen, or Pa Puaa o Pele, is the rim of a now buried spatter cone in the low pass between Halalii and Ka Moa o Pele.

As in the rest of Hawaii, the terrain is saturated in legend. The most famous connected with Haleakala, of course, are those connected with Maui taming the sun.

HALE-AKALA OR "HOUSE OF THE SUN"

The Hawaiian people named the ten-thousand-foot volcano on Maui Hale-akala, or House of the Sun, from a legend about the demigod Maui. He is said to have climbed to the summit of Haleakala, snared the rays of the sun, and forced it to slow down in its daily course in order to give his mother, Hina, more sunlight in which to do her work.

But there are untold other stories stimulated by the old Hawaiian's awe of this stupendous spectacle. Maui himself almost didn't make it. Unwanted as an infant because he was scrawny and deformed, his mother wrapped him in a hank of her hair and threw him into the ocean. But jellyfish rescued him and the god Kanaloa took the unlucky child under his protection. Despite his cool familial reception Maui sneaked back to play with his four brothers, and only after the most eloquent pleading of the eldest was he allowed to stay with the family officially.

The roster of Maui's achievements doesn't do credit to the

unfriendly attitude of his mother. He made birds visible for the first time; until then they could only be heard as they sang and flew. He also invented the spear and the barbed fish-hook, technological break-throughs of great significance to his fishing society. We have already read about how Maui fished up the islands from the bottom of the sea, but have you ever stopped to ask why there were several islands instead of one continuous one? This was no problem to the Polynesian imagination. He had warned his brothers fishing with him not to look as he was working the magic. But their curiosity overcame them as they paddled. Looking up in the middle of his magic fishing, they kept Maui from getting the complete island all out of water and so only parts stayed above.

It was Maui, too, living then in a plain grass shack at Kauiki, in Hana, who pushed the heavens up above the highest mountains—Mauna Kea, Mauna Loa, Hualalai, and Haleakala—so that man could stand up straight and get out from under the ever-present darkness and fog. Before his great feat, the heavens were held up by plants. That is why their leaves are flat—mashed by the burden of what they had to hold up. The frequent bad weather in Haleakala is explained by Maui's being asleep. It was from Kauiki that Maui made his successful plot to snare the fast-moving sun.

Perhaps the most impressive Maui myth is the one about immortality. Maui was doomed to die because his father had not completed the ceremony necessary to ensure everlasting life. Maui hated the fact of death; he regarded it as an insult to man. When he found out that the secret of life was hidden inside the heart of the dread ogress of death, Hina-nui-kepo, he set out to secure it. This meant he had to sneak between her ragged basalt teeth, descend into the utter darkness of her stomach, and from there tear out the ogress's heart. Only the bravest man would even think of such a trial. Because this could only be done while Hina slept, Maui turned man into a little bird, so that no noise would possibly wake Hina up while Maui was inside. He got to the heart all right, and was on the precarious return journey when stupid, silly mankind outside couldn't control his laughter at seeing the fix Maui was in between the ugly teeth of Hina. Hina awoke and crushed Maui to death. Ever since there has been no recourse from death for man.

One thing you might suppose Maui did he didn't, viz., give his name to the island of Maui. The demigod is pronounced in three distinct syllables, Ma-oo-ee, with accent on the second; Maui the island is "Mow-ee." There are also alternative explanations of the etymology of Haleakala, which commonly is rendered "House of the Sun." Another variant is that it is a corruption of Alehe-ka-la, "Snarer of the Sun," which of course refers to Maui's great feat, as does still a third interpretation, Ahale-ka-la, or "Rays of the Sun."

Something you should do for a souvenir of Haleakala is to join the Society of the Silversword, Hui o Ahinahina. For a dollar you get a certificate and an assurance that you have helped expand the scientific study, interpretation, and display areas at the national park. If more of the sixty-five thousand annual visitors did join, it would help the National Park Service improve its function faster.

On your way down from Haleakala, take another long way home. Turn left where Route 378 ends onto Route 377. After you have joined Route 37, past Kula Sanatorium you will see an HVB marker on your right, marking the direction of Molokini Island. Get out and take a good look.

At Ulupalakua Ranch you can see the remains of the Makee Sugar Mill (1878). The road leads down to Makena Landing. Shortly beyond Ulupalakua is an interesting site—Poo Kanaka, the petrified head and body of a man who tried to palm off sour *poi* on Pele when she asked for a chicken; the hapless trickster's wife and children are turned to stone down at the shore of La Perouse Bay, named after the French navigator whose ship disappeared without a trace in the South Seas after having visited the place in May 1786: "At every instant [he wrote] we had just cause to regret the country we had left behind us; and to add to our mortification, we did not find an anchoring place well sheltered until we came to a dismal coast where torrents of lava had formerly flowed like the cascades which pour forth their water in other parts of the island." These sour remarks certainly didn't deserve geographical remembrance, but the Hawaiians are generous people!

The road to Makena and Wailea (Route 31) is rather rough, but it is a most refreshing drive, especially if you have the leisure to stop now and again at the groves of trees overlooking a little cove on the Alalakeiki Channel, between Maui and Kahoolawe, and the Kealaikahiki Channel between Kahoolawe and Lanai. Kalama Park is between Kamaole and Kihei. It's a fine place for a box lunch. Before you get to Kihei note the HVB marker showing where the Koa House and king's fishponds were, when ships bought their vegetables from farmers there in the nineteenth century. Just beyond the intersection of Routes 31 and 35 is the Kealia Bird Sanctuary, a private pond taken over by wintering birds, mostly the kolea, or plover, resting up there between October and April for the exhausting flight back to Alaska. You are now skirting Maalaea Bay, which has a good small-boat harbor. On the western side of the bay is the Pohaku Piko, where the umbilical cord of a royal infant was secreted to ensure his future by keeping it from being eaten by bugs or rats. Also there is the adz-grinding stone or Pohaku Hookala.

Turn right now onto Route 30, the Honopiilani Highway, back to Wailuku. Turn left on Route 32 and visit Hale Hoikeike, the headquarters of the Maui Historical Society, which holds relics from prehistoric times to annexation. It is open from 10 to 3:30 every day but Sunday. Hale Hoikeike was dedicated in 1957. Only about six thousand people visited it in 1962, which is a shame because it is a fascinating place.

From 1841 to 1848 it was the home of Mr. Edward Bailey and later the Wailuku Female Seminary. The seminary had been founded in 1837 by the Rev. Jonathan S. Green as a boarding school to take a group of girls "away in a measure from the contaminating influence of heathen society" and by instruction make them "examples of propriety amongst the females of the Sandwich Islands." When Mr. Green took over the pastorate of Wailuku Church in 1841, he asked Mr. Bailey to succeed him as head of the seminary. The house that Bailey built that year has walls twenty inches thick, made of stone and covered with plaster held together by human hair donated by the faithful lady parishioners! The beams are made of hand-hewn sandalwood. The kitchen was once separate from the house because it was considered a fire hazard.

The school was abandoned in 1848 because its building was in so dilapidated a condition. But Mr. Bailey continued his career of amazing versatility: a painter (see the three oil paintings of his hanging in the museum); a sketcher for engravings made at Lahainaluna; the introducer of the first plow to Maui, with which device he marked off Market and Main streets; founder of a sugar and a wheat mill; author of a study of Hawaiian ferns and a narrative poem *Hawaii Nei*; and at one time the postmaster of Wailuku.

From there drive to Konda Gardens, a tropical oasis that delights camera fans, three blocks from the Civic Center on Vineyard Street.

Double back now and go down Route 32 to the Iao Valley, where the Iao Needle pushes 1200 feet in solitary splendor from the base of the valley—its point 2250 feet above sea level. Like so many places in Hawaii, where poetic fecundity was more highly prized than scientific accuracy, Iao Valley has more than one legend. Iao, according to legend, was a daughter of Maui, born to Hina in the third year of her marriage to Maui. Because she was a beautiful child she was sought after by neighboring island kings before she was ten years old. Maui and Hina protected her because of her attractiveness; she was allowed only one visit to the seashore a day and nothing more. Her admirers didn't dare to approach her for fear of Maui. At a pool near her house, however, contact with the gentle girl turned the merman god of the pool Puuokamoa into a man. This experience wrought a considerable change over Iao, and Maui engaged a kahuna to find out why. He found the trysting pool where Puuokamoa had taught Iao to swim underwater. Maui went there one night and, imitating the voice of Iao, snared him in a throw net when the lover answered the love call. Maui and the kahuna returned to Iao's house to pass sentence—death by fire at the first ray of dawn—in her presence. Pele, who had been a lifelong friend of the philandering Puuokamoa, interceded on behalf of the merman. She urged that he be turned to stone to warn men forever what happened if they defied sacred law. The needle in the valley, then, is Puuokamoa, turned to stone.

The other story of Iao Valley is the more usual one. It is concerned with the Creation and the beginning of mankind at the Dawn of Time. Iao means "Of the Dawn Light" and is the name given to Jupiter as a morning star. This was regarded as the valley of inspiration, poetically symbolized by the dawn. A great chief named Ka Ka'e proclaimed the valley as a sacred burial place of worthy kings during the early 1100's. The needle is also referred to as Ku Moku, i.e., the standing or perpendicular precipice that forms a land division. The full name for this meaning is Ku' Ka e' Moku, meaning the "Projecting Fragment of a Hill Standing Upright." Another meaning connects the name with the god Ku. In this context, Mo-ku means "Stationary in One Place Where the Dawn Always Touches It." Ku was the god who controlled the organs of reproduction and the laws governing their use. Iao Needle hence is a phallic symbol created by nature or Ku. There is also an interesting Japanese garden on one of the switchbacks up to the Needle.

Back in Wailuku you should pay your respects to that redoubtable early convert to Christianity, Kaahumanu, Kamehameha I's favorite wife. There across from the courthouse is a church completed in 1837 and named after her. Its spire is the principal Wailuku landmark. Next door, the excellent Hawaiian room of the Maui County Library is also a source of greater insight and pleasure on your visit. There are ten branches throughout the island, some of them very interesting architecturally, especially the modern one at Lahaina.

North of Wailuku on Route 33 is the Waihee Sugar Mill, which was in operation from 1863 to 1905. It was managed before 1870 by S. T. Alexander, one of the great names of Maui, patronym of half the firm of Alexander and Baldwin, a Big Five firm that started business as a sugar factor. Returning to town by the Beach Road 341, you can see Hale Kii and Piihana Heiaus. Piihana was one of the most ancient war *heiaus* or *luakinis* on Maui. It is there that Kamehameha went after the great battle of Kepaniwai (1790). The first one is 300 by 150 feet, an impressive structure of gray stone carried from the stream below and fitted into the characteristic temple terrace. You can get the full story from a display case nearby. The chief's sacrificial *heiau* is 300 feet up the hill.

Next plan at least a day for a trip around the windward side of the island to Hana. "Heavenly" Hana is about fifty-three miles from the airport in Kahului, but it takes three hours one way because of the deeply eroded valleys on Maui's windward side. Route 36 is the Hana Highway. On your left you will find Spreckelsville, named after the California sugar speculator Claus Spreckels, who used to play poker with the Merry Monarch, King Kalakaua. There is the famous story about Claus holding four aces in a poker hand, which the king claimed he could beat with "five" kings—four in his hand, and himself! Also on the road to Hana is the Maui Country Club, founded in 1924. The caddie house and course are open to the public. Next is Henry P. Baldwin Park—named after the one-armed sugar pioneer who shamed his chickenhearted men into finishing a dangerous job in a sugar irrigation scheme by shimmying into a gulley himself despite his handicap. Until a 1960 tidal wave destroyed it, this was also the site of Hawaiian Commercial and Sugar Supervisors Clubhouse; it is still a good place to swim and play baseball.

Down Baldwin Avenue on your right on Route 39 is Maunaolu College, founded in 1861 as a female seminary but now a junior college with over a hundred students and twenty faculty members. Back on Route 36 you will see on your left just before Maliko Bay the Hamakuapoko Sugar Mill (1880–1906), where the first American flag was raised at the time of annexation, in 1898. Shortly after the sugar mill, you will see a turnoff to Haiku on your right, leading to a most interesting Japanese folk art garden.

The Road to Hana

Back on Route 36 you should notice Kaulanapueo Church, which dates from 1853 in Hueolo. A favorite picnic place is Kaumahina Park overlooking Honomanu Bay. Another old church on the road to Hana is Keanae Church, built in 1860.

According to local legend, the parishioners prayed for help to the patron saint of the parish, St. Gabriel, and he obliged by seeing to it that a storm washed up coral stone from the sea to construct the church with; and, even more obligingly, another storm cleared away the excess stone when construction was over, and was also washed in to mix the cement. To Hawaiians interested in a good sandy beach for swimming as well as getting into heaven it was an excellent arrangement! There is a fine view from the Keanae Peninsula Lookout at this point too.

Wailua Outlook is also a spectacular sight. If you want to see what old Hawaii was like, descend into the valley and get a close look at the taro patches here. There is also a shrine to St. Augustine in this village. Just beyond Puaa Kaa Park there is another old-time Hawaiian homestead, Nahiku Village. If your eyes are getting whirly from the curves your car has been taking, in and out, in and out of the valleys on the lush windward flanks of Haleakala, it may console you to know that some statistician has calculated over five hundred curves between Wailuku and Hana. Nahiku Valley was a famous canoe-building center for this part of Maui, mainly because it was one of the few places where you could launch boats, but also because there are big koa trees for making them in the forests above. David Kaahookele, who lives here, claims that his grandfather made a one-week trip to Tahiti in a canoe in the 1880's.

Puaa Kaa Park, by the way, is a good picnic spot, too. And it means "Place of the Rolling Pigs," from the days when plump wild pigs were supposed to have rolled down the slick, steep, grassy hills here.

Just beyond the Hana Airport, on your left, there is a turn-off to Wainapanapa Cave. Look for the HVB marker. This was a legendary trysting place for lovers who were brave enough to dive into a pool and swim underwater to a cave. Inside there is a natural rock throne where a Hawaiian princess once hid in fear of her life. She had a jealous husband who threatened her life when she saw too much of another lover. She fled with a faithful servant to Wainapanapa Cave. They came out from their underground chamber only at night to search for food. The husband searched everywhere until one day when he stopped to rest by the cave he saw the reflection of his wife's servant sweeping the fly-dusting kahili over his wife. He slew them both in a rage; the water in the pool turned blood red. And it still does every April, because of algae that forms there. If you listen carefully, you can hear the sighing and sobbing of the murdered princess as the water rushes in and out of this old lava tube.

In Hana you should also look at Kauiki Lighthouse. In 1768, Kaahumanu was born there, and her mother hid her in the cave while the great battle between Maui and Hawaii was going on. If you look at the map you can easily see why this point would figure in battles between the Big Island and Maui. At the base of Kauiki Head, children hunt on the beach for the rounded stones with pointed ends that ancient warriors used to aim with lethal accuracy at each other with slingshots. Kauiki Head is an old cinder cone. On the *makai* side there is a plaque showing where Kaahumanu's mother had her labor pains. The fact that a royal princess was born in such an underdeveloped delivery room only attests to her high rank, for secret places were sought to keep contenders for the throne from switching infants! Kauiki Hill is also the site of the giant wooden image that intimidated the invading Big Islanders in the army of Umi until one of his men discovered that it was just a figure.

While in Hana don't fail to look at the old Congregational Church, Wananalua, built in 1838 on the site of an ancient war *heiau*, one of the first such pagan temples on the island of Maui. The parishioners made it out of solid lava rock over a twenty-year period of reverent dedication. Services are still given there Sundays in both Hawaiian and English. There is also a superb Buddhist temple on the left toward Hamoa Beach.

Hana itself remains untouched by most of "Progress." The road over the thirty-three gulches from Wailuku (by HVB count) was opened only in 1927. When the sugar plantation closed, millionaire Paul Fagan decided to turn it into a luxury resort so that the thousand or so people living in the area could have work. But nobody had even heard of this isolated spot. Fagan owned the San Francisco Seals baseball team. As a publicity move, he brought them to Hana for spring training. Then he brought in people to train the natives in the specialized skills needed at the luxurious Hana-Maui—one of the most exclusive places on the island. A large lava rock cross now dominates one of the hills overlooking the village in that community's tribute to its benefactor.

Hana to Lahaina

Out beyond Hana, on Route 31 toward Kipahulu, is another place sacred to the ubiquitous Pele. It is called Ka Iwi, or Pele's Hill, and it is supposed to be where Pele left her bones when she went to the Big Island in another form. Kuula's sacred fishpond is also nearby. Next is Hamoa Beach; although the beach is exclusively for hotel guests at the Hana-Maui, there is an excellent picnic area available to all.

Then look for Hale o Lono Heiau, which was dedicated to the god of growing things, life, and rain. There were no human sacrifices taken by the priests of this *heiau*, who were considered inferior in status to priests of the war god, an interesting index to the severity of life in old Hawaii. Then if you go almost to the end of the Waiohono Stream you can see some pictographs under a ledge. These were drawn, not carved, and probably show chiefs working and playing. Between Puuiki and Kipahulu look for an HVB marker showing the direction of the Big Island. Stop here on clear days and look for Mauna Loa and Mauna Kea (which will be snow capped in winter months) as well as Hawaii's third peak Hualalai.

At Wailua Falls a large concrete cross commemorates Helio Kawaloa, a lay Catholic Hawaiian who converted four thousand of his fellows while waiting impatiently for Honolulu to send a priest! The Catholic missionaries were persecuted and opposed for about eleven years after they first arrived in Hawaii in 1827. Some Catholics were arrested and put in jail; a few were even chained together and used for prison labor. The story of the new religion finally drifted back to this isolated Wailua Valley. Helio was so taken by the new religion, to which he was converted in 1849, first man in 1841, that he traveled all the way to Honolulu to get the complete gospel. He immediately asked the astonished priests to ordain him. Undaunted by the news that he would need a great deal of training for the priesthood, he paddled back to Maui and walked from Lahaina to Hana, spreading the new gospel as he went. He became known as the Lay Apostle. There is a touching story told about Helio's funeral. When he realized that he was about to die, he knew that, as the only baptized Catholic in Wailua Valley, he was going to have to be resourceful if he were to have a Catholic burial. He taught the other, non-Catholic villagers the burial service he had memorized in Honolulu. The day he died, so the legend goes, the first priest landed in Lahaina. Helio's grave is in Wailua Gulch about fifty yards from shore. Over the ridge on which the concrete cross divides the valley you can find the remains of the hidden village of Wailua, where he lived (if you can stand the mud and mosquitoes!). Noticing the lei-draped state of the Virgin of the Roadside, you can conclude that Helio's influence still lives in the valley.

The next sight to see is a favorite frolicking place of the old Hawaiian chiefs: the Seven Sacred Pools. Maui's mother, Hina, used to wash tapa here (only the sunlight didn't last long enough until Maui extended its day); now tourists bathe in the pools below the bridge or picnic by the sea.

Kipahulu Falls, about a mile farther on toward Ulupala-kua, is another favorite scenic attraction. It is also the site of Kipahulu Sugar Mill, active between 1890 and 1922. The village also has an attractive Hawaiian church built in 1857. But one of the most poignant spots in all the islands is Hui Aloha Church, just before you get to Kaupo. It was built on a spit of land jutting bravely into the Pacific, with the gulches of the Hana Coast and the majestic slopes of Haleakala as a backdrop. Closer to the sea is a ruin that could have been an outbuilding of the lava-rock church. Inside the deserted church, which once was a thriving center of Christianity, the attendance sheet hanging from a clipboard near the back of the church revealed that only a handful of people showed up every other week for services. If the weather is good, try driving off Route 31 down to this churchyard for lunch.

You will see an HVB marker showing where King Piilani's Highway ran here, going through Haleakala Crater. It was finished by Piilani's son, Kihapiilani, who achieved a great reputation as an early public-works sponsor. Some parts of the road he laid down are still clearly visible. At Kaupo there is a trail some hikers use to enter Haleakala from the south.

Now you're in for a ride, jiggling and jouncing for miles until you'll swear that neither you nor your car can take another rut. The scenery is unique—places like Waiohono Stream, a dry river bed carved out by aeons of flash floods. (You'd better not be there when it's wet, because then this road is the original Mire, and you'd better be ready for a sloshing hike and a big towing bill.) I've never made the trip, but there's supposed to be a goodly collection of petroglyphs and caves by a pool at the head of the isolated canyon. The whole stretch of arid desert between Kaupo and Ulupalakua is in a class by itself—cinder cones, exotic trees and wild flowers, the incredible juxtaposition of deep Pacific blue and lava that flowed into the sea just beyond the old burial caves at Waiakapuhi and the last known lava flow (about 1750) on Maui near La Perouse Bay, the immense cinder cone of Puu Olai, just southwest where Route 31 meets Route 37 and goes down to the sea.

Keep on Route 31 (which you've already been on if you came back this way from Haleakala). You are headed to Lahaina now, which most satisfied my historical sense of all the attractions in Hawaii. After you've turned Maalaea Bay, you will see an HVB marker pointing out Kahoolawe Island, which is studded with undetonated naval shells and bombs from its use as a World War II practice range. It's no longer safe to go there, but it is an interesting island to look at, especially flying over it. On your right up Route 30 you can see Ukumehame Canyon, one of a number of routes through the West Maui mountains, which has a pass lower than the others. At Olowalu, six-tenths of a mile off the HVB marker through a sugar-cane field, are the Olowalu petroglyphs. I give you the precise mileage so that maybe *you* can find them. Three times I tried, once with my young son as a navigator, once going and once coming solo to Lahaina. And I never found them! More's the pity, since from the description of them in the forty-eight-page *Lahaina Historical Guide* (an excellent dollar bargain, by the way, from the Maui Historical Society) they sound fascinating.

The Hawaiians carved petroglyphs on dense slabs of basalt lava rock. Some of the figures are simple matchstick types, whereas others are more sophisticated, with triangular chests and the details of fingers and toes. It is estimated that the rock carvings at Olowalu are between two and three hundred years old.

The early Hawaiians, while traveling overland from one area to another, would stop for food and rest. At such way stations, usually close to a sheltered cliff or beside a stream, one would record his mark on a rock slab. The type of figures, it is believed, depicted their position or station in life; divers, fishermen, soldiers, canoe paddlers, fathers with children, and boats and animals.

Try to find them! On my next trip to Maui I'm going to even if I have to hire a tour guide (which, for all my own predilection for solo tourism, may be an argument for going with a *kamaaina* after all).

A short distance above the petroglyphs of Olowalu is Kaiwaloa Heiau, a *luakini* class temple, which has been described by Hawaiian antiquarian David Malo as "the highest class war temple, in which human sacrifices were offered." The name *luakini* comes from *lua*, pit, and *kini*, many, from the fact that the smoking remains of the sacrificial victims were thrown into a pit. When a king was about to make war on another monarch or if he heard that he was about to be attacked, he built such a *heiau* to keep Ku, the god of war, on his side.

Olowalu is also the site of a massacre in 1790, when Simon Metcalfe, commanding the American ship *Eleanora*, resorted to a most uncivilized stratagem to punish the natives of Olowalu for stealing a small boat and killing the sailor in it. When Metcalfe learned that they had torn the boat apart (for the nails they loved inordinately), he had all his ship's guns put on the starboard side and loaded them with musket balls and shot. He put a *kapu* on the port side of the ship and invited the natives out in their canoes. When they all got bunched close together within range, he commanded his gunmen to fire. More than a hundred natives were slaughtered in this fierce barrage.

Soon you will be in Lahaina itself. During the early 1800's Lahaina was a favorite place of Hawaiian royalty. Then from about 1840 to 1865, until the discovery of petroleum, a diminished whale population, and the Civil War put a crimp in the whaling industry, Lahaina was the Whale Capital of the World. The name Lahaina means, some say, "Unmerciful Sun," from a legend that tells of a chief who started walking from Launiupoko to the valley of Kauaula during the hottest part of day. Stopping to rest and wipe his brow by a large rock where Lahaina is today, he is supposed to have said, "Kau keia ka la-haina," or "What an unmerciful sun." An alternative explanation for its meaning has been to consider it the two words la and haina, or "the answer." In olden days subjects of the chiefs gathered there to find out what the day's work was going to be. There they got their answers.

Lahaina actually was the capital under King Kamehameha III (1833–54), where the missionary preacher who was bombarded by girl-seeking sailors gave the king wise counsel on how to make his country more democratic through a written constitution. You can see where many of the Rev. William Richards' parishioners are buried in Waiola Cemetery, which dates from 1823.

This used to be named Wainee (Moving Water) instead of the more Christian Waiola (Water of Life). It was changed at the dedication of the new church in 1953. The missionaries as well as their most famous royal converts are buried here. Wandering among the headstones is a most interesting exercise in Hawaiian history.

The Episcopal Church in Lahaina is interesting because of its Hawaiian Madonna. The Anglican Church was not organized in Hawaii before 1862, when the Anglophile sentiments of Kamehameha IV (and his experience of racial discrimination in America) led to the encouragement of much Britishness. The present church building was dedicated in 1927. The altar painting of a Hawaiian Madonna as well as several other paintings were executed in 1940 by Delos Blackmar, a New York artist and friend of the vicar, Mr. Horton.

The Hongwanji Church in Lahaina was built in 1957 (the small columbarium dates from 1959) although the congregation can be traced to a group that started meeting in 1904 in the Mala District after Japanese immigration had been considerable and before it was cut off by the Gentleman's Agreement of 1907. This largest Buddhist group holds a midnight celebration on New Year's Eve, an April feast to commemorate the birth of Buddha, and its Bon dances during the last weekend in August, against an outdoor background of paper cherry blossoms and lanterns.

Toward the Napili end of Lahaina, just beyond the business district, is a most charming building representing another Oriental tradition in Hawaii—the Wo Hing Society. The Chinese commonly refer to it as the Chee Kung Tong; haoles merely say the Chinese society. It was organized there in 1909 as an offshoot of what was originally a secret society in China founded three hundred years ago during the Manchu dynasty. Its many world-wide branches had as their main purpose overthrowing the Manchu or Ching dynasty and restoring the Ming. The fraternity known as Hoong Moon affirmed the principle that everyone was equal as brothers in a family; it was also a voluntary association for mutual protection, relief, and support of deserving members and their families. Hoong Moon societies were set up early in the twentieth century wherever large numbers of Chinese migrated. There are three more such fraternities on Maui: Luen Hing in Keanae, Kwock Hing in Kula, and Chee Kung Tong in Wailuku. The way the Oriental architect has modified a simple New England box (adding the deeper lanais to provide for the Hawaiian climate), with Asian Carpenter's Gothic, is the kind of East-West intellectual and aesthetic interchange that makes Hawaii an exciting place to be.

As we learned on the road from Hana (where we saw the memorial to Helio), the first Roman Catholic priests to reside permanently at Lahaina in 1846 found four thousand catechumens on the islands. At least two native Hawaiians had been sent to Paris for training as lay teachers at the monastery of the Sacred Heart Fathers, the small French order that had been given French Polynesia as a mission. A bronze tablet on Front Street in a residential district memorializes the first place where Mass was celebrated on Maui. The first permanent church replaced a temporary one (1846) in 1858. In 1928 Maria Lanikila Church duplicated the frame one in concrete; the ceiling is supposed to have been transferred from the old to the new.

Hale Aloha, now used as a parish house for Wainee Church, was built in 1855 "in commemoration of God's causing Lahaina to escape the small pox, while it desolated Oahu in 1853, carrying off some 5 or 6,000 of its population."

The presence of all this religious architecture did not impress the visiting whalers sufficiently, so Lahaina had to have one of those indispensable appurtenances of an advanced civilization, the jail. Hale Paahao (Place of Confinement) is interesting to visit even today, and it is easy to imagine the bare cells reeking of hugely hungover sailors in close quarters. In 1851 Lahaina's superintendent of public works wrote that the fort doctor said that the town needed a place where prisoners could sleep above the ground so they would avoid chills and fevers and other diseases plaguing the lawbreakers in confinement. The prison house of planks was done by 1852, but funds for the surrounding coral stone wall were not made available until 1853. The prisoners made their own medicine by carting the coral from the old fort. In 1957 the legislature approved the reconstruction of the old prison building, and the one you visit (this one too put up by prisoners from Olinda Prison) was dedicated as recently as November 1959.

Healing Rock, or the Hauola Stone, is a curiosity that interests many tourists in Lahaina; it is near the Napili end of the stone wall that separates Wharf Street from the ocean. Look for some large rocks that stand out over the waves, especially a big one that looks something like a modern chair with a small back and a wide seat. Hawaiians believed that if you sat in this seat and dangled your feet in the water the waves would make you well again. Notice how the sick in search of well-being have worn the seat hollow. Because they looked upon the place as sacred, it meant that it was also a good place to hide the *pikos*, or umbilical cords, of newborn children. Such a place was called a *pohaku piko*, and cords were jammed into crevices and secured with pebbles. The cannon in Lahaina, by the way, were salvaged by Kamehameha's divers from the brig *Arthur*, which cracked up off Barbers Point, Oahu, in 1796. The king had them brought over to guard his two-story Brick Palace.

Back on shore in the center of town, where the Lahaina Branch Library now stands, there used to be part of the king's taro patch. Kamehameha III proved to his subjects the dignity of common labor by working this patch himself. Back of the library today is the old Baldwin House. It was built in 1834. Its original tenant, Ephraim Spaulding, left the mission for ill health in 1835, and his place was taken by Dr. Baldwin, medical missionary and father of the sugar baron who was later to become such a power on Maui.

The Pioneer Hotel, in Lahaina Square, was restored to its present state in 1956, when Don the Beachcomber, a Pan American executive named Bill Mullahey, and Stewart Fern, then a public relations man but now publisher of the Beach Press, saw the potential of the old hotel as a tourist attraction in a historically revived Lahaina. It had been built in 1901 to capitalize on the then thriving Inter-island Steamship business. Since most of the arriving ship passengers didn't want to face a long, uncomfortable horseback ride to central Maui right away, the hotel never lacked for customers, until travel fell off and prohibition cut off a hefty revenue in grog. The hotel has been used as the locale for movies based on Jack London's tales of the South Seas.

The huge Banyan Tree in the central square was planted by the sheriff of Lahaina in 1873 to celebrate the fiftieth anniversary of the founding of the Protestant Christian mission at the request of Queen Keopuolani. It was a gift to the sheriff's family from missionaries in India. The tree measures almost a quarter of a mile in circumference, is sixty feet high, and its shade is fully two-thirds of an acre in extent! At sundown every mynah bird in town makes a sentimental journey to this Indian tree, and the noise that results is really something. The name of the tree comes from the Hindu traders called banians, who used to spread their goods under these open-air-bazaar umbrellas. The tree manages to cover so broad an area because it drops down aerial roots for support; many of the shoots of this one have been amputated to discourage juvenile Tarzans.

While you'll not be able to see whale ships in Lahaina Roads, if you visit between November and May there is a good chance you will see humpback whales cavorting for your pleasure. When cold closes up their arctic lobtailing grounds, they swim south to mate and breed in the warm water around the islands. More rarely the sperm whale is seen, occasionally even a Moby Dick white whale. You can recognize the humpback whale from his short, fat body and enormous side flippers. The humplike knob that gives this whale its name is actually a dorsal fin. This species of whale likes to jump clear of the sea and stand on its tail, or lobtail, i.e., its flukes. It feeds by rushing a school of crustaceans with an open mouth and then using its tongue to force the water out of its mouth.

A landmark you will notice first as you drive to Lahaina is the stack of the Pioneer Sugar Mill Company, *mauka* of the historical sites that are on the ocean. James Campbell founded the company, which became Pioneer in 1860. You can get a sense of how sugar has developed in the islands when you compare Pioneer's assets of ten million dollars today with its need to mortgage all its assets in 1860 to secure a loan of three hundred dollars. What began as a two-mule-power, three-roller mill is now a steam-driven apparatus of seventeen roller grinders. Its nearly five thousand acres are irrigated; in 1957 their productivity was 13.21 tons of sugar per acre. Pioneer gets some of its water (it takes a ton of irrigation water per pound of sugar) from the West Maui mountains and eighty-five million gallons a day from wells.

Back behind the mill, high on the slopes of the mountains, is a monument to the New England spirit of learning that you shouldn't miss, Lahainaluna High School. The palm trees you see lining the route to the school are the royal palms native to tropical America. They grow seventy-five to a hundred twenty feet high and have a whitish straight trunk characteristically swollen in the center. They are often used to give elegance and dignity to an avenue. The view of the town is superb from Lahainaluna; the view it gives of the missionaries is even more valuable to the historically inclined. The school's motto is *"Ka ipu kukui pio ole i ka makani Kauaula,"* or "The light of knowledge never will be extinguished by the fierce wind of Kauaula."

In Lahainaluna's cemetery lies Sheldon Dibble, who founded the Royal Historical Society of Hawaii with Kamehameha III. Dibble left for the islands at the age of twenty-one and died tragically at thirty-six, having left a considerable *History of the Sandwich Islands* and translated parts of the Bible and other books into the native tongue. Also buried there is the Rev. Samuel Whitney, one of the original missionary company. He spent twenty-five years on Kauai and died shortly after he came to Maui in search of relief from his failing health.

Hale Pai (or House of Printing) is another important part of your Lahainaluna visit. In 1833 the seminary secured a creaking Ramage press and some badly worn type from Honolulu and started to translate textbooks into Hawaiian. In 1834 they printed the first island newspaper *Lama Hawaii* (Lamp of Hawaii). It was also the first newspaper west of the Rockies.

Coming down the mountain and starting out on the seaside road to Kaanapali, you will see one attempt of the "foreign invaders" that came to naught—the Mala Wharf. The sugar plantations as they developed found the Lahaina Landing used by both missionaries and whalers inadequate for their purposes. Then Pioneer Sugar built a dock at Kekaa or Kaanapali Landing in the late 1890's to take care of freight and sugar. In 1922 a deep-water wharf was finally completed for a quarter million dollars, but only two big ships ever tied up there to unload passengers. The flagship of the interisland line with a full complement of visiting Honolulu dignitaries aboard got such a buffeting from the powerful currents and big swells that only one other ship ever tried to use the wharf for discharging passengers. Until after World War II, when passenger traffic shifted to the airlines, passengers still had to transfer to a small motor launch from the big interisland steamers. Freighters managed to load and unload if tied up a few feet away from the dock. The wharf has been condemned as unsafe by the state, but fishermen, who still find it a good place for sunrise catches, aren't concerned by the bad planning that was responsible for this folly.

Other historical sites of interest in Lahaina include Malu-ulu-o-lele Park, which was the site of Kamehameha III's private island residence, the old coral stone courthouse, built in 1858 and restored in 1925, used as a customhouse and government office building when it was the capitol of the kingdom, and the Old Spring House where whaler crews filled water casks at an old hand pump.

When you've had your fill of historical lore, take out your pocketbook and start shopping. Tops on my list is the Lahaina Art Gallery. It's just Napili of the Central Square on the *mauka* side of Front Street. I should warn you that Mrs. Peggy Hartman, who runs the place, is an indefatigable world traveler with an eye for the superlative in every nook and cranny of world culture.

The Whaling Port, next door, has exceptionally attractive native jewelry made out of various kinds of volcanic rocks, and a few authentic Polynesian things mixed in with the standard Waikiki Beach exotica, which doesn't appeal to me. As for jewelry, I've found that things like bead leis are significantly cheaper when bought from stands in the Outer Islands than in the "high rent" districts where most tourists go. Down the same street are some hole-in-the-wall places that give you good value and interestingly offbeat cuisine. Around on Lahainaluna Street there is an interesting curio store, too. With the exception of the Maui Divers, the rest of the tourist craft and fashion stores are clustered on the *mauka* side of the Banyan Tree, where the Banyan Inn also is, reputedly the best restaurant in Lahaina. There you can find the same complement of standard Polynesia in all the other big shopping centers on the islands. I don't say this to discourage you from visiting them, which I did and enjoyed; they just didn't seem to have as many superlative things for sale as the Lahaina Art Gallery. You should try to hit the Maui Divers place, right across from the library, when they show their films on the underwater "mining" of black coral. The jewelry itself is often outstanding, but I found it too high for my limited pocketbook. (The movies are free!)

Moki's Inn is a good place for lunch; I like the coconutty kind of doughnuts the Lahaina Bakery has fresh every morning as well as the Portuguese linguesa sausages for those who don't mind a mouth on fire; and almost at the corner, a Japanese delicatessen or Okazu-ya, for snacks.

THE LAHAINA WHALING SPREE

If you plan to be in the islands around Labor Day, be sure to attend the Whaling Spree Weekend at Lahaina, the old whaling capital. It is important to have hotel reservations ahead of time, however, because facilities will be jammed from Kula to Napili. Some of the festivities in the past have been a Lahaina–Lanai–Lahaina canoe race, an all-morning canoe regatta, a beard and Polynesian costume review at Banyan Inn, a no-host cocktail party for yachtsmen at the Whale's Tale, a luau at the Canoe Club, an evening wharf dance next to the ocean, all this on Saturday. On Sunday, the Rev. Abraham Akaka, leading Hawaiian minister in the islands, conducts "missionary" services, and then awards are made for the best missionary costumes. In the afternoon you can watch the intricate art of throw-netting on the wharf. There is also a spinner and reel-casting contest for accuracy and distance. El Toro class boats race in the afternoon. A highlight of Sunday afternoon is a canoe tug of war in front of Lahaina Wharf. On Monday morning the Lahaina–Honolulu yacht race starts off the Kaanapali resort area. Don't miss the special art exhibit at the Lahaina Art Gallery sponsored by Hui No Eau from start to finish of Whaler's Week. Genuine whale meat will be served throughout the festivities. Concessions are open Friday evening and Saturday and Sunday. There are special places to park at the National Guard Armory and Malu-ulu-o-lele Park.

If you have time left over, you might go over to the good-looking branch library in Lahaina and ask to see the "Lahaina Historical Restoration and Preservation" brochure, prepared by Honolulu's Community Planning, Inc., 1961. It is fascinating to see the city planners propose a program for making this now sleepy village the Williamsburg of the Pacific. The way Community Planning has used the techniques of urban design to reconstruct historical values at the town is a very impressive example of enlightened combination of old values with new techniques.

Beyond Lahaina

Down the road at Kaanapali, the State Department of Planning has succeeded in its dream of the future for Hawaii: as sugar cane and pineapple production employ fewer and fewer people on the Outer Islands, "destination resort" areas far from saturated Waikiki Beach will gradually shore up the dwindling economies of the Neighbor Isles. The Sheraton-Maui is concrete evidence of how that farsighted strategy is paying off. Kaanapali Beach is four times as wide as Waikiki and three miles long. The seven-story, 212-room Sheraton-Maui, which opened in the winter of 1963, is built "like a series of ivory ruffles" against the legendary Black Rock of Kaanapali Beach.

Kepaa, the legendary Black Rock of Kaanapali, against which the Sheraton-Maui was built by architect George Wimberley, is supposed to be the final departing place for the souls of the dead. Its lobby (dominated by an extraordinary sculpture by Edward Brownlee), dining room, bar and terrace are situated on top of "Black Rock," providing a stupendous view of the ocean and the West Maui mountains.

You should also try a new place to eat in the old house of a pineapple plantation manager, just beyond the Mauian near Napili Bay, off Route 30 up an avenue made grand by Norfolk pines on both sides of the road. Pineapple Hill was built in 1912 at Honolua atop a hill with a magnificent view of the surrounding country and ocean by David T. and Martha Fleming. The Baldwin Packer's manager called his place Makaoioi (Sharp Eyes) because of the thrilling prospect from his front door. Al and Mary Jane Holmes have taken over the home as a restaurant. They have left everything the way it was except for the addition of a lanai overlooking the sunsets, and I recommend that you have at least one early dinner there. Save some time to look at the old Pacific charts in the Chart Room, made up to look like an old ship's saloon, and the Makaoioi Room, with its interesting stone fireplace. While the place did not yet have a liquor license when I was there, you could pour your own at a do-it-yourself bartender array just inside their front door.

Just beyond Honolua there is a HVB marker pointing out Molokai Island. The light green *kukui* grove, Lanikaula, sometimes visible from here, was the site of an important *kahuna* seminary in old Hawaii. Napili Bay and Fleming Beach, along the northwestern coast of Maui facing Molokai and Lanai, are valued as among the best beaches in all Hawaii.

Route 30 becomes Route 33, an ominously dotted line beyond Honokahua. My U-drive car couldn't be taken over that route because insurance coverage rates were too high for the owner to afford, so he said. But people do navigate the "hard way" to Wailuku from Napili Bay around the northeast coast of West Maui, and the HVB lists some sights to be seen there: Pohaku Kani—the bell stone, seven or eight feet around, which rings with a metallic tone when struck with rock; Puu Koae, the nesting place for white sea birds, in Kahakuloa Valley, a tiny Hawaiian community where homesteaders farm and fish in the ancient ways; Kahekili (Leap Over Cliff), where the Maui king reputed to have been Kamehameha I's father and who was tattooed on one side and plain on the other died, according to legend; and down near Waihee the Kapuna fresh-water springs in deep sea—artesian springs formed by lava flowing over alluvial clay from one of which fishermen still get drinking water. If you didn't come up from Wailuku to see the Hale Kii and Piihana *Heiaus*, stop in now on your way by them.

If you have some time to kill before your plane, I suggest two things: shopping for Oriental foods like the famous Korean "Kim Chee" at Ooka Supermarket in Wailuku or at Ah Fook's in Kahului. Crafts Kahului drugstore luncheon counter has a reputation for the fine things it does with island-fruit pies. Or try the hot pastrami on sour-dough bun at the Hukilau Hotel.

The other thing I recommend is browsing at the old junk and antique store on your left just a block or so from the airport. In addition to a cavernous shed in back with Aunt Minnie's discarded lamps and furniture, the friendly woman in charge has a locked case of authentic Polynesiana—poi pestles and other lava rock implements. In fact, if you have an eye for interesting local variations on standard furniture, you can find charming chairs, tables, and bureaus cheek by jowl with everybody's kitsch. If after this much looking around the Valley Isle, you can't understand why the native motto is "*Maui no ka oi*" (Maui is the best), then you're indeed a hardhearted tourist.

Chapter VI

KAUAI

Kauai's ancient name, "Kauai-a-mamo-ka-lani-po," is as tongue-twisting as the island is green. It means the "Fountainhead of Many Waters from on High and Bubbling Up from Below," all of which water makes things grow. Getting a good look at nature's bounty is perhaps easier touristry on Kauai than on any other island. Think of (1) Lihue, where the airport is, as home base and make sorties (2) first around the east and up to the north at Haena, with a side trip up (3) the Wailua River, then around the coast (4) to Mana on the west, with (5) a lovely long detour up Waimea Canyon. More intrepid souls brave the Na Pali Cliffs, between Haena and Mana along the unpaved, northwest "frontier," but most save that for subsequent trips.

Lihue

If you have only one day, a ludicrously short stay (but it happens every tour), I'd recommend taking the Haena route. Stick to the seaside sights on the way up, and see the *mauka* attractions on the way back. And don't forget, in your enthusiasm, to spend some time in Lihue itself. I can think of no better way to get in the mood for the island than a visit to the Kauai Museum, next to the public library. The architecture of the new building is a superb job of blending a modern design, using lava-like materials, with that of the library, which is a strange medley of classic and Victorian. Housed in this handsome center are fascinating displays of Kauai antiquities. If you have a historical bent, ask the generous and co-operative librarian next door if you can look at the proceed-

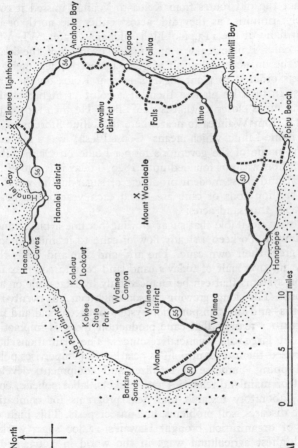

KAUAI

North

Kilauea Lighthouse
Anahola Bay
Kapaa
Wailua
Nawiliwili Bay
Poipu Beach
Lihue
Falls
Kawaihu district
Hanalei district
Hanalei Bay
Mount Waialeale
Haena
Caves
Kalalau Lookout
Waimea Canyon
Kokee State Park
Na Pali district
Waimea district
Waimea
Mana
Barking Sands
Hanapepe

0 5 10 miles

56
56
50
55
50

ings of the Kauai Historical Society, the conscientious collections and publications of the local history buffs.

Lihue itself didn't have much of a history until the 1830's. In fact the old routes from Koloa to Wailua missed it completely, running, as they did, across either the north or the south flank of the 1134-foot-high Kilohana Crater. When the high chief Kaikiowea was appointed governor of the island after the unsuccessful revolt of 1824 against Kamehameha II, he was ordered to plant sugar cane near Koloa on the royal lands. Instead he planted them at a point of higher rainfall several miles closer to what is now Lihue. He then moved the capital from Waimea to near where the Lihue Store is today. The name Lihue, which means "Goose Flesh," was a reference to the name of the governor's former home on Oahu. Lihue Plantation was not founded until 1849. Today it is one of the largest and most modern producers of sugar in the world. A half million tons of cane are raised each year on its nearly fourteen thousand acres.

It was inevitable that sugar growing became a big business in Hawaii. To keep a steady flow of cane to its mills, processors grew their own cane. The arid and semiarid lands that make up over half of today's cane land require complex irrigation systems that can be financed only by large-scale organizations. The long growing season—eighteen to twenty-two months—and the transportation system between field and mill are further reasons that cane production today is impractical without large-scale financial resources. The plantations have organized themselves into an association that supervises policy in shipping, purchase of fertilizer and equipment, development of mainland refineries and markets, labor policies, common laboratory research and field programs for combating plant diseases, soil problems, and insect pests. This high degree of organization brought Hawaii's 12,800 sugar workers the highest agricultural wage in the world in 1963, and it gave Hawaii itself almost nineteen million dollars in revenue to make it the biggest single civilian sector of an economy that employs a quarter million people. Its productivity (10.3 tons of sugar per acre) is the envy of a hungry world.

To Haena

On Route 56 is a Lihue Plantation town, Kapaia. Its mixed population has many Portuguese. If you take the left turn, you can reach Wailua Falls through the cane fields.

The next village on Route 56 is Hanamaulu, also part of Lihue Plantation. Paul Isenberg, from one of the most famous families on the island, founded a mill there in 1875. Before motorized transport replaced the oxcart, it was cheaper to mill the cane near the fields. Now it is all carted to Lihue for processing, and the Ahukini Landing no longer is used for a railroad wharf to ship sugar. Kauai Hardwoods, Inc., has a retail woodcraft shop just beyond Hanamaulu on the *makai* side of the overpass.

A mile beyond Hanamaulu on the *makai* side is Wailua Plain. During World War II the Marines had an advanced training camp there for the Pacific invasions. Unfortunately in leveling this land they uncovered a commoners' burying ground as well as a site of an unsuccessful invasion from Oahu. When an ammunition dump blew up there, Hawaiians respectful of the old ways were certain that this was a punishment for violating the sanctity of the cemetery.

Lydgate Park is named for the Rev. John Lydgate, who was an authority on Hawaiiana. You can see the remains of a City of Refuge in the coconut grove in the park. Drive on beyond the turnoff to the Wailua River, and if you stop to savor the surf opposite the Coco Palms Hotel, be very careful with your car on the turfy-looking grass. It's much more sand than green, and we got stuck!

As you are about to enter the next town, Kapaa, get a quick glimpse of the Sleeping Giant and listen to one of the *two* explanations we came across for this feature. Legend "explains" that the giant Puni was always getting in the way of the fast-moving nocturnal *menehunes*. A gigantic bull in their tiny china closet, he kept tromping down their houses and stone walls. He was such a likable clod, however, that the *menehunes* didn't ostracize him. Once when a flotilla of canoes was invading from Hawaii they tried to put their Big Friend to use for once by asking him to lob boulders at the attackers. But you might know, they found him asleep along the ridge you're now looking at. They tried their best to arouse the giant as the fleet got closer and closer. They built bonfires, they threw boulders on his *opu*, some of which caromed off into the sea and did some damage to the invading canoes, but they didn't break Puni's sleep. However, the rocks plus the apparition of the giant outlined against the bonfires frightened the Oahu attackers away. The next day the *menehunes* found to their dismay that Puni had swallowed many of the rocks that had fallen into his open mouth, and these had killed him. That's why he has such a big *opu*.

As you approach the town of Anahola, you can see a Hawaiian Homes project started in 1956. The first response of many Hawaiians to progress was one of utter demoralization. A sense of responsibility to the people who first owned the islands has led to several steps, of which the Hawaiian Homes Act is one, to help the "Indians" of this part of America get back into the white man's race. Through Hawaiian Homes, proceeds from land rentals go to a fund that gives up to six thousand dollars to pure or half Hawaiians to build houses. Anahola's Hawaiian population was hurt badly by a failure of its taro crop and the decline in their fishing grounds in the bay. But Orientals who replaced them in the tiny village have been able to make good.

Kilauea, up Route 56 from Anahola Bay, is the headquarters for a sugar plantation by that name. You also really shouldn't miss Kilauea Lighthouse, which is a short and not too bumpy ride off the main road to your right. Turn in where you see a quaint Episcopal church on your left. The lighthouse is on the northernmost extremity of the island and the view is one of the best on the islands. Between 8:00 A.M. and 4:00 P.M., except on Sunday, the Coast Guard will take you to the top of the light, which has a unique clamshell lens. And when you're there don't forget to let the children hunt for nests in the basement window boxes. The sea birds apparently like these crevices because they protect them from the often severe winds.

Kalihiwai Bay is the next attraction on Route 56. Tidal waves in 1946 and 1957 carried most of the houses in this gentle valley out to sea. Beyond Kalihiwai a side road will take you to the small Hawaiian settlement of Anini, known for its torchlight reef fishing. The Anini Beach and Princeville Ranch are supposed to become a "destination resort" area financed by American Factors, one of Hawaii's so-called Big Five corporations. Princeville Ranch was named in honor of Kamehameha IV's and Queen Emma's Prince Albert Edward, when the royal family visited the estate of R. C. Wyllie, the British Resident Minister, in 1860. Most of Kauai's beef is raised in its upland pastures.

One of the most photographed scenes in Hawaii (it is almost impossible to take an uninteresting picture of its grandeur) is the Hanalei overlook. When you look at the neat geometry of the taro patches and vegetable crops where once rice paddies flourished, you can understand why another name for Hanalei is Hanohano or "Most Beautiful." In the 1850's this lovely bay was the center of much agricultural experimentation. Oranges grown from seeds left by George Vancouver, for example, were exported to California long before they were grown commercially in the Golden State. There is also a story behind the willows seen along the banks of the Hanalei River. A certain Mr. Brown took slips of willows surrounding Napoleon's first burial place on St. Helena and grew them in his shaving mug as he shipped around the Horn to Hawaii.

On the way into Hanalei don't fail to stop for a short visit to St. William's Roman Catholic Church. It is one of three glorious modern churches on Kauai sponsored by a farsighted priest Father John MacDonald. The one in Hanalei has a simple A-frame construction of unpainted, stained logs. It has art work by Jean Charlot of the University of Hawaii, as do the other MacDonald churches, St. Sylvester's at Kilauea (this one is done in the round and has a glassed-off crying room for babies), and St. Catherine's at Kealia, where the Hawaiian Joseph and the Wise Men have gifts of bananas, taro, and coconuts, a classic Chinese rubbing-style fresco by Tseng Yu Ho, and Charlot's altar painting *The Compassionate Christ*. Father MacDonald raised some of the money for these superlative modern churches by taking a children's choir to the Coco Palms Hotel to sing the *Ave Maria* in Hawaiian. You can still hear them on the AV (Ave Maria) label. I count these three churches among the most interesting structures on Kauai.

Waioli Mission, founded in 1834, is also interesting, especially as the first meetinghouse in which the thatched roofs of old huts were imitated to form the steeply pitched Hawaiian-style roof. It's much more attractive aesthetically than the "better" church next door, with its cliché stained glass. The missionaries taught the native Hawaiians industrial arts long before the idea caught on in mainland United States, another instance of the vitality of those spiritual pioneers.

Hanalei Bay is a favorite watering hole for Kauai families, and they have vacation places along the shore. The swimming can be dangerous in the bay during winter because of undertow and strong currents, but it is always safe at the dock beyond the public pavilion, which has dressing rooms and picnic facilities. Of course the show place at Hanalei is the old Plantation House, which has become a luxury hotel since its use as a locale for the movie *South Pacific*. The circular cocktail lounge, the House of Happy Talk, has handsome carved beam ends that deserve close attention—*before* engaging in the increasingly happy and circular talk inside this architectural conversation piece. For the purse-poor I would recommend an early Sunday-morning breakfast at the Plantation House. Pick a table near one of the doors that open out on the pool and the Pacific.

Lumahai Bay Beach is next off Route 56. It is strictly for Kodachrome, not for swimming. If you're wondering how the spit of black rock protruding into the sea from beyond the Lumahai River got there, it is the tongue of the foulest-mouthed giant in Kauai's history. One day he called the wrong giant by a dirty name and was slain. His killer flung his body to the sharks, who ate all but his tongue because they found it too tough and bitter for even their tastes.

You must drive through Wainiha Valley to get to the Haena Flats. Kauai's little Spouting Horn is found on the left side of Wainiha Bay. Wainiha means "Wild Water," a title that makes sense only near the river's source, where there are many steep falls. Next to the blowhole is a small beach called Kaumaka, or the "Weeping Eye." The story goes that in olden days two brothers in Wainiha loved fish eyes. When a shark came close to where they were fishing one day, they got in a hot argument over who would get the shark's eyes to eat. So big an argument in fact that the shark lunged onto the beach and devoured them both. The amused shark laughed so hard he cried that day, according to those who watched the foolishly selfish brothers.

The beach near the Haena dry cave was used as the Bali Ha'i setting in the film *South Pacific*. The dry cave is actually a lava tube that runs several hundred yards back into the mountain. The hole gets smaller and smaller the deeper you get into it, until it becomes a small opening on the top of the mountain. The cave is named after the head fisherman of the *menehunes*, Manini-holo. Just before the small ones left the island forever, they made a huge catch of fish and piled half by the seashore while they took the rest to their people camped on a nearby mountain. When they returned they found that an evil *akua* had swiped the rest and taken them to his den. Half the party followed him into the hole at the top of the cliff; the remaining half of the party dug out a cave from the other side and a hole to bury him in after they had trapped him. To this very day there are times when the epithet *kahuana* ("smell of decay" from his dead body) is appropriate.

The wet caves are farther on. The cold water that fills the first, called Waikapalae, offers an opportunity for a very bracing dip. A mile farther on is the second wet cave, called Waikanaloa, a deep pool you must climb a hill to reach. Here in old days the Hawaiians used to play the sport of *lele kawa*, or jumping into the pool after a thirty-foot climb, sploosh. These caves were supposed to have been dug by Pele, who, looking for fire but finding water, had to leave this part of the island. A triangular peak known as the Fire Cliff, or Makana, towers over the Haena region. In olden times a specially trained group of men learned how to hurl burning brands of the lightweight hau wood into air currents so strong that they would carry the flaming torches far out to sea, to the delight of the crowds who came in canoes from all over Kauai and Niihau to watch.

A little beyond the second wet cave is the end of the road. There is a day-long hike across the winding valleys of the Na

Pali Coast, but don't try it if you're not the outdoor type. The week we were there a Kekaha lady fell fifty feet from a washout on the Kalalau trail onto a ledge and had to be rescued by the Waimea Fire Department. If you walk about three hundred yards down the beach *toward* Hanalei, however, you can get a good look at the Na Pali Coast. The beach here is safe for swimming. And why not try the pool that forms at the right side of the road just beyond the caves as you drive back toward civilization on Route 56.

To the Wailua River

On your way back also look for the Moloaa region, just past Kilauea on your right. The word means "Tangled Roots" and refers to the thick growths of mulberry from which tapa cloth was made in the old days. Moloaa was the principal source of tapa in Kauai. Moloaa Valley natives never want to drive through this valley at night and will refuse to do so with fresh pork in their cars. The reason is that Kamapuaa, a part-pig, part-human demigod, lives there. When he smells freshly killed pork he is enraged and turns into various shapes in his attempts to wreck the car. He has been known to be outwitted if the pork is camouflaged in ti leaves.

Next on the *mauka*, or mountainside, part of your tour back on Route 56 to Lihue are the Anahola Mountains. The sharp peak of Kalalea in this short, picturesque range is a landmark. There is a *heiau* on its tip with three terraces twenty to thirty feet wide. Look for Hole in the Mountain at the base of the sharp peak. The hole has a romantic origin. Kapunohu, a great spear thrower of Kohala, Hawaii, came to Kauai to challenge the Kauai chief who was famed for sling throwing. The Kauai chief slung prodigiously: all the way from Lawai, near Koloa over the Haupu Mountains, across the Wailua River and on to Anahola. But Kapunohu's spear was stronger and he became chief of Kauai with a throw that not only went to Anahola but poked a *puka* in Kalalea and ended at Hanalei.

Waipahee Slide is an interesting side trip except after a

strong rain. You get there by taking the inland road that leads from Anahola to Kealia and watching for a sign near the Spalding Monument. The slide is three miles beyond this sign. At the end of a miserable road is a short, clearly marked trail to the mountain stream, where you can slide down an eroded lava tube into the stream. A second and larger pool is down the stream a few hundred yards more.

Your next stop is the Wailua River region. Before you take the standard boat trip up the river, stop for a few minutes at a fascinating shop. This side of the road from the Coco Palms Hotel is a training center for Kauai's disabled, and their handsomest products are on sale at most reasonable prices. I bought my daughter a really striking muumuu for a few dollars under what we had been paying for dresses of equal value in Honolulu. There is a lot of stereotyped tourist bait there too, but even that is for a good cause. And the careful shopper can find first-rate crafts at unusually fair prices.

If you drive a few miles up Route 58 you will come to Opaikaa Falls, plunging over a high cliff. The name means "Rolling Shrimp" and refers to the fact that shrimp once rolled in the water and on the rocks there while laying eggs.

The Wailua River region is supposed to be the place where the Tahitians first reached Hawaii, about A.D. 1000. The great chief Puna resided there, and for years to be able to trace one's ancestry back to Kauai *alii* was the greatest honor. *Wai-lua* means "sacred water," a fact duly confirmed by the presence of no less than seven *heiaus* from the river's mouth to Mount Waialeale, where the river rises. The Coco Palms is on historic ground too. There Queen Deborah Kapule, wife of the last deposed King of Kauai, lived for a score of years to 1850. She lived in a set of large thatched houses near the lagoon, which then was a series of fishponds. Her subjects paid taxes in ocean fish, which were gradually shifted from less salty to more sweet-water pools while being fattened for her delectation.

Boat trips up the river to the Fern Grotto are accompanied by the recital of legends about the royalty buried in the caves along the river bluffs. A short walk from the end of the three-mile boat ride is the Fern Grotto, a cool cavern festooned with ferns and other subtropical vegetation watered to luxuriance by an eighty-foot cascade of water. Also in this area is the Holo-Holo-Ku Heiau, one of the oldest temples on the island and one of the few places in Hawaii where human sacrifices were offered. It is the easiest site to get to and was restored by the Bishop Museum and the local historical society in 1933. Once every month, on the fourth night of the god Ku (as the Hawaiian calendar ran), captives of war were sacrificed. If there were no such victims available, the executioner would go out at night and strangle someone with a special coconut fiber cord.

Nearby you can also see the famous Birthstones of Kauai. There are two birthstones in the islands, one near Wahiawa, Oahu, which was the center of a healing cult in the 1920's, and the more famous one on Kauai, at Holoholoku. There is a Hawaiian saying about the latter:

> The child of a chief born at Holoholoku is a high
> chief;
> The child of a commoner born at Holoholoku becomes
> a chief, also;
> The child of a high chief born outside of Holoholoku
> is no chief, commoner, he!

The rules surrounding Holoholoku were rather complex. If a pregnant mother got there too soon, she was regarded as a cheater and her child could not be royal. She had to arrive with her entourage *in labor*; they made the proper shelters for her and engaged in the proper rites. Thunder and lightning were supposed to accompany the birth of a really great chief. Sharkskin drums announced the birth for miles around, and the sex of the infant was announced with the same device. The final detail is moderately gory: the umbilical cord had to be stuffed into a certain hole in a rock; if rats ate it, the child would turn out to be a thief!

As you drive back toward Lihue from Wailua on Route 56, note on your right the slopes of the Kalepa range. This was once covered with sandalwood, which the chiefs cut in a frenzy of greediness for Western baubles early in the nineteenth century. Kalepa means "Signal Hill." In ancient times sentinels stood on these heights to warn of attackers approaching from Oahu. As if in solemn confirmation of the strategic intuitions of those old warriors, World War II observation posts were set up there, and today an airplane beacon as well as Hawaiian Telephone's wireless station are located on Signal Hill.

Back in Lihue, look for Route 50 and follow it to Nawiliwili Harbor. This little port a mile south of the county seat is named for the wiliwili trees that once were abundant there. Their wood was suitable for surfboards. Their red berries are still popular for necklaces. At one time this was a thriving village with good fishing and water for the taro patches. Now it is the principal port of Kauai. It can accommodate ocean-going ships that take on bulk sugar by conveyor belt. A night club, the Jetty, and a restaurant, Hale Aina, afford a pleasant view of the bay and the mountains. There is a lighthouse on Ninini Point, the Lihue side of the bay. You can also swim at Kalapaki Beach at Nawiliwili. When we were there John Ford, the movie director, was making *Donovan's Reef,* and his yacht, against the backdrop of the Hoary Head Range, made you almost forget that you were in a commercial sugar port; it was more like Tahiti or some other remote South Sea lagoon. At the crest of the hill you can see the charming Huleia stream as well as the historic Alekoko Fish Pond. This was the second one-night feat of the *menehunes,* cutting off part of the Huleia with a nine-hundred-foot wall for their shrimp-a-night wages. The wall is four feet wide and five feet above water. Unlike most fishponds, this was made of fitted "bricks" purportedly passed by a human chain of hands from Makaweli, twenty-five miles away. The princess and her brother, for whom the pond was made, were turned to stone for observing the *menehunes.* See if you can see the twin pillars above the road.

Nawiliwili has had its share of history too. A Japanese submarine lobbed fifteen shells into the town on New Year's Eve, 1941. One hit a large gasoline storage tank but failed to explode. This is also where in 1925 Lieutenant Commander John Rodgers and his exhausted crew were brought after their first flight from California fell three hundred miles short of the Hawaiian Islands.

Easily my happiest recollection of this area is supper at the Kauai Surf. Many tourists in a hurry overlook this place, to their loss. Set on Kalapaki Beach, the dining room opens onto the surf, and the flaming torches and the trade winds afford a dining pleasure as memorable as the cuisine. If you can afford a luxury hotel, stay here, a few miles from Lihue Airport. You will awake refreshed for the second leg of your Kauai trip: the trip along the western shore.

To Waimea and Mana

My advice would be to take the Waimea Canyon side trip, on Route 55, *before* you follow Route 50 to its conclusion at Mana because Barking Sands is not really much.

But to begin at the beginning. On your right as you drive down Route 50 from Lihue will be Mount Waialeale, the wettest spot on earth; its crest is usually wreathed in rain clouds. Seven rivers radiate from this watershed. Its highest peak is Kawaikini, at 5170 feet. Its name can mean either "Myriad Waters" or "Forty Thousand Radiations of Light," meanings that are extremely apt if you look at its contours on the topographic maps you can get free at any gas station. The winds are so fierce and prevalent at the summit that the lehua trees are dwarfed to an astonishing four inches! Compensation for this is the fact that the lehua blooms carpet the ground itself. The most sacred of the chain of *heiaus* leading upward on the Wailua River is on Mount Waialeale's summit.

At Puhi you will see the community of the Grove Farm Company, Ltd. It is the only sugar plantation that also produces pineapples. Grove also produces lichees, macadamia nuts, beef, crushed rock and limestone, and agricultural lime.

Pass now through Koloa Gap, which is the so-called gateway between the eastern and western parts of the island. As you cross the Huleia, you can see above it the plain where the U. S. Army decided to defend the island during World War II in case of any invasion. The road from here to Kalalau Overlook is almost precisely the trail used in ancient times (as opposed to the eastern circuit, where the ancient trail was much higher up the mountainside). Mount Kahili, on the right, is one of the places where the old chiefs used to watch for approaching attackers. From the so-called Tower of Silence they could see armies coming from either side of the island. After the islands were unified, this peak was the stronghold of a bandit who sent his men to rob travelers as they went through the then densely wooded Koloa Gap. His evil reputation lingered on so that missionary children riding on horseback from Lihue to the Koloa School used to prod their steeds energetically through this area because of the wild tales their young Hawaiian friends told them about the bandits.

As you go down an avenue of eucalyptus trees, you should cross a narrow bridge over Weoweo Pilau, which literally means "Bad-smelling Fish." Thereby (naturally, in Hawaii) hangs a tale. It seems that a man returning with a catch of *weoweo* fish from Koloa Beach was accosted by an ugly old woman who wanted some. He told her to catch some herself, because they were running well and he had a lot of children to feed. After committing that unforgivable sin of lack of hospitality he sat down for a rest. When he picked up his sack, he saw, not his catch of fresh *weoweo*, but a smelly mess of decaying fish. The unlucky sinner had made the mistake of refusing Pele in the guise of an old woman.

Because fishing was so important to the early Hawaiians, a great deal of lore and custom grew up around the occupation. Related to the Pele legend at Weoweo Pilau is the tradition that at a *hukilau,* or communal fish gathering, everyone who pitches in the least bit must be rewarded with part of the catch. Otherwise the fisherman will be plagued by bad luck for the rest of the season. If you should run into a man with a pole, net, or spear obviously on his way fishing, don't, for heaven's sake, make small talk by asking him if he's going where it's obvious he's going. The fish will overhear your lame attempt at conversation and not bite for him. Neither should a person ever turn back once he has set out on a fishing expedition, even to pick up forgotten things. (So be sure that you have your bait and beer cans set before you leave!) No bananas, either. Even seeing them on the way to go fishing is bad luck. Dangerous night fishing has its own religious safeguards. When you hunt the rare *upapalu* fish on moonlight nights, don't talk about dead persons, or about anything frivolous, for that matter. This interdiction applies to your whole family, for if you don't watch out in this way, you will get caught at sea or will see nothing but the fire of your torch in the water, or eels will crawl over you. If you feel like I do about eels in the daytime, let alone at night, you'll probably curl up with one or the other volume of Ethel M. Damon's *Koamalu* (borrowed from the Kauai Public Library) and read about more Kauai lore instead of going night fishing.

Save the side trip to the town of Koloa for the way back (or even for another day). At the foot of the hill and to the right of the intersection you can see a rise called Puuohewa, or "Hill of Punishment." This is where the old Hawaiians played a Stone Age variation of chicken. The game was called the *holua* slide, and the X of darker green vegetation shows where they used to coast, at the risk of crossover collisions, on long narrow sleds. They rode these vehicles lying, standing, or sitting; the main thing was the thrill at the danger of the sport.

Kalaheo is the territory of McBryde Plantation. In 1860 an energetic Scot named Duncan McBryde leased land here for a cattle ranch. He later served as judge and acting governor, becoming one of the historic citizens of the island. The Army took over the public park in Kalaheo, on your left as you drive to Waimea, during the war, and since then it has been in decline from its former magnificence. Local citizens are trying to restore it to its original glory. On your way back, don't forget to save time for a side trip here to see famed Nomilo Pond, which is associated with the ubiquitous Pele, who lived here before moving on to less green and more volcanic pastures on Maui and the Big Island.

Next on your way to Waimea is Hanapepe Valley. This is where the vivid red soil of Kaumakani begins. The name Kaumakani means "Wind-swept." (If you were to drive a jeep through Kauai, as I did with my children, you would still see a film of red dust on your notes and the color would remain on your clothes even after several washings!) It was this rich red soil, however, that established the world's record for sugar productivity in 1955—15.52 tons per acre. The Olokele Sugar Company not only specializes in agricultural innovations, but its little community is worth a quick side trip

TO WAIMEA AND MANA 245

off the road. It is one of the pleasantest little villages on Kauai.

The next town is Waimea. Save the Russian Fort, on your left as you enter the town, for a good look on your way back from the canyon. Looking at the town today, you'd never guess that it was the center of government before the white man came. Waimea is where Captain Cook made his first landing in the islands. It is where Liholiho was received, and whence King Kaumualii was shanghaied (for all practical purposes) to Oahu. The first missionaries to Kauai set up their mission here, the only such on the island until 1835. Waimea was also the center of the sandalwood trade. Traders and whalers were provisioned here.

Take a road off toward the Makaweli Valley to get to the Menehune Ditch. At the second swinging bridge, made of creaking wood and wire, about two and a half miles from the mouth of the river, you will find the fabulous Menehune Ditch. The legend of the Ditch says that in the old days King Ola wanted to help his people bring water more expeditiously to their taro patches in the Waimea Flats. His *kahuna*, Pi, told him to put a total *kapu* on the community at night. Pi made a great pile of identical stones on a cliff above the valley and then asked the *menehunes* to build it. They did in one night, protected from the sight of others, who had been forced to stay in their houses. The builders did so precise a job fitting the stones that not a drop leaked through what came to be called Ola's Water-lead, or Kiki-a-Ola. The people of Waimea were so happy with the new irrigation device for their taro that they threw a huge blast for the *menehunes* with mounds of shrimp, which was the favorite food of the dwarfs. The little men whooped it up so that night they scared the birds on Oahu. And they didn't finish all their shrimp, either. The mound you see there is called Puuopae, the Shrimp Hill, the excess crustaceans turned to stone. Waimea itself, by the way, means "Red Water."

Beyond Waimea before you turn off on the Canyon Road, Route 55, is Kekaha. This whole area used to be dotted with small settlements, the most noted of which was Pokii, which you can locate south of the mango trees just before you turn onto the Canyon Road, or Route 55. There is where the heroine of Hawaii's Orpheus and Eurydice story lived. According to this story, a Hawaiian chief sought the soul of his dead lover in Po, the land of departed souls. Po was supposed to be a huge cave under the sea beyond the Na Pali Cliffs. At the end of the road past Mana is Polihale Heiau, sacred to Milu, the god of the dead. The sea here is treacherous most of the year, but the old Hawaiians thought that swimming there brought them luck.

Also just beyond the turnoff to Waimea Canyon is a *holua* slide where the annual February Makahiki sports festival was held. During a Makahiki period, you had a brief surcease from death in war or work, but taxes took the edge off your pleasure. To this slide young chiefs came from all the islands, even as far away as the Big Island. Its paved rock, covered with dried pili grass, was sudden death to a rider who lost control of the sled, a platform nine inches high on two runners that could be as long as eighteen feet.

One of the first things you'll notice on your right as you climb into the cool highlands of Waimea Canyon from the dusty, dry flats around Kekaha and Mana is the crest of Puu ka Pele. This Hill of Pele is an extinct sulphur vent. It is here that Pele got a good foothold for her jump to Oahu (volcano goddesses broad-jump a hundred miles with the same facility that they engineer earthquakes and lava flows). The pit is her footprint. It has been filled with small stones by travelers who have made such a small offering to the goddess. Some authorities believe that the hill should be rendered Puka-Pele, or the hole through which Pele left Kauai for Oahu.

You can get your first (and, some think, best) view of Waimea Canyon by taking a side road to the right at the bottom of Puu ka Pele. The canyon itself results from a great fault in the rounded dome of the island; thousands upon thousands of centuries of erosion by wind, rain, and river have brought it to its present scenic splendor. When we were there John Ford was directing *Donovan's Reef* on the rim of the canyon, and I felt then, and even more so when later screening the films I took of his movie making, how infinitesimal man's activities look in such a natural formation. All that self-important hustle and bustle, and yet it didn't seem to touch the imperturbability of that place. The gorge itself reaches an elevation of about 3657 feet, is nearly a mile wide and ten miles long. Since one of the main features of this canyon is the shifting panorama of its colors, to get the full flavor of Waimea Canyon, one should see it at different times of the day. If you went up in the morning, lolled around over lunch at Kalalau Lookout, and spent some time at the interesting Kokee Lodge Museum, you could return to a quite different view of Waimea Canyon in the late afternoon.

Koaie Canyon enters Waimea at a right angle. Five miles up Koaie there is a village site where a large, 180-foot-high temple was constructed against the cliff in five terraces. Below this village was a pool called Kamalio, after the nymph who was supposed to reside there. There is an eerily romantic legend connected with this pool and this lady.

The next outlook to view Waimea from is at Kaana Ridge, where the county has a pavilion for tourists. Old Hawaiians believed that this was where the souls of the dead gathered while waiting their turn to go to the land of Po.

You will then enter a new zone of vegetation, the dense "wet forest" of the Kokee region. Halemanu (literally "Home of the Birds") is the beginning of this area. Its history is a fascinating study in human interruption of a natural ecology. This used to be a prime source of the feathers needed for the royal cloaks and helmets. You will remember that the *kahunas* whose job it was to catch these birds were conservationists at heart, for the most part pulling the precious few colored feathers they needed and freeing the birds to grow more. When Captain Vancouver gave King Kaumualii cattle and goats, the king wisely put a ten-year *kapu* on them to allow them to multiply. Unfortunately the *kapu* was on too long, and by then the wild cattle and goats so denuded the forests of vegetation that the birds could no longer live there and moved higher into the mountains. Hunting these wild beasts became one of the most thrilling sports on the island, but in 1916 the wild cattle were killed because they were doing too much damage to the watersheds and forests. There still are wild pigs and goats loose in the canyon region, but they can be controlled within safe limits. Now the deep, wet forests are returning, and with them the birds. A happier result of human intervention is the rich summer plum harvest from the trees planted by the state forestry people. Since each person is entitled to twenty pounds, the local people fill their cars with boxes and line up at the ranger station the evening before the season opens in August to get a flying start at picking the following morning. The ranger station at Kokee, beyond Halemanu, controls the forestry preserve, which encompasses the entire mountain area. To enjoy this region at greater leisure, you can rent mountain cabins and camping facilities for large parties through the manager of Kokee Lodge.

The Kanaloa-Holuhulu Meadows have a fascinating legend to explain the absence of trees there. The story, like that connected with Koloa Gap bandits, reminds us how silly it is to think of the "good old days" of Hawaii as a kind of primitive Golden Age in Eden. In very ancient times these meadows were covered with a very heavy forest where lived a most evil *akua*, or spirit, who harassed and even robbed and murdered people traveling through his turf. The travelers in desperation prayed to Kanaloa, Kauai's most ancient god; and he answered their prayers by chastising the bad *akua*. But the *akua* so ignored the god that Kanaloa in a rage came to the place, rooted up all the trees there, heaped them up, and set them afire with a lightning bolt. He cursed the ground so that it could never grow trees any more, behind which evil *akuas* could hide! And it doesn't to this day. Look for yourself! Kanaloa itself means "Engaging in Angry Actions." One doesn't know which was worse in the "good old days"—the precariousness of life or the vindictiveness of the gods.

The Natural History Museum at Kokee is not the greatest in terms of modern exhibition techniques. It has the rather ragged look of the energetic but untidy scholar's office. However a most garrulous and engaging old man who seemed to know every square inch of Kauai's territory and history was on hand when we visited to look at the exhibits of natural history. The museum is run by a society with the charming name of Hui O Laka, Laka being the goddess of the forest in Hawaii and the term *hui* meaning an organization or combine. A half hour in this organization's orbit will enhance your understanding of the island's scenic splendors.

After such a cram course in flora, fauna, and lore, unwind your mind before the awesome splendor of Kalalau Lookout. I frankly was moved a great deal more by this vista than by the vest-pocket version of the Grand Canyon at Waimea. A brilliant sun, intermittent clouds and fog patches, and the incredible blue of the Pacific seen from this height make the view a gasper, destroying with one scan of the eyes every Kodachrome cliché about natural beauty. This valley was cultivated by Hawaiian families as late as the 1920's, when the last ones moved out to Haena and elsewhere. Only goats, wild pigs, and chickens dumbly share its glory today. Peacocks, which once flourished there, have been exterminated by the hunters who boated in by sampan or climbed in over the trail to hunt wild animals.

The Hawaiian tradition of explaining natural formations with myths is nowhere more compellingly put than in the story of the two small stone figures visible on one of the many hogback ridges at the left of Kalalau Valley. In the old days some demigods lived in this valley. They remained immortal as long as they lived in the shade. One of them who lived in the upper Kalalau forest was called Naiwi. He was a cranky customer who believed that he could drink only water that came out of a spring near sea level in the valley. But he was too lazy to fetch his own drinking water, so he used to send his two small children, -the girl named Hikimaunalei and the boy Kua, down the almost mile-long trail to do his dirty work. One night the two children saw a group of mortal children playing in the full moonlight at the sandy beach at the mouth of the valley. They watched in amazement these happy mortal children singing and laughing, then they put their calabashes down to get a better look. Finally, before they knew it, they were playing themselves. So engrossed, they failed to note the passage of time. Hikimaunalei was first to see the red in the east, but before they could run to the shade of their home, the rays of the sun caught them and turned them into stone.

If you look to the right of the parking lot at the Kalalau Overlook, you can see the beginnings of a road around the inaccessible Na Pali Coast, which has been discontinued temporarily for lack of funds. Na Pali is the plural in Hawaiian for Kapali—the "Cliff." Unless you are a hardy hiker or lucky enough to get a rare sampan or canoe ride into one of the hidden valleys on the northwest Na Pali Coast, you will have to rely on those who have been there.

As you drive back toward Kekaha on Route 55 you should get a number of superlative views, of the Forbidden Island, Niihau if it is a reasonably clear day. Less than a hundred square miles in area, eighteen miles long and five miles wide, it lies about seventeen miles southwest of Kauai. The two smaller islands you may be able to see are Lehua, about a mile north of Niihau, on whose seven-hundred-foot heights the U. S. Coast Guard has its highest lighthouse. This is supposed to be where Pele first brought her family in her eastward Odyssey in search of a new home. Kaula is nineteen miles to the southwest of Kauai.

Niihau itself is semidesert, with little rainfall and no permanent streams of its own. What fresh water there is comes mostly from collected rainfall. Thus farming is impossible. But except for serious droughts there is enough water for the thirty thousand head of sheep and one thousand cattle and horses. Niihau has its own stories too. One concerns the destruction of the *akuas,* or spirits. On one end of the island, *akuas* often devoured men sleeping on the sand after a heavy day's work. One brave soul had had enough of this and decided to foil the spirits. He built a long house something like a canoe shed but with only one entrance. Inside this hut he put a great many *kiis,* or wooden images of men, using the gray and black *opihi* (limpet) shells for eyes. Then he hid and waited for the *akuas* to fall into his trap. Inside they saw the images with their shining eyes. Rather slow spirits, apparently, they inferred that Kauai men slept with their eyes open! They started to consume what they assumed were sleeping men. The *akuas* gave further testimony of their own low IQ's by exclaiming as they bit into the wooden images: "*Paakiki kanaka o Kauai*" (The men of Kauai are tough customers). With their teeth sticking to the wood, they could not extricate themselves, and the fisherman rid Niihau of *akuas* by burning his trap house down. Now they call this safe part of the island Kii.

As you leave Waimea on Route 50, stop for a while at the

Old Russian Fort. This was built in 1817 in the form of a six-pointed star overlooking both the river and the sea. It was one of two forts built for the Russian Fur Company of Alaska by the German doctor Georg Anton Scheffer. The one overlooking Hanalei Bay is no longer in existence. The stone fort, which is now practically buried under *haolekoa* trees, overlooks the same place where Captain Cook's arrival so amazed the natives, who breathlessly told the other natives about the men on the "floating islands" who had "white foreheads," "sparkling eyes," "wrinkled skins" (clothing), "angular heads" (hats), spoke a strange language and "breathed fire from their mouths" (smoked).

Driving east again on Route 50, you will see on your right Port Allen, which is the shipping center for plantations and towns on the west side of Kauai. The tall smokestack is the McBryde Plantation mill. The first shopping center on Kauai was built there recently and has caused a great deal of concern among small merchants in nearby Hanapepe.

As you pass by Kukui-O-Lono on your way back, you can drive down a side road toward the sea to another of Pele's places. Nomilo Pond is what remains of a crater two hundred feet wide and three hundred feet long. It is connected underground with the ocean two hundred feet farther on. The brackishness of water in this pond gives it a unique shade of green; it is full of fish, including the fierce barracuda. The strange, unearthly atmosphere of the crater makes it easy to understand why the Hawaiians ascribed it to Pele. The legend has it that she came here after having failed as a fire maker at Haena, coming up with wet caves instead of volcanoes. She got very angry when the very next abode she tried to create turned out wet too. Immediately she started island-hopping until the hot and dry Kilauea struck her fancy on the Big Island. There is a belief among local people that whenever Kilauea erupts Nomilo Pond turns yellower and gets warmer, "evidence" that Pele is visiting her old Kauai home.

Kalaheo has the distinction of being the residence of Isamo Doi, one of the most interesting local painters. Doi has his studio behind the general store in Kalaheo. Also of aesthetic interest in this area is the warehouse of James Sakimae, an unheralded craftsman of unique flower arrangements. He uses as his raw materials dried leaves, berries, pods, stalks, and plants both exotic and ordinary. His designs are recommended for those who want to go beyond the monkeypod salad bowl in the gifts they take (or have mailed) home.

In Lawai you should visit the Buddhist shrines called the 88 Holy Places of Kobo Daishi. They are set on a steep and rocky hillside in a grove of old eucalyptus trees. Kobo Daishi was an important teacher of the Shingon sect of Buddhism over a thousand years ago in Japan. Each shrine celebrates a Buddhist saint and reveres sacred sands placed under each image from the original 88 Holy Places erected by Kobo Daishi in Japan. Each place represents a particular virtue, and making the circuit shrives you of 88 sins.

Leave Route 50 at Lawai and take Route 53 down to Koloa for another interesting side trip. Koloa was the center of affairs in Kauai from about 1840 to 1880. The name itself means "Long Cane," a reference to an experimental variety that was tried many places but only really thrived to be harvested successfully here. Forty strong men used to pull the plantation plows in the beginning. When the missionaries showed them how to use draft animals for this backbreaking work, in gratitude for this marvel they called the yoke *maile*, after the precious lei. In the old days Koloa Landing was the third most important port in the entire chain; only Honolulu and Lahaina were more so. At its peak fifty ships might lie at anchor at one time. On your way to Poipu Beach you can see the Poipu salt pans on either side of the road. Hawaiians were the only Pacific island people to make salt for preserving fish and meat.

Beyond the salt pans of Poipu is one of the showcases of all the islands—Moir's Gardens. At popular request, Mr. and Mrs. Hector Moir have opened their private garden to public viewing daily between 9:30 A.M. and noon and between 1:30 and 4:30 P.M. The Moirs are on hand themselves to explain the collection they have assembled in a landscape of striking Hawaiian rocks; it includes unusual dry-land tropicals; for example, the largest private collection of African aloes in the world; the largest planting of plumerias; tree cereus, cacti, yuccas, and other desert plants; water lilies and lotuses on lava rock pools.

Poipu's beaches are the favorite ones on the island. Picnic facilities and the bathing pavilion are always crowded on the weekends. Their popularity is due to their excellence and to the choice available: shallow water for the timid in front of the pavilion, body-surfing down the shore, and quiet waters beyond the sandspit to the right of the pavilion. Near the beach there is a very attractive hotel, too: the Waiohai Hotel, in which striking new architecture has been built around two old homesteads. At Makahuena Point, beyond the end of the Poipu road and beyond the U. S. Coast Guard loran (long range and navigation) is a commoners' burial ground. You will remember that chiefs were buried in inaccessible places (with, like as not, the two unlucky commoners who carried them killed to protect the dead man's secret resting place). The chiefs were afraid that their bones might end up in disgrace as someone's fishhooks. The commoners had to risk that indignity, and Makahuena Point is one such "open" cemetery. At the far end of the beach there are petroglyphs on sandstone ledges. Actually you might better spend your time studying them carefully at the Kokee Natural History Museum, since they are often buried by sea and sand at Makahuena. Still farther is a long beach with a great deal of historical value to Kauaians—Mahaulepu. For there in 1796 those who weren't forced by a great storm to turn back to Honolulu in Kamehameha's invasion flotilla were clubbed to death, according to Kauaian legend. A Big Island tradition confirms this story. There in Kawaihae a canoeload of ancestors who managed to launch one canoe, while their colleagues lay in exhausted sleep from their struggle with the storm, went straight back to Hawaii, afraid of Kamehameha's wrath should they report back to him in Oahu. Kauaians make a big thing of their island never having been conquered, as Maui, Molokai, Hawaii, Lanai and Oahu were. This tradition gives them a shred of evidence for their vain boast.

Mahaulepu is also famous because it receives great redwood and fir logs regularly from the northwest coast of America. Prevailing winds and currents introduced Hawaiians to bits of iron in driftwood. This is how they developed their passion for the material before Captain Cook "discovered" them for the West, and in the process brought this Stone Age people in steady contact with iron technology.

Turn around now and drive past the Koloa Route 52 and down the road that brought you to Poipu Beach. At the other end of it is the Spouting Horn. This curiosity was caused by the sea having forced itself under great pressure into an old lava tube the top of which was pierced by interior erosion.

On your way back to Koloa stop for a minute or two in Kuhio Park. Prince Jonah Kuhio Kalanianaole was born here in 1871 of royal parentage and later became the Hawaiian delegate to Congress, an election that political scientist Lawrence Fuchs thinks was dreamed up in the haole panic that home-ruling Hawaiians might actually run the territory when U.S. annexation gave the Hawaiians great voting power. The Hawaiian Homes Commission was his most signal victory in Congress.

There are *two* handsome Buddhist temples in Koloa. We found it very restful to stop in these places of worship. The parishioners were more than willing to chat informally with visitors about their religious traditions. The weekend aloha can very easily end up with their providing free cans of beer on the church lawn to make the comparative religious judgments flow more freely.

As you drive back onto Route 50 to return to Lihue, take a good look at the Hoary Head Range on your right. The highest peak, Haupu, means "Excitation of Thought." On its slopes grows the mokihana berry, which goes into Kauai's emblematic lei. Notice also the spitting image of Queen Victoria with a prim finger up in mute admonishment. The ethnological punsters have developed an outrageous topographical play on words that I will beat the tour driver to (only so you'll be prepared to groan more deeply at its offensiveness). She is said to be chastising her obstreperous grandson, William II, "Now, Willy, Willy" (Nawiliwili). By the time you recover from that pun, you'll be in Lihue.

If there's time before your plane to spend in Lihue, drive over to Lihue Lutheran Church and look at its ornate pulpit and altar. This congregation dates from 1883 to serve the German immigrants who came to work sugar. Isenberg is a historic name in Kauai; many of the *lunas*, or overseers, were

German back in preunion days. In the nearby cemetery you can see the monument celebrating the Rev. Hans Isenberg and his wife, Dora Rice Isenberg. Isenberg Memorial Square and Isenberg Field at Kauai High School further attest to the importance of those Kauai pioneers.

Another interesting place to browse in is the Bookmark, on the main street. You can buy the Hadley-Williams booklet on Kauai there, for example. The Lihue General Store is also worth a browse if you savor the pleasures of casing the heterogeneity of such omnium-gatherum places. Get to the airport a little early and relax at the Menehune restaurant there. Try to get into the front of the line for the plane back to Honolulu so you can choose a window on the left side of the plane. The view of Oahu coming in early in the evening is a rare pleasure. You'll see Kaena Point, the Waianae range, a good view of Pearl Harbor as the plane descends to land. (The same view is entirely different if you fly out to Kauai early in the morning, when you should of course sit on the right side of the plane.) Unless you've been in an unbelievably cantankerous mood during your Kauai visit, you should agree with the old *mele* "*Maikai-Kauai*" that you have seen "most beautiful, most blessed Kauai." I like it best of all old Hawaii.

Niihau

Niihau you'll just have to read about. It took years for even former Governor Quinn to get invited there.

Over a hundred years ago, the *Bessie* sailed from New Zealand en route to Vancouver with a wealthy and intrepid widow aboard. She stopped in Honolulu to winter. Kamehameha IV heard about her and offered to sell her Niihau and part of Kauai that faces the smaller island for $10,000 (and, the story goes, her piano). One of her daughters married a man named Robinson and their son became the "lord" of Niihau. When he died, he gave the island to his wife, four sons, and a daughter. The Robinson family still owns it and lives there.

Once a week a boat brings provisions. Two hundred fifty native Hawaiians live a most strict life there. While English is taught in their eight grades of school, most prefer to speak Hawaiian. They tend the cattle and Merino sheep, make fancy leis and hatbands for Honolulu shops from the peacocks and pheasants that abound on the island.

The Sabbath is kept with all the severity of the early missionaries. Everyone must go to the Congregational church there. No swimming, hunting, or fishing is allowed on Sunday. Prayers must be said every day by the family. If your father has to go to work early, you have to get up too and say your prayers and sing hymns before he leaves. The native Hawaiians can leave the island only if they have a good reason. If they go without permission, they can't return. The Robinsons are very firm about this: "It is better that way. What they don't know won't tempt them."

Chapter VII

MOLOKAI

Molokai Mileage Guide

Distances from Kaunakakai to:

Airport	8.0 miles
Kualapuu	6.2 miles
Kalae	7.7 miles
Kawela	6.0 miles
Kamalo	10.5 miles
Mapulehu	15.5 miles
Pukoo	16.7 miles
Waialua	20.6 miles
Halawa	28.8 miles

Molokai

I almost didn't visit Molokai. I kept asking *kamaainas* whether they thought it would be worth my while, and a surprising number said to skip it. I think they were wrong. Spend a day there if you can. If you're pressed for time, though, you can so arrange your flight from Maui back to Honolulu to stop off for a half day and pick up the early-evening flight on to Honolulu. It's just about a twenty-minute flight from Wailuku-Kahului Airport, on Maui, and the scenery, if you cut through the central valley of Maui, is splendid with sparkling images of the offshore coral reefs and the lush West Maui mountains. Our pilot also gave us a good look at the islands of Kahoolawe and Lanai on his way into the airport—in the center of the island eight miles from Kaunakakai, where you can stay overnight at the Seaside Inn,

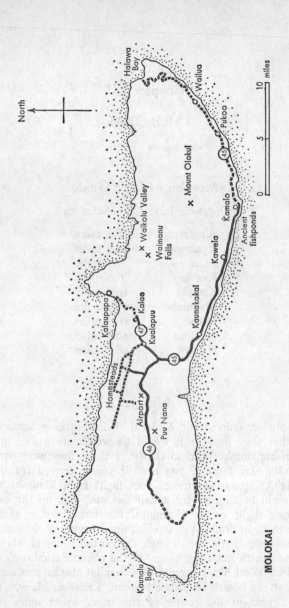

MOLOKAI

an unpretentious motel with food and drinks and weekend entertainment.

Molokai now has over 4500 people on its 260 square miles. At one time, around the turn of the century, its population was down to a little over a thousand, and it became known as the Lonely Island. When the Hawaiian Homes Act, of 1921, offered forty acres to all those who were at least 50 per cent Hawaiian, those who qualified came back to places like the Hoolehua Homesteads. Now there are more pureblood Hawaiians on Molokai than on any other island. The founding of the pineapple industry there brought still more to the island. The big problem has been water. The western mountains are hard up for water, while the abundant rains of the eastern forest lands run off, useless, into the ocean. If a way could be found to trap that water, Molokai might become, as C. Montague Cooke of the Molokai Ranch predicted, the breadbasket of the fiftieth state. As Oahu's truck farmers give in to suburban developers, Molokai's days as a Polynesian retreat may be coming to an end. In November 1960, a five-mile, nine-million-dollar irrigation tunnel was completed. Some interesting steps have also been taken with saline agriculture, using brackish water to irrigate alfalfa, asparagus, papaya, and other crops.

You can rent a car at the airport, after having stashed your grips and gear in care of the airline you will take into Honolulu (they're very helpful about this on the Friendly Island). Head east along Route 45, the ocean road for about forty miles for a really isolated retreat in Halawa Valley. The last ten or fifteen miles of this route is still pretty much a wish in the mind of a highway engineer.

Halawa Valley is about three or four miles deep and a half mile across. At one time it used to be covered with taro patches, but now only a half-dozen families fight a losing battle with the jungle that is reclaiming the valley. The tidal wave of 1946 convinced almost everybody that it was time to leave. At the head of the valley is Moaula Falls at the foot of which is a pool about a hundred fifty feet across. The story is that it has no bottom. Hawaiian lore counsels you to test the safety of the water by throwing in a ti leaf. If it floats, you're in. If it sinks, so may you! Another legend connected with this place is that the way you placate angry gods given to shagging rocks down on visitors is to take a gift (say a coin), put it on a boulder under a ti leaf, and anchor the symbolic gift with another rock. Do this (and keep an eye out for falling boulders) and the rocks may all miss you.

Bob Krauss, Honolulu *Advertiser* columnist, suggests that the *kukui*, or candlenut, trees along this trail are worth an experiment in early Polynesian illumination. (The *kukui* trees are the gray-barked trees with light green leaves on mountainsides.) If you string a handful of kernels on the center of a coconut frond and light the first kernel, it will burn for three to five minutes and then ignite the next *kukui* nut. Krauss says that you can tell the combustible nuts by shaking the kernels: if they rattle, they'll burn.

On the trip back, there are several interesting places to see with the time you have left. (It took me two hours to make the round trip from the airport.) Just after you leave Halawa, on your right you can see Molokai's sacred *kukui* grove, which Hawaiians fear as the home of Kahuna Lanikaula, a powerful priest. At the Paikalani Taro Patch, it is possible still to see the bare outline where Kamehameha camped with his troops as he prepared to invade Oahu. Since the small island of Molokai was in no position to provision his troops, he had his men plant a huge patch of taro. There will be several interesting churches on your right as you drive back to Kaunakakai: Father Damien's Our Lady of Sorrows, white with a green steeple; and the oldest church on the island, the red-steepled stone Kaluaaha, with a Bible in Hawaiian on its lectern, as in so many of the old, nearly abandoned Congregational churches on the Outer Islands.

If you like the feel of old country general stores, and if you're as thirsty as I was when I got back from Halawa, without having had the foresight to bring a canteen, stop at the only store between Halawa and Kaunakakai—Ah Ping's. As I wetted down my own parched throat with several root beers in a row (do bring water along!), I found the proprietor as interested in the Philadelphia Phillies as I was in the royal fishponds I had seen driving down to Halawa. He taught me a great deal more about those ponds than I was able to tell him about the Phillies, I'm afraid.

Keawanui Pond was made, probably over five hundred years ago, by closing with a stone wall the open end of a natural cove reaching out from shore in a half-circle. The pond is still being used. You may notice, by the way, as your plane sets down from Maui, that this southern coast seems to be very shallow, conducive to creating such places to keep fish alive, and the very opposite of the sheer, almost two-thousand-foot cliffs on the northern side of the island. Just beyond the pond you will see where two intrepid aeronautical pioneers, Ernest Smith and Emory Bronte, almost *didn't* make the first nonstop transpacific flight. In 1927, twenty-five hours and two minutes out of California, en route to Honolulu, they settled for a *kiawe* grove when their craft ran out of gas.

When you get back to Kaunakakai, you should have enough time left over to drive up to the Kalaupapa Pali (an hour round trip to the airport) where you can get a spectacular view of the Hansen's disease (leprosy) Settlement. The leper colony's name, Kalaupapa, means "Flat Leaf." Look at the map to see why, or, better, look from the Kalaupapa Overlook. Until the miracle sulfone drugs brought this disease under control in 1946, the very word leprosy was terrifying. And that is why the lepers were isolated on this flat seven square miles of land backed up to the steep cliffs. You can fly into the colony, where over two hundred cured patients prefer the limited but assured freedom among fellow victims to the ambiguous results of returning to society. Although you need a clearance from the Health Department, the Andrew Flying Service (Honolulu 825-225) can arrange this with your ticket. Mail flights leave Honolulu every morning at nine. You can also take a flight from Molokai's main airport.

To hear about the heroes of Kalaupapa and Kalawao, like Father Damien and the Rev. John Hanloa and Deacon Kamahalo of Siloama, or Rev. "Mother Alice" Kahokuoluna, who devoted their lives to the lepers, you can take tours directed by inhabitants of the tiny peninsula, Isaac Keao (phone 37195) or Winifred and Paul Harada (phone 37297).

Should you go there you would find a sleepy village with many mementos of a tortured past when the Belgian Father Damien gave up his life for the unfortunates, most of whom were not Catholic. His letter to his brother, in Belgium, is very eloquent, I think:

Kalawao, November, 1873

My Dear Brother—God has deigned to choose your unworthy brother to assist the poor people attacked by that terrible malady, so often mentioned in the Gospel—leprosy. . . .

Leprosy, as far as is known, is incurable; it seems to begin by a corruption of the blood. Discoloured patches appear on the skin, especially on the cheeks; and the parts affected lose their feeling.

After a time this discoloration covers the whole body; then ulcers begin to open, chiefly at the extremities. The flesh is eaten away, and gives out a fetid odour; even the breath of the leper becomes so foul that the air around is poisoned with it.

I have had great difficulty getting accustomed to such an atmosphere.

One day, at the Sunday Mass, I found myself so stifled that I thought I must leave the altar to breathe a little of the outer air, but I restrained myself, thinking of our Lord when He commanded them to open the grave of Lazarus, notwithstanding Martha's words, *jam foetet*. (He is rotting already.)

Now my sense of smell does not cause me so much inconvenience, and I enter the huts of the lepers without difficulty.

Sometimes, indeed, I still feel some repugnance when I have to hear the confessions of those near the end, whose wounds are full of maggots.

Often, also, I scarce know how to administer Extreme Unction, when both hands and feet are nothing but raw wounds.

[From Honolulu *Star-Bulletin*, Progress Edition, *Hawaii 185*, II, 15.]

There are two other interesting but hard-to-get-to spots on
the way back to the airport. One, off Route 47, is Kauleona-
nahoa Phallic Rock. This is a carved gray basalt rock six feet
high. It is near the cliff coastline of northern Molokai. According to legend, a barren woman who spent the night there went
home with child. And people who defaced the rock became
barren. There is also a female counterpart of the phallic rock
formed by two parallel eroded grooves running up and down a
large boulder.

Another interesting and inaccessible sidelight is the sandalwood pit, which is nine and a half hard-to-drive miles off
Route 46. What's so great about a sandalwood pit? What *is*
a sandalwood pit? It seems that the first white traders found
sandalwood growing in the mountains. This aromatic timber
was highly prized in China for making chests. Hawaiian chiefs
were offered whiskey, muskets, gaudy uniforms, and other
trinkets calculated to dazzle the untutored, if they would fill
the traders' ships with sandalwood. This became Hawaii's
first export until greediness razed the trees entirely. Unfortunately, the chiefs had no scales. So when the white man said a
"shipload" of sandalwood, the only way the canny, if uncom-
plicated, chiefs could measure their hauls was to dig a hole
the size of a ship's hold and bring the timber there for "weighing in."

Molokai has some of the best hunting in the state. Axis
deer, birds, wild goats, sheep, and pigs can be found in profusion. Permits and information are available from Department of Agriculture offices in Honolulu and Kaunakakai. Fishing is also excellent off the Penguin Bank, a part of Molokai
that lies submerged at an average depth of 180 feet for
twenty-seven miles to the southwest. At the edge of this submarine shelf is a sheer cliff plunging 1800 to 3600 feet. It is
the largest submarine shelf near the main islands.

Lanai

The word *lana'i* means "hump" not "porch." The island of
Lanai is only eight miles away from Maui across the once famous Lahaina Roads and, on the north, only seven miles

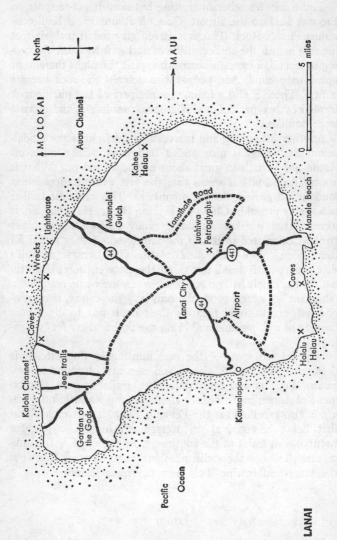

LANAI

from Molokai. Most visitors do not take time to visit Lanai, but the island has its own special attractions. Lanai City is a company town of the Dole Pineapple Corporation. You can see workers in the "pine" fields dressed in heavy clothing and leggings with gloves and goggles to protect themselves from the thorny pineapple leaves. If Lanai doesn't have palm-lined beaches, it does have many mountain roads and beautiful views. Water sports are less crowded there. Manele Beach is one very popular place for the aquatic loner. At Shipwreck Beach you can see old ships rusting and rotting. There are also many traces of early Hawaiiana: fishponds, *heiaus*, burial caves, and ruins of old villages. The "Garden of the Gods" awaits the hardy jeep hiker: it is a deep canyon filled with weird stone figures. Kamehameha the Great spent much time in his old age on Lanai, where he built a home near a small village on a bluff overlooking the bay on the southern coast.

Kahoolawe

Kahoolawe is called the "Island of Death." It is no longer possible to visit this small island, seven by eleven miles, because there are too many undetonated naval shells there accumulated through years of target practice. Try to get a good look at the island as you fly over on your way to Kona from Honolulu or on your flight from Maui to Molokai. Early in the morning the island looks pink; by noon it has turned to red; in the evening the colors become purple. When the trade winds are blowing strong, the island seems like it has a red plume, which is really a dust cloud of the reddish soil being blown off the island's highest point.

INDEX